CELEB 2.0

New Directions in Media

Blogging America: The New Public Sphere
Aaron Barlow

CELEB 2.0

How Social Media Foster Our
Fascination with Popular Culture

Kelli S. Burns

New Directions in Media
Robin Andersen, Series Editor

PRAEGER

An Imprint of ABC-CLIO, LLC

A B C ☰ C L I O

Santa Barbara, California • Denver, Colorado • Oxford, England

99113

Library of Congress Cataloging-in-Publication Data

Burns, Kelli S.
  Celeb 2.0 : how social media foster our fascination with popular culture / Kelli
S. Burns.
       p. cm. — (New directions in media series).
  Includes bibliographical references and index.
  ISBN 978-0-313-35688-9 (alk. paper) — ISBN 978-0-313-35689-6 (ebook : alk.
paper) 1. Celebrities in mass media. 2. Social media. 3. Popular culture. 4. Mass media
and culture. I. Title.
  P96.C35B87   2009
  302.23'1—dc22   2009034104

13 12 11 10 9   1 2 3 4 5

This book is also available on the World Wide Web as an eBook.
Visit www.abc-clio.com for details.

ABC-CLIO, LLC
130 Cremona Drive, P.O. Box 1911
Santa Barbara, California 93116-1911

302. 231
BUR.

CONTENTS

Acknowledgments

This details the intersection of two areas I enjoy both professionally and personally—social media and popular culture. I am extremely grateful to the people who helped me during this journey.

First, I would like to thank my colleague and friend Bob Batchelor, who shared his professional connections and advice. I would also like to thank my editor, Dan Harmon, for believing in me and giving me this opportunity. Dr. Joe Moxley also deserves credit for motivating me to write the proposal for this book and providing me with helpful writing techniques. I would like to thank Ashlee Alstrom for her research assistance and perspective. Elle Galerman also contributed significantly to the chapter on celebrity bloggers. Andi Kuhn provided much of the background for the chapter on promoting movies using MySpace. I would also like to thank my parents, Will and Astrid Staples, for providing me with an incredible education and much encouragement throughout my entire life. Finally, I especially wish to thank my husband, Corey, and my son, Griffin, for supporting me in this endeavor and allowing me to carve out time for this project.

INTRODUCTION

"The new Web is a very different thing. It's a tool for bringing together the small contributions of millions of people and making them matter. Silicon Valley consultants call it Web 2.0, as if it were a new version of some old software. But it's really a revolution."

—Lev Grossman, *Time*, 2006

The impact of social media has been observed in the domains of business, politics, religion, social movements, and interpersonal relationships. The most significant consequence of social media, however, may be the influence on popular culture, as social media affect our consumption patterns and our creation of popular culture products, possibly changing the very meaning of popular culture. This book provides an overview of key social media applications, namely blogs, video-sharing sites, social networks, message boards, and social news sites, and describes the synergistic relationship between these applications and popular culture.

The use of social media has grown from a fringe activity to a mainstream passion. Forrester Research's 2008 Social Technographic Profile found that about 75% of U.S. adults use social media to connect and share with others, an increase from 56% for the same time period in 2007.[1] Although a vibrant part of youth culture, social media are also used extensively by middle-aged adults. The Forrester study documented that the largest gains in adoption were among 35–44-year-olds.[2] Even seniors are part of the trend. A study by AARP and the Center for the Digital Future at the USC Annenberg School of Communications found that 70% of AARP members surveyed (age 50 and up) consider the AARP online community to be "very" or "extremely" important to them, and 58% reported visiting the online community daily or several times a day.[3] Data from RapLeaf shows an increased presence of older adults on social networking sites, but that the sites are still dominated by youth.[4]

The remarkable growth of social media has amplified the public's appetite for popular culture products. We are watching video clips on YouTube of our favorite television moments, reading blogs for the latest celebrity news, and listening to tracks from our favorite musician's MySpace page. Likewise, our fascination with popular culture spills over into our personal expressions as we create mashups of music and movie trailers; list our favorite books, television shows, music, and movies on Facebook; and friend a favorite actor on MySpace. A 2005 Pew Internet & American Life Project found that teens are a prolific group for creating Internet content, with over half of those who were online at the time having already done so, a percentage that is likely to be higher today.[5] A 2008 survey by Mediamark Research and Intelligence of U.S. adults found that over 25% of respondents had shared photos online during the past 30 days, 4.3% had written blogs, and 4.1% had uploaded a video to a Web site.[6] On the consumption side, the same study showed that over 23% had watched online videos, almost 22% had downloaded music, and 11% had visited blogs. Social media, therefore, has fostered both our consumption and production of popular culture products, upending the bandwidth assumption that people would download more than they upload. Sites like BitTorrent with almost symmetrical uploading and downloading rates demonstrate the falsity of that assumption.[7]

Although consumption and production are easily distinguishable within traditional media (hence the terms consumers and producers), a digital culture blurs the two processes. As David Beer and Roger Burrows explain, "Perhaps the key-defining feature of Web 2.0 is that users are involved in processes of production and consumption as they generate and browse online content, as they tag and blog, post and share."[8] When a blogger, for example, posts a video clip from another source, the blogger becomes both producer and consumer.

The introduction of social media also changes the nature of popular culture. The mass communicators of the past who are increasingly concentrated into media conglomerates are taking a backseat to the new mass communicators who are decentralized over the various platforms for social media. This shift thus changes the notion of mass communication. The delivery mechanism of our shared culture has begun to move away from mass media to the much smaller and intimate settings that are found online. We are witnessing signs, however, that the pendulum of popular culture may be swinging back toward control by media organizations.

German sociologists Theodor Adorno and Max Horkheimer referred to popular culture as the "culture industry," contrasting it with "a matter of something like a culture that arises spontaneously from the masses themselves, the contemporary form of popular art."[9] Adorno described the culture industry as imposing profit-seeking onto cultural forms, thus transforming art into commodities. He further criticized the culture industry for manipulating the public as it produced and distributed cultural products, thereby making people passive consumers, a concept challenged by social media today. Adorno, particularly concerned with loss of artistic modernism, wrote that "the culture industry is the purposeful integration of its consumers from above. It also forces a reconciliation of high and low art, which have been separated for thousands of years, a reconciliation that damages them both. High art is deprived of its seriousness because its effect is programmed; low art is put in chains and deprived of the unruly resistance inherent in it when social control was not yet total."[10] While the culture industry creates false needs addressed by capitalism, Adorno argued, people are distracted from their true needs of autonomy and creativity. Critics have challenged this theory, arguing that reality is more diverse and dynamic than Adorno believed and that people are not as manipulated as Adorno proposed.[11]

Considering Adorno's perspective in today's environment, the culture of social media emerges from the culture industry of mass media as well as organically from the masses. In today's world, the mass culture consumer is an active participant in creating and redefining culture, reinterpreting the text that has been presented. The digital age has provided consumers with many methods for communicating with others and thus becoming active, rather than passive, participants. The proverbial water cooler populated by a handful of fans has been replaced by a virtual conversation among thousands with no restrictions on time and place.

The social media revolution may strengthen popular culture as we can now more fully engage in its products. We all have a chance to witness a television event when video clips are shared online. We engage with others about our favorite celebrities through blogs, MySpace pages, or message boards. We disclose our favorite books or movies, thereby encouraging others to consume, and hopefully like, these as well. Social media, in this way, foster our fascination with popular culture.

Social media may, however, cause the decline of a shared popular culture. As people congregate in small pockets online, a strong subculture may develop among those members who may be creating their own content instead of downloading the content produced by traditional media organizations. These online subcultures, however, may fail to gain attention or relevance outside this realm and thus not enter into mainstream popular culture. Culture becomes decentralized as authority and hierarchy are defied. As *New York Daily News* culture critic David Hinckley writes, "[W]hile we have more pop culture than ever, we have less of it in common. Huge chunks of pop culture today, from hip hop to instant messaging networks, might as well exist on a separate planet from the other chunks."[12]

Our shared culture is further threatened as social media applications blur the line between public and private spaces. We can access a stranger's vacation photos on Flickr, watch a school performance on YouTube, or read the travails of a couple adopting a baby from China. As we gain admittance to these private spaces, we may lose interest in the celebrities, politicians, musicians, and athletes who exist within the public sphere. Traditional mass media organizations are certainly questioning whether they will eventually face a significant decline of interest in their products.

It remains to be seen whether traditional media conglomerates will eventually dominate in social media spaces. They have demonstrated their power and financial resources in purchasing social networking sites (or starting their own), offering production or recording contracts to breakout MySpace stars (or creating their own), or ordering the takedown of their copyrighted video clips from YouTube (to establish control on their own sites). Traditional media organizations will need to be both flexible and innovative to assert their authority among social media players.

The popularity of social media may have broader implications for popular culture if participating in social media taps into and fosters innate desires of self-expression. Although Americans are reading fewer books, according to a study by the National Endowment of the Arts, we are certainly writing more.[13] Industry tracker Bowker reported that in 2007, 400,000 books were published in the United States, up 100,000 from 2006.[14] Social media have likely spawned a creative revolution that impacts all cultural products, and not just those that can be read, watched, or listened to on the Internet.

FROM MEDIA TO SOCIAL MEDIA

When we think of the concept of *media*, print media such as newspapers and magazines or electronic media such as television and radio may come to mind. The term *new media* refers to the use of the Internet to deliver news and advertising. Now, we have *social media*, which describes the collaborative process that creates meaning and community online through the exchange of text, photos, or videos. The term *social media* is often used interchangeably with Web 2.0, which more specifically refers to the "second generation of Internet-based services," as stated on Wikipedia and often cited by other scholars.[15]

Tim O'Reilly provided a comparison of Web 1.0 and Web 2.0 to demonstrate how Web 2.0 represents a new mindset. "Web 1.0 was the era when people could think that Netscape (a software company) was the contender for the computer industry crown," wrote O'Reilly in 2005. "Web 2.0 is the era when people are recognizing that leadership in the computer industry has passed from traditional software companies to a new kind of Internet service company."[16]

The personal Web sites, Ofoto, and directories of Web 1.0 are now blogs, Flickr, and tagging in Web 2.0.[17] The Britannica Online is now Wikipedia, the collaborative encyclopedia. In a *MediaPost* commentary, Rob Crumpler describes social media as being "socially-charged."[18] He continues by saying, "Because publishing power has been democratized and content is easily syndicated and shared with a few clicks of the mouse, it has become highly specific and meaningful to its readers in a way the old-school 'one-to-many' publishing model could never hope to achieve." Kevin Kelly, in a 2005 *Wired* article, declared Web 2.0 a "bottom-up takeover."[19] "This impulse for participation has upended the economy and is steadily turning the sphere of social networking—smart mobs, hive minds, and collaborative action—into the main event," Kelly writes.[20] The words Sun Microsystems's John Gage said in 1988, which have since become a Silicon Valley mantra—"the network is the computer"—provide a way of thinking about computing whereby the network, not the hardware, is relevant.[21]

This introduction will describe the software developments that made social media possible and define the many forms of social media to be discussed in the following chapters, including blogs, video-sharing sites, social networks, message boards, and social news sites. It is important to remember that although these social media forms are being discussed separately, the lines between them are often blurred because one application can be combined with another. For example, bloggers often post videos from video-sharing sites, and social networkers often write blogs and post videos. The various social media applications provide users with ways to easily integrate content from many different sources.

BLOGS

Web logs, now commonly referred to as blogs, are characterized by reverse chronological entries of text, video, audio, or photos. The number of blogs tracked by Technorati was more than 70 million in April 2007,[22] but it is likely that only 15.5 million are active.[23] In 2006, Technorati reported that 175,000 new blogs were being launched every day.[24] Technorati lists 4,822 blogs about pop culture alone.

Long before Merriam-Webster named *blog* the word of the year in 2004, early forms of blogs existed, often as compilations of Web links.[25] Catapulting the explosion of blogs was the release of free blogging software by Pitas.com and Blogger.com, both in 1999.[26] These services offer users a free and simple interface for coding and designing a blog. The Pitas.com story begins with Toronto programmer Andrew Smales, who sought to build a community of online diarists in 1999. His blogging software was a by-product of this vision, as it was intended to help facilitate the journaling process. In December 1999, Smales's online community Diaryland had 4,600 members with about 100 new members joining every day.[27]

Although Pitas.com debuted just one month before Blogger, it was Blogger that skyrocketed to the top of the most popular blogging software list. Created in August 1999 by Evan Williams, Paul Bausch, and Meg Hourihan, Blogger differentiated itself from Pitas.com by allowing the option of storing the blog on the user's own server, rather than a remote server. Blogger is now owned by Google.[28]

Blogging would not have flourished today if not for the development of RSS, an initialism for really simple syndication. RSS allows for data broken down into discrete items to be syndicated on the Web, and RSS feeds make it possible to receive news stories, blog entries, and podcasts in a news aggregator.[29] Using XML scripting, RSS emerged in 1999 as a blend of Dave Winer's "Really Simple Syndication" technology and Netscape's "Rich Site Summary."[30] Netscape, not interested in further pursuing RSS development, left Winer to develop the technology through his company Userland.[31]

VIDEO-SHARING

After the video-sharing site YouTube was founded by PayPal employees Chad Hurley, Steve Chen, and Jawed Karim in 2005, it became the fastest growing site on the Web for the first half of 2006, according to Nielsen//NetRatings.[32] YouTube allows its users, whether amateurs or professionals, to post videos for public viewing and commentary, and videos are downloaded at a rate of 100 million per day.[33] In just a little over a year after the public preview of YouTube in May 2005 and less than a year after its official debut in November 2005, YouTube was purchased by Google for $1.65 billion in stock.[34]

A comScore Video Metrix report revealed that U.S. users viewed almost 15 billion online videos in January 2009 with Google properties, including YouTube, representing almost 43% of that total.[35] YouTube alone accounted for 6.3 billion videos viewed by 101 million viewers, surpassing 100 million viewers for the first time. Trailing significantly in second place is MySpace, where 54.1 million unique users viewed 473 million videos. Across all sites, the average user watched 101 videos during the month, spending an average of 356 minutes watching videos.

Although YouTube has the largest market share among video sites and receives a great deal of media attention, other video-sharing sites are establishing a niche in the marketplace. Google already had, and still maintains, a video site called Google Video prior to its purchase of YouTube. Other competitors include Blip.tv, Vimeo, Hulu, Yahoo! Video, CollegeHumor.com, imeem, Veoh, and Funny or Die.

Technology advances helped spur the creation and uploading of user-generated videos, providing more content to entertain the growing user base. Prior to the launch of YouTube and other sites, videos would have to be hosted on a user's own Web site, a process that required technical sophistication, or on a site that charged monthly fees for the service. Lower costs for Web site operators that host videos sparked the launch of many sites, such as YouTube, that host videos for free.[36]

The introduction of smaller digital video cameras also changed the industry. The pervasiveness of digital cameras has led to more digital video being shot— 34 million gigabytes in 2005 as compared to 24 million gigabytes in 2004, according to research firm IDC.[37] In 2007 Pure Digital introduced the Flip Video camera, a reasonably priced camera that records about 30 minutes of video and has a USB port that plugs directly into a computer.[38] This product, with its built-in software allowing a video to be uploaded directly to YouTube, is targeted to adults not as comfortable as the younger set at filming from their cell phones.[39]

SOCIAL NETWORKS

Although MySpace and Facebook hold the two top spots for social networking sites in terms of members, hundreds of social networks are in existence, including LinkedIn, Bebo, Tribe.net, Cyworld, and Friendster.[40] Nicole Ellison and danah boyd (lowercase intentional) provide a definition of social networks: "We define social network sites as Web-based services that allow individuals to (1) construct a public or semi-public profile within a bounded system, (2) articulate a list of other users with whom they share a connection, and (3) view and traverse their list of connections and those made by others within the system."[41]

Launched in 1997, Sixdegrees.com was the first social networking site to combine all the features of modern social networks within one platform, although many of these features were previously available on other sites.[42] Earlier dating and community sites had user profiles; AIM offered a way to keep track of friends; and Classmates.com allowed users to connect with alums from their high schools or colleges, adding profiles and friends lists years later.[43] Sixdegrees.com met its demise in 2000, possibly because the extensive networks of its users' offline friends were not likely to be online.[44]

Between 1997 and 2001, several social networks followed in the footsteps of Sixdegrees.com by combining profiles and publicly-available friends lists, including Community Connect's AsianAvenue, BlackPlanet, and MiGente, which all target a specific racial or ethnic group. LiveJournal allowed people to "friend" bloggers and follow their posts shortly after its 1999 launch. The social networking phenomenon exploded worldwide as the Korean Cyworld and the Swedish LunarStorm were launched.[45]

Ryze, Tribe.net, LinkedIn, and Friendster were all founded by various people connected personally and professionally. Although Ryze floundered, Tribe.net attracted a niche community, and LinkedIn became the predominant business networking site. Friendster had significant initial success, but later lost ground to new competitors. Before attracting press attention, Friendster had already acquired 300,000 users.[46] Boyd described the downfall of Friendster as a result of server and database issues that caused site problems and the change in culture created by the blitz of new users after the site received media attention.[47]

Social networking has exploded in popularity since 2003, dominated by the growth of MySpace. Founded by Tom Anderson and Chris DeWolfe, MySpace went online in August 2003 and had its official launch in early 2004.[48] The site's popularity skyrocketed through 2004 and by July 2005, when Rupert Murdoch's News Corp paid $580 million in cash for the site, MySpace had 17 million unique monthly visitors.[49]

Just one year later in July 2006, with 46 million unique monthly visitors, the social networking phenomenon reached a milestone as MySpace became the most visited site on the Web, garnering 4.46 percent of all Internet visits.[50] By June 2007, the numbers reached 53 million visitors a month, according to Nielsen//NetRatings.[51] A March 2009 report by Nielsen estimated MySpace's global unique audience for December 2008 to be 81 million.[52] In August of 2006, MySpace registered its 100 millionth user, while the number of total users rose to over 116 million in October 2006 and to 172 million by April 2007.[53,54]

Facebook has also experienced a rapid rise to popular adoption, as it expanded its membership pool from Harvard students to Ivy League students, all college students, high school students, and then anyone who wanted to join. Founded by Mark Zuckerberg and several friends at Harvard, the site now has over 150 million active users, with more than 70% of those users residing outside the United States.[55] A 2009 Nielsen study found that Facebook surpassed MySpace in terms of the global unique audience in December 2008, with Facebook being visited by 108.3 million users that month compared to MySpace's 81 million.[56] Zuckerberg commented in an interview that if Facebook were a country, it would rank eighth in population worldwide, ahead of Japan, Russia, and Nigeria.[57] The site generated over $210 million in advertising revenues in 2008, according to eMarketer.[58]

Social networks allow users to build profiles to express themselves with a strong emphasis on networking with friends. Many social networks incorporate other social media features, including shared video or photos and blogging. Similarly, many social media sites have added social networking features, including video-sharing site YouTube and photo-sharing site Flickr.

MESSAGE BOARDS

Predating the emergence of the World Wide Web by more than 10 years, the first bulletin board system (BBS) was founded in 1978. Other common names for BBSs are message boards, Web forums, discussion boards, electronic discussion boards, discussion forums, or forums. Characteristic of message boards are threaded discussions, which contain a topic and its subsequent replies. Although bulletin boards are not generally included in Web 2.0 lists, they have evolved to include such social media applications as member profiles and are sometimes a tool themselves on blogs or social networks such as MySpace. Message boards continue to serve as important online communities where much conversation about pop culture is occurring.

Developed by Ward Christensen and Randy Suess during the Great Blizzard of Chicago, the Computerized Bulletin Board System was patterned after the standard cork bulletin boards used at their computer club meeting place.[59] Suess developed the hardware, and Christensen managed the software, but the idea was

Christensen's.[60] Bulletin boards required a modem, and Dennis Hayes, who later formed the companies D.C. Hayes Associates and Hayes Microcomputer Products, had invented a computer-controllable internal modem that was available at the time. Christensen's development of the file transfer protocol MODEM.ASM, later modified by Keith Peterson and renamed XModem, was also necessary for BBS implementation.[61]

Usenet groups followed in 1980 and offered threaded discussions similar to bulletin boards, but with sequentially stored posts. Unique to Usenet groups is that posts are not stored on a central server, but among a large conglomeration of servers that store and exchange messages. Messages are read from and posted to users' local servers by their ISPs and then exchanged with other users as requested.

Posts to Usenet are placed in categories called newsgroups. The 1987 restructuring of newsgroups led to the establishment of the following seven hierarchies: comp.* (computers), misc.* (miscellaneous), news.* (current events), rec.* (recreation and entertainment), sci.* (science), soc.* (social), and talk.* (controversial topics). In the mid-1990s, humanities.* (fine arts, literature, and philosophy) was added to the Big Seven to accommodate the surge in Internet traffic. Another newsgroup, alt.* (specialized discussions), was added shortly after the 1987 restructuring, but it is not subject to the rules of the Big 8 Management Board. Usenet is still in existence today, but uses the Internet as its transfer system instead of UUCP (Unix to Unix Copy Program) architecture. As dial-up modem speeds improved, bulletin boards grew in popularity. In the early 1990s, BBSs allowed access to Usenet, ftpmail, and SMTP (Simple Mail Transfer Protocol).

SOCIAL NEWS

Social news sites like Digg and Reddit allow users to not only submit stories or other content from the Web, but also vote for stories that—in the terminology of Digg—they "digg." Precursors to these social news sites include Slashdot, a site that primarily focuses on technology news and utilizes editors to select news stories submitted by users.

Digg, founded in December 2004 after Kevin Rose, Jay Adelson, Owen Byrne, and Ron Gorodetzky began experimenting with the concept in October 2004, allows users to "digg" or "bury" a user-submitted story, providing a means for stories with the most "diggs" to be featured as top stories.[62] Digg conveniently sorts stories with the most "diggs" and demotes those stories users want "buried." The site transforms news into a social media experience by cataloguing users' diggs onto their personal profiles and providing RSS feeds for users to share suggestions with friends.[63] Users can also participate in the friends system, whereby the stories of select fellow users are shared, followed, and trusted.[64]

The next year, recent University of Virginia graduates Steve Huffman and Alexis Ohanian launched Reddit, a social news site that uses an "arrow up" and "arrow down" system in order to raise or lower the prominence of a story.[65] Users who post stories that are popular with others acquire "karma points," which can elevate future postings.[66] The site was acquired by Condé Nast in October 2006 for an undisclosed sum.[67]

Digg dominates the category of social news sites. In January 2009, Digg had 24.2 million unique visitors, according to Quantcast. Digg's audience is also younger than other social news sites, with 38% of all users between the ages of 18–34, and has a higher percentage of males (59%) than females. The site is particularly easy to browse with the ability to divide content into a variety of categories, such as Science, Lifestyle, World, and Sports, and also see the top stories over a variety of timeframes. In 2008, the most popular story (with 47,734 diggs) was a blog post by Digg founder Kevin Rose about the willingness of Digg to continue to post stories with a single code to play HD-DVD videos in Linux despite the fact the Digg was facing a cease-and-desist order.

SUMMARY

The exponential growth of each of these social media applications can be tied to the point at which they reached critical mass. After early adopters shared their videos, profiles, stories, blogs, or comments with their friends, they inspired these friends to do the same. As more users create more content, they attract more people.

The early chapters of this book will introduce the practice of blogging and discuss blogs about celebrities and television shows, celebrities who blog, and bloggers who become celebrities in their own right. The next section will illustrate how video-sharing sites create celebrities, host mashups using popular culture content, and change television-viewing behavior. The next two sections on social networking and messages boards will add to the understanding of how fans connect with musicians, movies, and favorite television shows as well as other fans within the realm of the Web. The final section will discuss how social media define and influence news reporting and are situated into the plots of television programs and other cultural products. The implications of social media usage on popular culture will also be explored throughout all chapters.

This book includes many well-known and not-so-well-known highlights from the social media realm, interviews with players in the social media realm as well as with users who are engaging in social media, data and statistics from key industry organizations and research firms, and hopefully, provocative insight into the impact of social media on popular culture.

Chapter 1

THE STALKERAZZI:
STALKING STARS IN THE BLOGOSPHERE

Before the emergence of social media, the reputations of celebrities could be managed by publicists who provided fodder for tabloids, arranged exclusive interviews, and coordinated photo shoots. The rise of celebrity gossip blogs such as TMZ.com, Dlisted, Defamer, and PerezHilton.com heralded a transformation whereby the lives of celebrities are chronicled 24/7 with unbridled fervor and seemingly unabashed concern for privacy. As a result, publicists have less control over the public persona of their clients.

Celebrity gossip bloggers as well as media outlets, journalists, and photographers are on the rise. Consumers also have an expanded repertoire of technology for accessing celebrity news from the Internet to cell phones. As a result, celebrity reporting generates a great deal of revenue.[1] Paparazzi who photograph Britney Spears rake in approximately $4 million a year, about 20% of the total paparazzi revenue, while her escapades generate about $110 million to $120 million a year for the economy, as estimated by *Portfolio* magazine.[2] Celebrity reporting has become an accepted part of the news, with the antics of celebrities showing up in venerable mainstream media outlets, such as the *CBS Evening News* and the *New York Times*.

This chapter will review the evolution of celebrity gossip and entertainment news media, including magazines, television programs, and blogs. Reporting conventions of blogs and traditional media outlets will be compared. Key celebrity gossip blogs will then be examined to demonstrate the level of microdetail provided in the coverage of celebrities. Finally, the implications of gossip blogging will be discussed, including the creation of an environment where consumers feel a sense of entitlement to celebrity information and where celebrities no longer have any vestiges of privacy. This practice of presenting every move of celebrities may change public interest in following the lives of the rich and famous. When the public cannot escape into the fantasy of a fabulous celebrity life, the appeal of celebrity may be lost.

THE RISE OF CELEBRITY GOSSIP REPORTING

The reporting of gossip about celebrities and other important people has a long and sordid past, possibly starting as long ago as 1500 B.C. when the citizens of Mesopotamia documented on cuneiform tablets an affair between the mayor and a married woman.[3] The tale of modern celebrity gossip, however, begins with the Industrial Revolution and the penny press in the 1830s when reporters mostly relied on official sources and continues with society columns in the late 1800s when reporters described the fabulous lives of the wealthy.

In the 1920s, Walter Winchell introduced his *New York Graphic* column, which exhibited a combination of news in the style of society columns but with more scandalous, unofficial information. Reflecting his background in vaudeville, Winchell's columns focused on the New York City theater district.[4] The success of Winchell's column, which later moved to the *New York Mirror,* inspired other newspapers to follow suit. The People page was introduced in *Time* magazine in 1926 to chronicle the lives of celebrities, including entertainers. Although entertainment news had received attention in *Time* prior to 1926, it had not been contained in a special section of the magazine until then.[5]

When Italian actor Rudolph Valentino died August 24, 1926, tabloids such as the *Daily News* were criticized for covering this celebrity death much more extensively than that of former Harvard president Charles Eliot, who had died two days prior. As Simon Michael Bessie wrote in 1938, "To this group, as to the masses throughout the nation, Rudolph Valentino was a passionate expression of the glamour and romance so fervently desired and so hopelessly unrealized in their lives."[6] Tabloid coverage prompted more than 100,000 to attend Valentino's funeral, creating a need for riot police on horseback to control the crowd.[7]

By the 1930s and 1940s, celebrity gossip was reported alongside the news, with most papers carrying at least one gossip column and many carrying more.[8] Winchell's success blossomed after World War II, and his weekly reach at the height of his popularity extended to about two-thirds of all Americans who listened to his radio show or watched his television appearances on the new ABC-TV network.[9] In the 1930s, more than 49 tabloid papers flourished with news, features, gossip, and sports, lacking the sensationalism of predecessors such as Winchell's former employer, the *New York Graphic*, which closed in 1932.[10] Publicists worked with these gossip columnists, providing stories of romance or lavish lifestyles (whether true or concocted) to enhance the star power of a celebrity. By the 1950s, the ranks of full-time Hollywood reporters numbered more than 400.[11]

The 1950s saw the introduction of *Confidential*, a magazine known for its details about Hollywood scandals. Publisher Robert Harrison grew its circulation from 150,000 to 3.7 million an issue in three years, mostly through newsstand sales of magazines with sensational headlines.[12] Again, like with gossip columns, the popularity of *Confidential* spurred copycats such as *Inside Story, Top Secret*, and *Hush-Hush*. In sharp contrast to past reporting that exalted Hollywood players, these magazines reported Hollywood's scandals and secrets. Popular exposés of the day focused on homosexuality, race issues, and Communism.[13]

A turning point in celebrity gossip reporting occurred when the movie industry, so scandalized by the coverage of their stars in *Confidential*, sought help from public officials, prompting California Attorney General Edmund Brown and the State of California to sue *Confidential* for "conspiracy to commit criminal libel."[14] A deadlocked jury prompted the need for a new trial, but in the end, Harrison, who was both emotionally and financially drained, agreed to a plea bargain whereby he would publish only flattering stories of celebrities.[15]

In 1952, the *New York Enquirer*, purchased by Generoso Pope Jr., was revamped to detail the scandalous New York underworld. Although full of stories of grisly crimes and political dealings, the paper did not discuss any scandals related to the mob, CIA, or Sophia Loren per the request of Pope.[16] After taking the paper national in 1957, Pope renamed it the *National Enquirer*.[17] Imitators soon followed in the late 1950s and early 1960s, including *National Exposure*, *National Mirror*, and *National Limelight*.[18] The focus on the paper changed in the late 1950s to include stories of common people and celebrities among the horrific and shocking crimes and then again in the mid-1960s when stories of gore were dropped so the magazine would appeal more to the supermarket shoppers so critical to sales growth after many newsstands closed.[19] A growing threat by the Teamsters forced Pope to move his operations to Lantana, Fla., in 1971 where he had a printing press in nearby Pompano Beach.[20] The *National Enquirer* remains based in Lantana to this day, an area now referred to as "Tabloid Valley."

Movies released during the 1950s reflected public fascination with the gossip industry. *Scandal Inc.* and *Slander*, both released in 1956, criticized the gossip magazine industry. In *Scandal, Inc.*, Robert Hutton's character, Brad Cameron, threatens a reporter who has written a scandalous story about him. After the reporter is found dead and Cameron is charged with murder, the eventual trial leads to the clearing of the charges and restoration of the good reputation of Cameron. In *Slander*, the publisher of a magazine by the same name attempts to blackmail a children's television performer and the childhood friend of a female movie star with information about his jail time for armed robbery. *The Sweet Smell of Success*, released in theaters in 1957, depicted the sordid relationship between press agents and gossip columnists, including a Walter Winchell character played by Burt Lancaster.[21]

Television programs were also beginning to embrace the style of exposé magazines in their treatment of celebrity guests. *Night Beat*, hosted by Mike Wallace, premiered on WABC in New York in October 1956. As Jeannette Walls describes in her book *Dish: The Inside Story on the World of Gossip*, "Every morning, blurry-eyed New Yorkers were abuzz over what some stumbling, stuttering movie star or government official or society swell had confessed under Wallace's relentless interrogation."[22] After the program went national in 1957, Wallace doggedly interviewed his guests, including former mobster and murderer Mickey Cohen, who called Los Angeles Police Chief Bill Parker a "sadistic degenerate," and journalist Drew Pearson, who described how John F. Kennedy's *Profiles in Courage* was ghostwritten by speechwriter Ted Sorensen. Wallace's approach drew much ire, contempt, and threats of lawsuits from the people who were disgraced by Wallace's guests, finally dissolving into a lack of support for Wallace by ABC executives and the cancellation of the show in the summer of 1958.[23]

When *Time* covered the launch of its spin-off *People* magazine in 1974, *Time* founder Henry R. Luce declared, "*Time* didn't start this emphasis on stories about people; the Bible did."[24] The goal of the magazine was to cover people— the "famous," the "unsung," and the "neglected"—rather than the issues of the day.[25] Kurt Anderson of the *New York Times* describes *People* as "the first major American magazine predicated on the basic Winchellian (and later Warholian) principle that fame—15-minute Baby Jessica fame, Ken Lay fame, Jay-Z fame, John Ashcroft fame, Julia Robert fame, whatever—differs only in magnitude, and that fame is inherently interesting and desirable."[26] *People* has been described as the most successful magazine to be introduced in the United States in 70 years and today has the highest subscription rate of any magazine.[27] Jeff Jarvis described in a *New York Times* article how *People* heralded a shift where "gossip stopped being mere gossip and became an industry."[28] Gossip had indeed become a commodity traded between publicists and journalists. The *New York Post*'s Page Six column, for example, deals with publicists who are willing to provide salacious tidbits about celebrities who are not their clients to earn positive mentions for their own clients.[29]

Also in 1974, Rupert Murdoch launched *Star*, after an unsuccessful bid to buy the *National Enquirer* from Pope. The retooling of the magazine in 1976 resulted in an increased focus on celebrities, but in a less garish manner than that of the *Enquirer*. Pope responded by introducing a full-color format, spending $30 million on an advertising campaign that spawned the "Enquiring Minds Want to Know" slogan, and introducing the *Weekly World News* for the more bizarre stories, freeing the *Enquirer* to report more celebrity stories.[30]

The television equivalent of celebrity magazines emerged in the 1980s. *Entertainment Tonight* has enjoyed decades of success since its 1981 introduction as the first daily entertainment news program.[31] The program also holds the title of the first syndicated program to be delivered by daily satellite feed to local stations.[32] In recent years, *ET* has been criticized for being more salacious and sensational, reporting on Chelsea Clinton's love life or Hollywood's reaction to the discovery of Capitol Hill intern Chandra Levy's body. *Access Hollywood* and *Extra* soon joined the ranks of television entertainment programs.

The 1990s saw the launch of several new entertainment magazines. Targeted to a younger, more smart-alecky generation is *Entertainment Weekly*, which debuted in 1990. Joining *InStyle*, which coves the fashion, beauty, and home styles of the stars, and *Vanity Fair*, known for its breathtaking photography and more in-depth reporting, *Entertainment Weekly* is one of the five most successful new magazines of the past two decades.[33] The 1990s also saw 24/7 coverage of entertainment news on networks such as E!, which offers red-carpet coverage, daily entertainment news programs, and programs that focus on celebrities.

Some predicted that after 9/11, the reign of celebrity journalism would crumble as our attention would be focused on more significant matters. As Anderson writes, "It was going to be impossible henceforth for any thinking, feeling American to watch the Golden Globes or even think about the *National Enquirer*."[34] Ken Baker of *Us Weekly* pointed to 9/11 as a critical time for celebrity journalism in an interview with *Christian Science Monitor* reporter Ethan Gilsdorf, "[Readers] didn't go away from escaping. They embraced escaping . . . I don't know if you can tie it to 9/11, but that's when our business took off."[35] Now, years after 9/11, we have been thrust into an even more celebrity-focused world within the realm of social media.

ENTERTAINMENT MAGAZINE TRENDS

U.S. sales of *Life and Style*, *In Touch*, *Star*, and *People*, four popular celebrity magazines, were flagging the second half of 2007, according to the Audit Bureau of Circulations.[36] Weak sales may indicate a declining interest in celebrity gossip or the hemorrhage of readers to other sources of celebrity gossip. Popular celebrity gossip blogs may be gaining traction at the expense of the old guard of gossip journalism, providing a reason for declining circulation numbers. Amidst difficult economic times for the magazine industry, *People* and *Us Weekly* lost staff and reassigned others to their Web sites. When *People's* owner Time Inc. faced cuts in January 2007, for example, *People* lost four bureaus and 40 employees.

The ABC numbers for the second half of 2007 show an upward sales trend for *Us Weekly* and *OK!*[37] The way *Us Weekly* has responded to industry changes may explain how it thwarted the declining sales trend of the industry. The magazine maintains an active Web presence at usmagazine.com, where in addition to celebrity news and videos, users can also participate in quizzes or polls, play games, or watch videos. The site attracts an estimated 1 million viewers a month.[38] Others have credited excessive coverage of Britney Spears in *Us Weekly* and *OK!* for their strong circulation in the midst of the declining sales of competitors' magazines. The pop star landed on the cover of *OK!* 54 times in the 103 issues between January 2006 and January 2008.[39]

These two magazines also heralded a new approach to celebrity photography that differed drastically from the white glove treatment their predecessors offered the stars. As *New York Times* writer Virginia Heffernan explains, "[T]hey didn't only go for red-carpet fashion photos, or the gotchas that come along once in a lifetime: Gary Hart with Donna Rice, Kate Moss with cocaine. Instead they focused on the mundane: stars in supermarkets, dog parks, parking lots. In all that natural light they looked indistinct, sometimes homely."[40]

The weekly entertainment magazine industry faces the challenge of weekly news cycles and products that are printed days before hitting newsstands. In the world of celebrities, much can happen in a few days. In February 2007, when former Guess model and reality show star Anna Nicole Smith died on a Thursday, *People* magazine hit the newsstands the next day with a lead story about Lisa Nowak, the NASA astronaut involved in a love triangle who drove from Texas to Florida to confront the other woman. *Us Weekly's* edition that week featured Reese Witherspoon and "Revenge Diets."[41] Consumers have begun to question the value delivered by weekly magazines in this age of lightning-speed online publishing. At one time, these magazines cornered the non-television market, offering in-depth coverage and color photography. Today, they will need to redefine their scope in order to remain relevant.

The print publishing world is now devoting more resources to Web sites as circulation and therefore, advertising revenues slump. As *New York* magazine writer Vanessa Grigoriadis explains, "This has made for wholesale changes within magazines, including our own, with Web departments, a few years ago considered a convenient place to dump unimpressive employees, now led by the favored."[42]

ENTERTAINMENT TELEVISION TRENDS

Entertainment television is also challenged to remain competitive in this new environment. *Access Hollywood*, for example, uploads its show daily to the satellite feed by 1 p.m. Pacific time. Any news in the intervening hours requires last-minute updates. In the case of the early-afternoon death of Anna Nicole Smith, *Access Hollywood* staff worked for two hours to add the story to their program, sending reporters based in Burbank to Florida and hiring stringers based in Florida.[43]

Programs like *Access Hollywood* and *Entertainment Tonight* are keenly aware of the eyeballs they are losing to irreverent blogs like TMZ.com and PerezHilton.com; in response, *Access Hollywood* revamped its Web site in January 2008 in an attempt to blend gossip blog-style reporting with television journalism standards.[44] The site also includes social networking, an improved video player, a variety of games, and more interactive features.[45] Additionally, breaking news is now posted online instead of being held for the program broadcast.[46]

The entertainment programs still draw higher ratings offline than daily, and even monthly, visits to the online products, and the leader in one arena is not necessarily the leader in the other. *Entertainment Tonight*, for example, had an average of 7.4 million viewers a night in November 2007, with *Access Hollywood* averaging 3.6 million viewers during the same time period. *Access Hollywood's* online efforts at AccessHollywood.com have given them an edge over *Entertainment Tonight*, however, with 1.5 million visits during the month of November 2007 (a number that had doubled during 2007), compared to ETOnline.com's 577,000 visitors.[47] In fact, AccessHollywood.com has more traffic than any other entertainment program's Web presence, according to comScore Media Metrix, including ExtraTV, The InsiderOnline.com, and InsideEdition.com, which all rank lower than both AccessHollywood.com and ETOnline.com.[48] AccessHollywood.com benefits from its links on MSNBC.com and relationship with Yahoo! where it maintains a content relationship with omg!, the entertainment channel on Yahoo!

With its high television ratings, *ET* does have a better opportunity than other programs to use its television program to promote its Web site; in contrast, *Access Hollywood* uses its Web site as a way to promote the television program.[49] As Brian Stelter notes in a *New York Times* article, "For years, television shows treated the Web as a secondary product to promote the daily broadcast, but it turned out that simply repackaging television segments did not prompt visitors to keep returning. What did work, it turned out, were bold photos, snappy headlines, and a sense of urgency, as conveyed through perpetually scrolling 'updates.' "[50] Page Albiniak of *Broadcasting and Cable* also advocates the use of fresh Web content to help television ratings.[51]

ENTERTAINMENT WEB TRENDS

The discussion of entertainment magazines and television programs naturally leads to a description of how the Internet has changed the entertainment business, particularly with respect to its impact on the growth of gossip reporting.[52] The Internet allows people to connect with celebrity content at any time of the day or night. The extensive availability of digital photography and video to everyone with a modern cell phone has further exacerbated the growth of content. Consumers are also using their cell phones and PDAs to receive breaking entertainment stories. Lawrence Mitchell Garrison of *PRWeek* described 2005 as the year we witnessed "the rise of the cult of celebrity to unprecedented heights."[53] Celebrity-obsessed blogs, Web sites, and even new magazines entered the scene and began to attract audiences. In 2007, approximately 19 million users were visiting entertainment sites every month.[54] This obsession soon led to an onslaught of entertainment blogs, many of which cover celebrities with snarky irreverence.

By September 2008, a total of 1,202 celebrity gossip blogs were in existence, according to Internet tracker Hitwise, a number that had doubled in the previous three years.[55] Some, however, were created as a hobby and compile information from similar sources, therefore not differentiating themselves in the marketplace to the point where the sites can command an audience and earn significant advertising revenue. A number of gossip blogs, however, are attracting a large following and generating income.

In February 2007, a sample of 19 celebrity gossip Web sites saw their unique audience size increase 40% from February 2006, according to Nielsen// NetRatings.[56] The top five sites in terms of unique audience were TMZ.com, People.com, E! Online, PerezHilton.com, and EW.com.[57] Some highly-trafficked entertainment blogs ranked by Web information company Alexa include PerezHilton.com (#444 in overall traffic rank for all blogs), TMZ.com (#575), egotastic (#1,058), the Superficial (#1,535), Dlisted (#2,215), Gawker (#2,282),

PopSugar (#3,299), IDontLikeYouInThatWay.com (#3,626), X17online (#3,799), Defamer (#6,693), justjared (#9,239), Pink is the New Blog (#10,531), and Jossip (#33,540).[58] Many of these blogs and their founders will be profiled in the next chapter.

Hitwise ranked PerezHilton.com as the sixth most popular blog in the Blogs and Personal Web sites category for the week ending June 21, 2008, but noted PerezHilton.com was the most visited individual blog Web site, following heavy-hitters MySpace Blogs and Blogger.[59] In terms of numbers, PerezHilton.com had 1.7 million unique visitors in the United States for May 2007, according to both comScore and Nielsen//NetRatings.[60] Technorati's list of favorite blogs in September 2008 places PerezHilton.com at #43 and competitor TMZ.com at #97.[61]

TMZ.com differentiated itself at the onset through video, a technique quickly followed by other entertainment blogs with an effect like "flipping through a live-action issue of *Star* magazine."[62] In November 2007, TMZ.com was drawing the highest number of visits among all entertainment news sites at 10.2 million, followed by omg! at 9.5 million.[63] The entertainment news category saw a 5% jump in visitors, up to 52.7 million, from June 2008 to July 2008, fueled by the celebrity news of Brangelina's twins and Christie Brinkley's bitter divorce proceedings. By July 2008, omg! had surpassed TMZ.com for the top spot with 16 million visitors (a 19% increase), followed by TMZ.com with 9.7 million (a 9% increase) and People.com with 8.8 million (a 4% increase).[64]

Gossip blogs are also important for niche audiences that do not get the coverage in mainstream media demanded by those audiences.[65] African-American audiences connect to Media Take Out, Concrete Loop, and Young, Black, and Fabulous for gossip about a spectrum of black celebrities and not just the superstars who receive coverage in other gossip blogs. These three blogs are among the 10 most searched gossip blogs by Yahoo! users, according to the Yahoo Buzz Index.[66] Gossip blog Jossip attempted to attract some of the African-American audience by launching its own spin-off blog, Stereohyped, as part of its network of blogs.

Media conglomerates are recognizing the potential of celebrity blogs and are starting to acquire them. CBS, for example, paid $10 million for Dot .Spotter.com, self-billed as "The Pulse of Pop Culture." This blog, which at the time was attracting just 350,000 visitors a month, does not even compare to the most popular celebrity blogs in terms of traffic.[67] In 2009, News Corp introduced gossip and entertainment site Daily Fill, and Microsoft's MSN with BermanBraun Interactive debuted a similar site called WonderWall.

Some of the pioneers of online news, mostly extensions of traditional news media products, are losing ground to relative newcomers, namely blog networks with lower overhead costs. Although some industry experts predict the recession will bring more advertising dollars to blogs, where the targeting capabilities and low advertising costs might be attractive to advertisers, others have noticed an advertising slump. Gawker Media, for example, made the decision in October 2008 to lay off 19 staffers as a result of declining advertising revenues.[68]

BLOG REPORTING STYLE

Blogs have been the recipient of much exaltation as well as denigration. Torill Mortensen depicts blogs in the following manner:

> A true-born child of the computer medium, the weblog may have its roots in the research journal, the ship's log, the private diary, and the newspapers, all at the same time. But like a mongrel hunting the dark alleys of the digital city, the weblog is nothing if not adaptive and unique at the same time. No fancy thoroughbred this . . . but a bastard child of all personal writing, breeding wildly as it meets others of its ilk online.[69]

In an essay, Gawker Media founder Nick Denton described how bloggers are not the first group to be denigrated for threatening civilized discourse. Media moguls who are now glorified for their shrewd business decisions as they built empires include Rupert Murdoch, who established the Fox network through trash television programming, and William Randolph Hearst, who used yellow journalism tactics to create political conflict surrounding the Spanish-American War.[70]

Several marked differences exist between gossip blogs and entertainment magazines. First, gossip bloggers are not journalists and do not have access to the celebrities in the same way journalists do. Although change is underway here, bloggers often need the mainstream media to do the fieldwork for them. Many bloggers link to stories from traditional media, adding their own commentary. Blogging also changes the relationship between the blogger and the publicist as bloggers do not necessarily treat celebrities with respect to gain access. Mark Lisanti of Defamer spoke with *CNN Presents* and described the relationship between bloggers and publicists, "The thing about dealing with publicists is . . . their job is to trade the access to their clients for coverage. And since we have no need for access to their clients, we don't have to do any kind of trades to get the information."[71]

A concept related to access is the exclusive. Several major entertainment magazines have paid millions for exclusive photo opportunities that typically fall into one of two categories: celebrity babies and celebrity weddings. When *People* magazine purchased the North American rights to the first photos of Shiloh Jolie-Pitt, the magazine provided a teaser photo to the tabloids knowing they would run it as a cover photo, a strategy designed to generate publicity a few days before *People* released its edition that included the full spread of intimate family photos.[72]

What *People* magazine did not anticipate was how bloggers would jump on the opportunity to obtain copies of the photos through less than ethical means.

Gawker, PerezHilton.com, and many other blogs and Web sites published the photos before the release of *People*, some stealing the photos from a bootleg *Hello!* magazine that owned the British rights and some reported to be taken from copies of *People* that were stolen prior to distribution.[73] Three outcomes of blogger use of exclusive photos prior to publication are suggested by experts in a *New York Times* article by Julie Bosman. One consequence is that the publication of photos by bloggers can drum up publicity for the magazine, thereby increasing sales. A second possible outcome is that the bootleg photos depress sales of the magazine because potential readers have already seen the photos. Finally, there might be no impact on newsstand sales because blog readers are not necessarily the same audience as magazine readers.[74]

After Carol Burnett successfully sued the *National Enquirer* for libel in 1981, the tabloid industry became cautious in its coverage of celebrities, shying away from statements that may be considered defamatory.[75] Many of the magazines approach celebrities with a starstruck perspective—showing their wonderful love lives, children, homes, and vacations. A 1988 study of the *National Enquirer*, *Star*, *Globe*, and *National Examiner* by Jack Levin, Amita Mody-Debarau, and Arnold Arluke found that the majority of tabloid stories examined had a positive tone.[76] Celebrity blogs are not as kind. Omar Wasow of the *Today* show explained in a *Boston Globe* interview how this practice works: "In the mainstream media there is often a sense of propriety. 'We don't want to offend a celebrity. We want that person to be on a cover' . . . You end up with the traditional media being co-opted to some degree by the industry they're covering. One of the things that the Internet offers is these outsider voices that can be much more critical and independent."[77] Many gossip bloggers, operating outside the institution of journalism, have different motivations and, lacking dependence on relationships with publicists, do not have an obligation to fawn over celebrities.

Although the tabloids hint "that those who are famous, rich, and beautiful have their problems too,"[78] the celebrity bloggers revel in schadenfreude, or the enjoyment of another's misfortune. The blogs offer the latest celebrity news, raw and unfiltered. The Smoking Gun, for example, is known for its mug shots and reproduced documents, such as a letter from a movie producer rebuking Lindsay Lohan for her bad behavior, the suicide notes of the D.C. Madam, or the catering rider for the Foo Fighters. After reading enough stories of celebrities who fall from grace, one may begin to realize that fame is ephemeral and that celebrities are not worthy of such unbridled adoration. As student journalist LaShelle Turner writes, "The good thing is celebrity bloggers can curb our envy of the rich and famous. At least the world cannot see all the mistakes us regular people make every day."[79] Others believe that scandals help us relate better to celebrities.[80]

The gossip bloggers also seek to expose the secrets of celebrities. Perez Hilton revels in his outing of gay celebrities, most notably 'N Sync performer Lance Bass and actor Neil Patrick Harris.[81] Private lives are difficult to hide when shutter-bugs are everywhere and publicists, through their relationships with key journalists, cannot provide a complete wall of protection.

The celebrity blogs also specialize in the reporting of the mundane, which raises the question of whether celebrities should be afforded some degree of privacy when they are performing such tasks as picking up children from school, walking their dogs, or grabbing a latte from Starbucks. Karen Von Hahn shares this viewpoint: "The puppetmeisters of this new art form are, of course, tabloid editors, whose fascination with images of stars picking their teeth or putting coins in the parking meter has reached such obsessive levels that we have lost all sense of what qualifies as newsworthy, let alone entertaining."[82] The sample of celebrity articles in the study by Levin, Mody-Debarau, and Arluke showed that 98% described mundane or insignificant events.[83] The focus on the mundane is even more prevalent on the Internet, with its limitless availability of screenspace for photos, videos, and text. But this emphasis is not without its critics, and TMZ.com is one blog that has been the target of much of it. As Jessica Coen explains in a *New York Times* article, "Detractors claim that TMZ is lowering the already low standards of celebrity journalism because it will show the most banal footage."[84] As long as blog readers continue to watch these videos, these non-stories will be a mainstay of online celebrity coverage.

Britney Spears, Lindsay Lohan, and Paris Hilton are among a select group of celebrities whose stories attract significant Web hits in the blogosphere, resulting is relentless pursuit by photographers and videographers eager to capture any behavior—whether mundane or outrageous. Spears has been caught on camera having her head shaved, being admitted to the hospital under psychological distress, and taking an impromptu Pacific dip in her underwear, but photos have also surfaced online of such ordinary activities as Spears walking to the bathroom while in a restaurant with her father.

Leo Braudy, interviewed for a *New York Times* article, notes that the more removed celebrities seem from ordinary life, the more the public is interested in the intimate details of their lives.[85] Virginia Heffernan describes how "the magazines taught me to care (about the mundane), and mistake the new unkempt images for intimacy, if intimacy is something I might achieve by rooming with a celebrity at a mental hospital."[86] However mundane, our appetite for details of celebrity lives may not be satiated, but perhaps we start to see them as regular people, and more precisely, people that we really know.

The subtext of the mundane celebrity photos may be that the stars are just like us. As Fred Schroeder indicates, "unflattering candid shots of disheveled beauties, of heroes caught off-guard in a scuffle and of close-ups disclosing warts, wens, wrinkles and overweight" show us that famous people are not as perfect as they seem on screen.[87] Emily Gould, in a *New York Times* article, explains, "Supermarket tabloids and gossip columns still sell the illusion that stars live in a different world from the rest of us; but the Internet has created a new reality, and we're all living in it together."[88] This reality helps us feel better about our unglamorous lives when we realize that the glamour of celebrities is often screen magic.

Unlike traditional journalists, bloggers do not shy away from rumor or hearsay. "Not so long ago, celebrity gossip was a moribund art form, domesticated by punch-pulling softies like Liz Smith, neutered by the red-carpet suckbots of *Entertainment Tonight*," writes Greg Beato in a featurewell.com article published in Canada's *National Post*. "But then the Web came along to resurrect it. Visual, voyeuristic, convivial to rumour and speculation, the Internet is to gossip what sheep dung is to azaleas."[89] Defamer's Lisanti described to CNN how Defamer will post rumor or hearsay, making fact-checking not as important as it is in mainstream media. He added, "You know, we don't need to spend the whole day fact-checking a rumor, when you can put it up. And then, if it gets debunked, you can immediately say, 'Well, we heard this isn't true.' "[90] In contrast to bloggers, journalists who work for news organizations often tread much more carefully in their reporting by confirming sources and checking facts, practices that take time. Syracuse University professor Bob Thompson, quoted in a *Toronto Star* article, offers a suggestion for traditional media: "The mainstream media has to keep its cool in light of all of this; they have to continue to do their jobs, to confirm developments with credible sources, and to give each story due diligence."[91] Although blogs can delete anything found later to be falsified, news organizations do not have that same option because the news is already in print or has already been aired.

The venerable gossip columnist Liz Smith declared in a 2006 article that "nobody can compete with the bloggers."[92] The challenge of keeping an item secret until the newspaper hits the newsstands is an idea of the past. Now bloggers are breaking and updating stories throughout the day. The stories are accessible on demand, include raw footage, and often lack the commentary or explanation that would be provided in traditional media.

POWER OF THE PEOPLE

The Internet erodes the relationship between celebrities and entertainment media that has existed comfortably since the beginning of celebrity coverage. Publicists provide information about clients to build relationships with media outlets in an attempt to garner positive news coverage of their clients. These tidbits might include vacation plans, love interests, favorite designers, beauty regimens, or preferred beverages. The blogs use the power of people to discover this information on their own, pushing publicists to the sidelines, with one widely-criticized tool being the Gawker Stalker Map.

The Gawker Stalker Map, spawned from popular blog Gawker, allows anonymous citizens to post celebrity sightings around New York City, often to much disdain by those who are stalked. Celeb-watchers can use Gawker Stalker, with its mapped, dated, and time-stamped postings, to monitor the movement of celebrities among the streets of New York City. On one day, for example, Heidi Klum and Seal were spotted walking down Bleeker Street, Mischa Barton was seen in a Duane Reade at Park Avenue and 22nd Street, and Alec Baldwin was found eating at Equinox on Broadway.

Emily Gould of Gawker, appearing on *Larry King Live*, was verbally attacked by fill-in host Jimmy Kimmel, who had been described in the Gawker Stalker Map as "visibly drunk and talking loud."[93] As Gould explains, "Our sightings anger the rich and famous because it's impossible for them to control their coverage by an unlimited number of anonymous writers the way they can with the smallish cadre of reporters in the mainstream news media."[94]

Some might question the veracity of such reports. Can the "truth" be found in the information provided by celebrity publicists and the staged photo opportunities that occur when publicists tip off the paparazzi? Or is the "truth" found in unexpected sightings by regular people who describe these experiences online? Maybe the "truth" is somewhere between. Adds Gould, "The stalker map sightings aren't verified or vetted by publicists, and we won't publish sightings that seem to come from publicists, though we receive many. Our posts are written by ordinary people with no obligation to tone down their insults in order to maintain access to a celebrity, as gossip reporters must."[95] This practice may hurt celebrities, who may expose a less-than-favorable public persona, and the publicists, who can no longer control complete access to their employers.

Photos published on celebrity blogs might also be the product of so-called *citizen paparazzi*, who are often granted access to celebrity events that keep professional photographers at bay or just happen to encounter celebrities in public places. These amateurs need only a cell phone camera, a great shot, and an interested media outlet to get published or broadcast, sometimes for cash and other times for no fee. The McDonald's patron in Toronto, for example, who captured a drunken Ashlee Simpson on his cell phone, sold the video to CTV in Canada.[96] The video popped up everywhere from entertainment news programs to blogs. The high demand for fresh content combined with the ubiquity of digital cameras that can handle large files has led to an attempt by many regular people to make a few bucks off these celebrities or possibly attract a great deal of attention for themselves should they capture a truly unique shot.

STORIES FROM THE BLOGOSPHERE

Reviewing some of the most popular celebrity blogs illustrates the stories that are captivating readers. A review of PerezHilton.com over several days in June 2008 revealed stories about Julia Roberts not cooperating with photogs while on the red carpet for a movie premiere, rapper 50 Cent being issued a restraining order by his baby mama, Jada Pinkett Smith on the red carpet being asked whether husband Will and Charlize Theron were having an affair, the desperation of

Brooke Hogan who sought bookings from her MySpace blog, Denise Richards walking toward a courtroom with her attorneys, and the chest infection of Amy Winehouse. Photos showed Rhys Ifans throwing a beer bottle at paparazzi, Sarah Jessica Parker walking on a New York City sidewalk with son James Wilkie, Khloe Kardashian in an unflattering sweatsuit, and a 60-pound lighter Kristen Johnson.

TMZ.com incorporates much stalkerazzi footage into its Web site, featuring a video of *Super Size Me* author Morgan Spurlock outside The Ivy in Los Angeles (yes, he had a supersized meal) and John Mayer walking to his New York City gym during September 2008. Also featured on the site are photos of celebrity dropouts; mugshots of Ryan O'Neal and son Redmond, who were both booked on suspicion of narcotics possession; and a mugshot of the son of Lauri Waring of *Real Housewives of Orange County*, who was arrested for possession of heroin and ecstasy and an intent to sell. In January 2009, featured stories included a Long Island home being rented by Brad Pitt and Angelina Jolie, post-baby bikini photos of Brazilian supermodel Alessandra Ambrosiok, and photos of Julia Roberts at the Taj Mahal with a bindi on her forehead.

The Superficial emphasizes our superficial obsession with celebrities. Kim Kardashian was the focus of several posts, including her appearance on *Dancing with the Stars* and some candid shots in tight pants. Stories about the future of Hugh Hefner and girlfriend Holly Madison with some red carpet photos, the delay of Britney Spears's upcoming album with candid shots of Britney walking outside, and Jenna Jameson's pregnancy were also featured on the site in September 2008. Back again in January 2009 was Kim Kardashian in a story about her Razzie nomination. Other posts included a story about an Oscar nomination for the late Heath Ledger, bikini photos of former Hefner girlfriend Bridget Marquardt, photos of Brad Pitt with an unzipped fly, and photos from a FILA modeling shoot featuring Paris Hilton.

IMPLICATIONS OF A CELEBRITY-OBSESSED SOCIETY

Celebrity blogs raise a number of questions for the future of gossip reporting. One issue is whether they lead to an oversaturation of celebrity news, which may curb demand. In contrast, the personal details shared in entertainment stories may fuel the perception of increased access to celebrities and a certain entitlement to know everything about their lives.[97]

Our culture is reflecting changing attitudes toward fame, but it is unclear whether media or consumers are driving this shift. A popular MySpace profile or YouTube video can bring instant fame as can an appearance on one of the many reality television shows. Fame has become a desirable characteristic among many young people of today, possibly because it seems so attainable.[98]

But celebrity coverage also shows the downside to fame. As Turner describes, "The one good thing is celebrity voyeurism does show us how effortlessly and fleeting modern day fame can be. One minute you're the Internet darling and the next day you're the laughing stock of the World Wide Web. Traffic tickets, bad relationships, or trips to rehab and jail are no longer personal and private matters that most of us get to keep private."[99] It is unlikely, however, that the potential problems associated with fame will deter those who aspire to be famous or end the practice of celebrity worship.

Chapter 2

THE BLOGEBRITIES:
WIELDING THE POWER OF THE KEYSTROKE

Celebrity news is a hot commodity in the blogosphere. Whether a break-up, make-up, hospitalization, suspected baby bump, drunk-driving arrest, or romantic rendezvous, bloggers chronicle the escapades of celebrities faster, more furiously, and often more flippantly than traditional media outlets. To stand out from the competition, a blog must create a distinct brand image. This image further helps parlay the online audience into an offline audience for brand extensions of the blog into traditional media content, such as a television program. Some of the top celebrity gossip bloggers have become celebrities in their own right as they have created a brand identity for themselves. In this way, they too have become a brand. This chapter will explore how these online and offline efforts are integrated to further enhance the brand of the gossip blog. What these examples show is that a personality or brand can be formed online that has appeal to not just a niche online following, but a mainstream audience as well.

Blogs are gaining respect as they attract talent from the realm of print journalism—including many former or aspiring newspaper and magazine journalists who have joined the blogging ranks. Recent graduates and out-of-work journalists are flooding the marketplace and are willing to be snapped up by a blog and paid the low wages of the field of journalism. The competitive and declining job market of journalism has forced aspiring journalists to publish their work online to get the clips needed to launch future careers in mainstream media. Some out-of-work journalists use blogging to stay in the industry. Others have chosen to leave successful journalism careers for new opportunities online. This chapter will also highlight bloggers who have made successful shifts between blogs and mainstream media and the resulting legitimization of the blog as an important medium. At the same time, as the distinction between bloggers and mainstream journalists is blurred, bloggers look less like mavericks, creating a new meaning for the practice of blogging.

THE EARLY DAYS OF GLITTERATI

Much like some bloggers in modern times, the gossip columnists and journalists who covered celebrities in the days before the Internet had a long tradition of becoming famous in their own right through their associations with celebrities. Columnist Walter Winchell may have been the first celebrity journalist to become famous himself.[1] Hedda Hopper and Louella Parsons are also among the early "glitterati," becoming known in the 1940s for moving among and writing about the famous in their gossip columns.[2] Celebrity editors, such as *Vanity Fair*'s Tina Brown and successor Graydon Carter, and television interviewers, such as Larry King and Carson Daly, are also famous by association.[3]

For the gossip columnists and journalists who cover the scandals of Hollywood, the stories behind the reporting of celebrity gossip are almost as scandalous, demonstrating the high stakes nature of celebrity reporting. Believing Parsons had orchestrated his firing from the *Los Angeles Examiner*, rival gossip columnist Sidney Skolsky bit Parsons on the arm.[4] Big-game hunter Richard Weldy shot *Confidential* publisher Robert Harrison in the Dominican Republic after a story ran that suggested John Wayne had stolen Weldy's wife.[5] During the *Confidential* trial, Polly Gould, who had gathered information about Joan Crawford's sex life, died from an overdose of barbiturates, and Mae West's former lover Albert White, who also provided details for the story "Open Door Policy" about West's sex life, was found drowned in a bathtub.[6] *Confidential* editor Francesca de Scaffa, who blabbed about her affair with Clark Gable, attempted suicide in Mexico.[7] Former *Confidential* editor Howard Rushmore, who became a witness for the prosecution in the magazine's libel trial, became depressed after the decline of the gossip magazine business and shot his wife and then himself in a cab while riding up Madison Avenue.[8] After *New York Enquirer* publisher Gene Pope spent the evening with family friend and "Prime Minister of the Underworld" Frank Costello, Costello was shot in the face outside his apartment on Central Park West.[9]

Other gossip columnists came onto the scene in later decades, including Liz Smith, former assistant to gossip columnist Igor Cassini. Smith emerged in 1976 in her own right with her *Daily News* column. Former beauty queen Cindy Adams launched her gossip column in the *New York Post* in 1981, a position she still has today. Richard Johnson, who has managed Page Six of the *New York Post* since 1985, still reports gossip in the old-school manner of his predecessors. Others following in this tradition include online journalist Matt Drudge, *New York* magazine's Michael Wolff, and *Variety* editor and columnist Peter Bart.[10]

BLOG POWER

Technorati's top blog list once included many tech bloggers; now those are dropping in ranking for blogs from the realms of politics and pop culture, according to CEO David Sifry.[11] Celebrity gossip bloggers have acquired some of the power over celebrity discourse that was once controlled by gossip columnists and entertainment reporters. As LaShelle Turner wrote for the Student Operated Press, "[Bloggers] can make or break a career with just a click of a mouse button. Celebrity blogger gurus, like Perez Hilton, get to say all the nasty things we want to say out loud, but are too afraid to because we do not want to be judged in same harsh manner. The best part of it is stars actually care what bloggers say about them. Bloggers brag how celebs call and plead them not to run stories or post pics."[12]

But what is it that celebrity bloggers are doing? Some blogs offer little more than rehashing and trashing as they pick up stories from mainstream media and add commentary. Some bloggers act like bullies who demean celebrities to make themselves feel better, while readers have fostered this behavior with their clicks. Sara Tenenbaum of PopMatters compares gossip blogs to literature from earlier times: "Blogs have become the online expression of American egalitarianism in relation to those placed on a pedestal by way of their participation in public entertainment. And just as Oscar Wilde and Voltaire lampooned the aristocracy in 19th and 17th century Europe, so too do Michael K, Trent Vanegas, and Perez Hilton sit down each day at their computers and turn their keen eyes to the celebrity aristocracy among us."[13] As mainstream media recognizes the ability of these bloggers to command an audience, some have achieved success in other media.

As Simon Dumenco of *Advertising Age* writes of the early days of blogging, "The best bloggers could become almost instantly beloved cult media figures. They were, it seemed, self-actualized mavericks who'd thrown off (or never even taken on) the shackles of media-conglomerate overlords. They were gutsy, outspoken, fearless, funny—the polar opposite of the MSM."[14] By 2008, however, "many pseudo-celebrity bloggers have finally figured out that they're as disposable—as cog-in-a-wheel-ish—as any of the cubicle-dwelling suckers populating old-media combines," writes Dumenco.[15]

FROM A-LIST TO C-LIST

Clive Thompson wrote of the fallacy of blogging democracy in *New York* magazine. "It doesn't matter if you're a nobody from the sticks or a well-connected Harvard grad. If you launch a witty blog in a sexy niche, if you're good at scrounging for news nuggets, and if you're dedicated enough to post around the clock—well, there's nothing separating you from the big successful bloggers, right?"[16] Yet, as Thompson is quick to point out, certain bloggers in popular niche categories have already ascended to A-list status, limiting opportunities for others.[17]

New York University instructor Clay Shirky has explored the social dynamics of the Web through a study of blogs. His research counts the links from other sources, known as inbound links, as indicators of a blog's popularity. Multiple blogs with inbound links to a certain blog will increase readers of the linked blog exponentially. This measure has been confirmed through other studies that have found that inbound links are 80% accurate as predictors of traffic.[18]

Shirky's research revealed that a small number of blogs enjoy a significant number of inbound links (A-List), while some blogs have a few sites pointing toward them (B-List) and many blogs remain virtually ignored (C-List).[19] Those A-listers will be able to command a large share of advertising revenue based on their large audiences, while the also-rans will never achieve blogging success. Plotting this relationship on a graph reveals a common phenomenon—a power-law distribution—that also applies to the world's wealth, employment of actors, or even sexual activity. Just as money begets more money and fame begets more fame, readers beget more readers. It's a natural tendency of human nature to believe that if enough people think a blog is worth reading, then it is. Shirky calls this phenomenon the preference premium, explaining that, "later users come into an environment shaped by earlier users; the thousand-and-first user will not be selecting blogs at random, but will rather be affected, even if unconsciously, by the preference premiums built up in the system previously."[20]

Shirky explains how, as the number of blogs increases, the gap between the top blog and the median blog grows. Additionally, because the power law curve is heavily weighted with top blogs, many more blogs are below average. He describes how the continuous entry of new blogs and new readers makes it increasingly more difficult to launch a successful blog. New readers will add more traffic to top blogs, and new blogs will receive increasingly less traffic. He predicts that the top bloggers will morph into broadcasters, distributing information but not being able to engage readers in two-way communication.

As much as the C-Listers envy the success of A-Listers, they also ride their coattails to try to lift themselves out of the gutter. If a C-lister provides an interesting tidbit to an A-list blog, which is then published, the C-lister might get an acknowledgment and link back to the C-list blog. Even better is a listing in a blogroll, which is a permanent link available from every page of the blog.[21]

The riches that come with being a well-known blogger are generally derived from one of three business models. In one model, a passionate blogger grows an audience and begins to sell advertising to support his or her blogging. Often a one-person operation, the blogger is responsible for locating the latest news, generating original content, and providing commentary. Almost anyone can start a celebrity news blog, and many who have done so have little formal training in journalism. The most successful example of this model is tech blog Boing Boing, staffed by four former *Wired* editors and writers, most notably Mark Frauenfelder and Cory Doctorow, all of whom work part-time. The most expensive ads on the blog cost $8,000 a week.[22] In a variation of this model, a blogger can partner with a mainstream media organization, bringing the blog's audience to the media organization and vice versa.

In the second model, a rather shotgun approach to blogging, a blogger develops many niche blogs with the hopes that one or two will build a following. Jason Calacanis of Weblogs, Inc. is recognized as being the master of this approach. The blog founder can easily pay cheap rates to writers eager to build their own portfolios while raking in advertising dollars. Calacanis struck it big with Engadget, which AOL later purchased for $25 million.[23]

The third model involves blogs designed for an upscale audience with the intent of attracting advertisers to this desirable target. The standard-bearer of this model is Nick Denton's Gawker Media, which has launched 14 blogs, all targeted to wealthy, educated readers.[24] Writers are paid notoriously low salaries and are given high productivity goals. The Huffington Post is also included in this category in which a marketer plans, launches, and promotes a blog.

Now that the A-list has been established for the celebrity gossip category, witty postings are not enough to attract a following. Attempting to stand out from the crowd of seemingly similar blogs to gain readers, advertisers, and future career opportunities for the blogger is much more difficult today. Just like any new mainstream media venture, a blogger must use public relations strategies to gain media attention. And just as branding helps to sell a product, it can also help to sell the blog. The blogger may be an integral, and for some the most critical, part of the blog's brand image.

David Hauslaib of the blog Jossip offers this advice in an interview with *PRWeek* to anyone who thinks they can compete with established blogs. "You have to bust your butt like any other media firm or outlet. I do think there is a lot of growth even in my category, the celebrity media category, there is still room for quality new blogs out there. So I think it's worth taking a stab. But it's foolish to think that if you give yourself 30 or 60 days you are going to be at the top of the game."[25]

Several A-list celebrity bloggers who have become celebrities themselves for mingling and reporting on celebrities are called blogebrities. Associated Press reporter Erin Carlson used this term to describe blogger Perez Hilton in a story on November 6, 2006.[26] These bloggers seemed to have cornered the market on celebrity dirt, making millions while others are scraping by. Gossip bloggers offer a somewhat snarky and irreverent treatment of celebrities, not something that would be found within mainstream magazines such as *People* or entertainment programs such as *Entertainment Tonight*, which tend to treat celebrities with more respect. PerezHilton.com, Pink is the New Blog, Jossip, PopSugar, and Gawker are just a few of the celebrity gossip blogs that have branded themselves through their unique blogging style as well as the founder's persona. Others include egotastic, IsThisHappening, the Superficial, Dlisted, IDontLike YouInThatWay.com, Defamer, and justjared. Other blogs, often corporate-owned, do not need to rely on the personality of the blogger. TMZ.com is one blog that falls into this category. An examination of these blogs reveals how a branded blog can be used as a springboard for additional opportunities for the blog or the blogger. The next section reviews several of these blogs, categorizing the blogger as a passionate maverick, a sophisticated marketer, or a corporate communicator.

Passionate Mavericks

Perez Hilton

Possibly the most well-known and eccentric gossip blog persona is the man known as Perez Hilton. After being fired from his writing job at *Star* magazine, Mario Armando Lavandeira Jr. focused his energy on a blog called pagesixsixsix.com, the name a reference to the popular *New York Post* gossip column.[27] After being sued by the *Post*, Lavandeira adopted the public persona Perez Hilton, and thus the blog PerezHilton.com was born.[28]

This self-described "Queen of All Media" and "Queen of Mean" differentiates his blog with his signature nasty scribbles on paparazzi photos and cruel monikers to refer to celebrities. Jake Gyllenhall is "GyllenHo" and Kate Moss is "Cokate," for example. *Rolling Stone* writer Erik Hedegaard describes PerezHilton.com as "lowest-common-denominator stuff, totally debasing, totally now, totally like he's getting even with those kids who pinched the fat on his back, and it's turned him into a sensation."[29] In 2005, *The Insider* named PerezHilton.com "Hollywood's Most Hated Web Site."[30] Even celebrities decry his modis operandi. Tara Reid, Nicole Richie, and *Desperate Housewives'* Jesse Metcalfe have all lobbed verbal attacks against him. In 2007, DJ Samatha Ronson was suing Lavandeira for calling her a "toxic" friend to Lindsay Lohan.[31] All this attention landed Lavandeira on *Time* magazine's list of the 100 Most Influential People and he was named the number one Web celebrity in *Fortune* magazine.[32]

Lavandeira's blog has catapulted him to international fame in a way that no other gossip blogger has been able to accomplish. He landed a deal with VH1 to host six specials related to awards programs called *What Perez Sez*.[33] He also made a guest appearance on FX's *Dirt*, a show about celebrity tabloids; guest hosted on *The View*; and appeared as a contestant on *Celebrity Rap Superstar*. He also worked the red carpet for the MTV Australia Video Music Awards show in 2007.[34] In 2008, ABC Radio Networks reached a deal with "C" Student Entertainment to syndicate a twice-daily Perez Hilton entertainment feature.[35] When the deal was announced with a press release, affiliates in 7 of the 10 largest radio markets had already signed on.

Lavandeira's status has awarded him other writing opportunities, including his own column on ITV.com, the Web site of the largest commercial network in London. The column coincides with the airing of *Gossip Girl* and runs alongside content for the program. He has done previous work for ITV, most notably conducting red carpet interviews at the Brit Awards, which ran on ITV2.[36] PerezHilton.com has also served as a springboard for Lavandeira to book and promote new artists. His first concert—promoted merely with a blog post—sold out in just four hours.[37] He is also influential in driving album sales after blogging about artists, most notably Lebanese-born singer/songwriter Mika, whose debut album sold 50,000 copies in the first two weeks.[38]

Pink Is the New Blog

Trent Vanegas of Pink is the New Blog (pinkisthenewblog.com), who hosted his blog at trent.blogspot.com until June 2008, uses his blog to post paparazzi photos and descriptions of his own celebrity encounters. Like Perez Hilton, Vanegas also has his own signature style, using large pink block letters to add commentary to paparazzi photos and photographing celebrities wearing PinkIsTheNewBlog.com stickers. Described as "an upbeat, outgoing gay man with a fondness for most of the celebrities he covers," Vanegas treats celebrities with a style that rests comfortably between vicious and indulgent.[39]

Launched in June 2004 from Detroit, Mich., the former teacher was barely attracting 200 viewers a day for his first two years.[40] When his blog was recognized by a few medium-sized New York blogs, traffic doubled and continued to grow to approximately 1 million page views a month.[41] Vanegas now resides in Los Angeles to be close to the celebrity scene. *Details* magazine bestowed upon him the honor of one of the "50 under 42" in 2006 and *Blender* magazine named him as one of their Hot 100 in 2005. He is attracting attention from mainstream entertainment media, including VH1, where he taped a guest spot for *Best Week Ever*, and E! and Bravo, from whom he is fielding offers.[42]

Jossip

David Hauslaib's blogging career began while a student at Syracuse University in 2004, where he created Jossip to post amusing commentary about the escapades of Paris Hilton. Initially, Hauslaib hoped the blog would be a springboard to a future magazine career, but, as he describes in an interview with *PRWeek*, "I said too many bad things about potential employers and nobody wanted to hire me."[43] After estimating competitor Gawker's annual revenues from page view approximations and their advertising rate sheet—his guess about $1 million to as much as $2 million at the time—and noting the low overhead (e.g., journalist wages and Webhosting fees), he was inspired to move to New York City in June 2005 and make blogging his full-time job.[44] Jossip, with its slogan "the gossip's gossip sheet," is targeted to media insiders.

Although Hauslaib believed he was mimicking Gawker in many ways—the same celebrities, the same response time and frequency, and the same tongue-lashing tone—his audience was a mere 30,000 visitors a day, about 15% of Gawker's back in 2005.[45] Today, Alexa's traffic rank three-month average score (a combined measure of page views and users) for Jossip is approximately 33,000, where Gawker is ranked higher at almost 2,400 for a three-month average. These numbers demonstrate the difficulty of competing with established blogs.

In December 2005, Hauslaib moved beyond the realm of being a passionate maverick, as he is no longer in charge of daily blogging on Jossip.[46] Instead, he serves as the editorial director for his growing blog network, which now also includes Mollygood (the celebrity gossip blog), Queerty (the gay blog), and Stereohyped (the black blog). Corynne Steindler, his initial replacement who had previously served stints at *Star* and the *Daily News*,[47] took a job nine months later with the *New York Post*'s Page Six.[48] Unlike other bloggers who have used their blogging experience to launch print careers, Hauslaib expressed in an interview with *PRWeek* that he has moved away from his college dream of entering mainstream journalism because new media offer many more opportunities.[49]

Sophisticated Marketers

PopSugar

San Francisco-based PopSugar delivers news about fashion and celebrities minus the snarky attitude. Founded by Lisa and Brian Sugar in March 2005, PopSugar is now part of the Sugar Network, which includes 16 additional sites and a social network, primarily targeted to "young, hip women."[50] Sugar Publishing built its empire on a core group of loyal readers of PopSugar, who then could be targeted for the brand's other services. With Lisa Sugar now the editor-in-chief for Sugar Publishing, Molly Goodson, formerly of the blog Mollygood, now serves as the editor of PopSugar. (Interestingly, Mollygood, even without namesake Goodson at the helm, continues under the leadership of Cord Jefferson.)

PopSugar has received a nod from mainstream media in its successful recruiting of print magazine talent. Associate managing editor Nancy Einhart, for example, was previously a senior editor at the now-defunct *Business 2.0*. Other sales and editorial talent has been recruited from magazines such as *Vanity Fair*.[51]

In October 2007, TechCrunch's Michael Arrington reported that a Series A round investment from Sequoia Capital raised about $5 million for the blog network. Arrington also noted the network receives a rumored 3 million unique visitors and 20+ million page views per month.[52]

Gawker

Edited by Nick Denton, the self-described tabloid of media gossip and culture-around-the-clock is Gawker. The Gawker blog is part of Gawker Media, which now also boasts a collection of 14 blogs, with some covering the popular topics of games (Kotaku), cars (Jalopnik), and gadgets (Gizmodo) and others focusing on the gossip of the prominent industry of an American city, such as Defamer (Hollywood) and ValleyWag (Silicon Valley). The Gawker empire gets millions of page views a week, with Gawker.com alone receiving about 2.5 million, and profit estimates from advertising sales are in the range of $10–12 million a year.[53]

Founding editors Denton and Elizabeth Spiers "didn't exactly invent the blog," as Vanessa Grigoriadis writes in a *New York* magazine article, "but the tone they used for Gawker became the most important stylistic influence on the emerging field of blogging and has turned into the de facto voice of blogs today."[54] Thompson was equally as complimentary when he noted that "(Spiers) is arguably the most famous professional blogger, since she invented its dominant mode: a titillating post delivered with a snarky kicker, casual profanity, and a genuine fan-girl enthusiasm—sonnets made of dirt."[55]

Since December 2002, Gawker has focused on the rage felt by members of the creative underclass of New York City with some celebrity gossip on the side. Shaila Dewan of the *New York Times* describes Spiers's style, "Her raised-eyebrow approach to the sacred syllogisms of Manhattan culture and gossip made a blog called Gawker.com so popular that *Entertainment Weekly* called it the It blog and *The Guardian*, a British newspaper, quoted a fan as saying it was 'like living in New York without paying the rent.'"[56]

As a native Alabaman, cheerleader, and the daughter of parents who worked for the Alabama Power Company, Spiers seemed an unlikely candidate to become an outspoken critic of Manhattan media. After graduating from Duke University, she considered working for the State Department or the CIA, but ended up in New York analyzing the business plans of dot-commers. Her foray into blogging began with a blog called Capital Influx, focusing on the world of investments.[57]

Unlike Spiers, Denton's background was in journalism, most notably as a reporter for the *Financial Times*, and he had started two Web businesses prior to Gawker.[58] Finding Spiers among the ranks of financial bloggers, Denton approached her with his idea to fill a niche in the blogging landscape with a new kind of blog.[59] The result was a resounding success. Gawker received mentions as a top 50 Web site in 2003 by *Time* magazine, a best media blog in 2003 by *Forbes*, and a "Best of the Breed" online news site by the New York Media Association.[60] Spiers's many honors include being named "Best Gossip" by the *Village Voice* in 2003, a "30 Under 30" by *Institutional Investors* in 2006, and a member of the "Pop A-List" by *Interview* magazine in 2007.[61]

Although Spiers wrote about media celebrities, she did not generally mingle with them, bucking the tradition of many gossip columnists.[62] She later left Gawker to join the ranks at *New York* magazine, writing a blog called The Kicker and editing the magazine's gossip column, the Intelligencer.[63] Her next stop was as editor-in-chief of mediabistro.com, launching six new blogs for the site,[64] and then she jumped to *Fortune* to serve as a contributing writer and columnist.[65] She also founded Dead Horse Media, which publishes DealBreaker.com, AbovetheLaw.com, and Fashionista.com, targeted to the Wall Street, legal, and fashion industries, respectively.[66]

Other Gawker editors have left for positions in mainstream media, with many heading up an online component. Spiers's successor Choire Sicha left to be senior editor of the *New York Observer*, writing posts for the Daily Transom and Media Mob blogs among other duties, then returned to Gawker before leaving again to serve as editor-in-chief of *Radar*'s Web site.[67,68] His replacement after his first stint at Gawker, Jessica Coen, left for *Vanity Fair* to serve as deputy online editor and also held the position of senior news editor at *New York* magazine.[69]

Another Gawker blogger, Emily Gould, also left to explore other writing opportunities. As a hired gun for Gawker, she has been described by Dumenco as being "unwittingly cast, at 24, as an emotional exhibitionist in Nick Denton's highly profitable (for him) online version of *Survivor*." The notoriety she achieved at Gawker, Dumenco continued, left her "humbled, damaged, and bewildered."[70]

Gawker Media's other properties have spawned illustrious editors. Until February 2008, the editor of Gawker Media's Hollywood industry gossip blog Defamer was Mark Lisanti. Lisanti originally moved to Los Angeles to pursue a writing career, and his personal blog ramblings caught the attention of Gawker Media.[71] His resulting tenure at Defamer lasted four years and included about 10,000 posts.[72] Described by Rachel Abramowitz in the *Los Angeles Times* as "the newest and hottest foot soldier on the front lines of the celebrity takeover of modern culture," Lisanti gained attention for Defamer with his Tom Cruise couch-jumping montage.[73]

Will Leitch, formerly of Deadspin, the Gawker sports blog, has also attracted attention. Deadspin reached new heights of cultural influence in 2006 with Leitch's story of a supposed Chris Berman pick-up line directed to a woman wearing leather pants.[74] The story launched an inside joke of "you're with me, leather," a phrase now emblazoned on T-shirts sold on the site. Leitch is now a contributing editor for *New York* magazine, a popular destination for Gawker editors. Gina Trapani of Lifehacker, Gawker's technology and personal productivity blog, has written two Lifehacker guidebooks that serve as collections of the best tips.

The Huffington Post

Once considered a "social climber, intellectual lap dancer, and political opportunist," Arianna Huffington was married to an oil heir politician and later struck out with her own attempt at political office.[75] The author of 12 books is now best known for her blogging empire. Huffington first went online with the Web site Resignation.com, from which she launched attacks at then President Bill Clinton. Her next venture was the site ariannaonline.com.

But it was the 2005 launch of her news blog, The Huffington Post, with former Time Warner executive Ken Lerer that attracted attention and quickly became one of the most influential blogs on the Web, racking up 18 million page views a month by the end of the year and becoming the fifth most-linked-to blog worldwide.[76] The concept was to offer a liberal counterpoint to the Drudge Report, and Huff Po now receives more unique visitors than Drudge (3.7 million a month vs. 3.4 million) according to Nielsen Online, has moved up to the fourth most-linked-to blog as ranked by Technorati, and was ranked as number one on a list of the world's most powerful blogs by London's *Observer* magazine.[77]

The Huffington Post has demonstrated the power of linking and placing A-list bloggers on the blogroll. The blog also counts celebrities among its bloggers, such as John Cusack, Jamie Lee Curtis, Nora Ephron, and Ryan Reynolds, a decision that attracted attention from mainstream media. The blog is organized into sections similar to that of a newspaper, counting politics, business, and entertainment among its offerings. As the blog has grown, journalists have been brought on board to do original political reporting.[78]

This blog has not been without controversy, as most of the 1,800 bloggers are not paid, a business model that the blog defends. Some have argued that this practice is bad business, particularly in light of the fact that the blog received $10 million in funding in 2007 and earns a great deal of revenue from advertising sales.[79] Additionally, estimates of the value of the blog are as high as $200 million.[80] As Josh Wolf wrote on CNET News, "These talented writers have helped make the Huffington Post into the economic success it is quickly becoming, and to suggest that they should never share in that success seems shameful."[81] Dumenco reacted to Lerer's statements in a *USA Today* article about the financial model.

> Instead, in a moment of delusional grandeur, he chose to announce that his and Arianna's celebrity-blogger serfs will always plow for free—in exchange for not even for a bit of gristle and cold porridge, but for the PR! Excuse me?!? First of all, arguably, it's the other way around: Despite Arianna's cable-news omnipresence, it's the excellent work of such regular bloggers as Harry Shearer, Nora Ephron, and Bill Maher that gave HuffPo visibility, promotion, and distribution.[82]

The practice of paying bloggers helps to ensure that the quality of writing remains high and that the best bloggers have a reason for staying, setting up a financial model for long-term success of the blog.

Corporate Communicators

TMZ.com

The name of gossip blog TMZ.com is a reference to the "thirty mile zone," a part of Los Angeles used for location shooting. This joint venture by AOL and production company Telepictures Productions launched in November 2005 and quickly moved into the number one position among gossip blogs and even more broadly, among all entertainment news Web sites.[83] Monthly tracking data from comScore Media Metrix consistently places TMZ.com in one of the top spots for entertainment news, with approximately 9.9 million unique visitors in May 2009.[84]

TMZ credits itself with the breaking of several entertainment stories, including the end of the marriage of Britney Spears and Kevin Federline, Mel Gibson's DUI arrest, Anna Nicole Smith's sudden death, and Michael Richards's racist comments at the Laugh Factory.[85] One of the most popular TMZ videos involved an oil family scion who made a derogatory reference about a young starlet. Captured by TMZ cameraman Josh Levin, the video of Brandon Davis calling Lindsay Lohan a "firecrotch" was streamed over 1 million times.

TMZ was awarded the distinction of "one of the coolest Web sites" by *Time* in 2006 and the "Breakout Blog of 2007" by *Newsweek*. But the site is not without its detractors. The Web site Tabloid Baby facetiously named Harvey Levin as its "2007 Journalist of the Year." Tabloid Baby asked, "Who did more damage to entertainment reporting in 2007 than Harvey Levin? . . . he and his gutter operation. . . almost singlehandedly transformed Hollywood entertainment reporting into a gutter-level street battle fueled by self-hatred, jealousy, and anger, with no concern for what once determined greatness, excellence, or fame."[86] Despite the critics, the blog has become an oft-cited source by entertainment and news programs, both at the national and local levels.

TMZ.com added a feature whereby users can respond to some of the blog entries with their own audio or video comments, a tool that traditional media organizations are also exploring. *USA Today* reporter Jim Hopkins describes how the *New York Times* is allowing video letters to the editor and the *San Francisco Chronicle* is posting audio files of voice mail letters to the editor.[87] For TMZ.com, audio comments are not available for every post, only the ones likely to generate the most discussion, and are limited to 30 seconds. After some initial refining of the system, the audio comments were reintroduced for a post about Clay Aiken. They have also been used for posts about Britney Spears's "comeback" appearance on the Video Music Awards.

In a 2007 deal with Fox and Warner Bros., TMZ.com evolved into a half-hour weekday and hour-long weekend syndicated television program that premiered September 10, 2007, which was a good turn of fate as it coincided with the day after Britney Spears's embarrassing opening performance at the VMAs. *TMZ TV* features managing editor Harvey Levin as a key element of the show, serving as executive producer and host. Although many traditional news outlets have successfully established an online presence, TMZ represents the first attempt to move a successful online brand to television. Other successful online brands have attempted to delve into television, most notably eBay and iVillage, but shelved the projects.[88]

This move positions *TMZ TV* as a direct competitor to other entertainment news programs, including *Entertainment Tonight*, *The Insider*, *Access Hollywood*, and *Extra*. "*TMZ* is the new bad boy in a neighborhood that includes the more fawning *ET* and *Access Hollywood*," declares *Washington Post* reporter John Maynard.[89] *TMZ TV* differentiates itself from the other entertainment programs by not doing press junkets, red carpets, or sucking up to any other celebrity publicity attempts, according to an AP interview of Levin.[90] Although the television program toned down the snarky online persona, it still covers celebrities with humor and irreverence.

On the air six days a week, *TMZ TV* is in 98% of U.S. television markets, mostly on Fox affiliates, but also carried on other network outlets. In a unique packaging deal, the show provides entertainment content to the Web sites of the affiliate stations that air the program, which further serves to promote the show. By the end of the first month, *TMZ TV* was the top-rated show in syndication, receiving a 1.7 household rating, according to Nielsen Media Research.[91] The established *Entertainment Tonight*, in comparison, delivered a 4.8 household rating during that same period.[92] This venture has been able to translate the younger online readers of TMZ.com into a younger television demographic for *TMZ TV*. Compared to *Entertainment Tonight*, of which 61% of viewers are 50 or older, *TMZ TV* captures that same percentage of viewers aged younger than 50. *TMZ TV* also performs better than other entertainment programs among men, an often elusive television audience.[93] Now Telepictures Productions is attempting to find similar success by targeting a different demographic—moms—with the Web site MomLogic.com, from which a television show is possible.

THE FUTURE OF CELEBRITY BLOGGING

The revolving door between the journalism industry and the world of blogging has provided legitimacy for bloggers and created opportunities for them in traditional news organizations. Other bloggers have found substantial success online and have abandoned the dream of pursuing a career in traditional media. This chapter has provided countless examples of writers who have moved between the realms of blogs and traditional media organizations, with demand for online experts increasing as media organizations have recognized the importance of their online properties.

Blogs that attract a significant audience may eventually be purchased by media conglomerates. We are already witnessing entrepreneurs who are turning their blog portfolios into successful media operations as well as media organizations that are starting their own entertainment blogs. For prospective bloggers, the prospect of attracting a substantial number of readers and advertisers is bleak. The bloggers who have already established an online presence or those backed by media conglomerates are just too powerful.

Chapter 3

REALITY TELEVISION BLOGS: MAKING REALITY MORE REAL

Television is the first truly democratic culture—the first culture available to everybody and entirely governed by what the people want. The most terrifying thing is what people do want.

—Clive Barnes

B logging adds another dimension to reality television, making the programs even more real as bloggers and their readers debate the onscreen drama in the online world. As contestants are voted out for bad singing, cooking, modeling, or dancing; fight or fall in love; or form secret alliances, bloggers are online, sometimes "live blogging" (blogging as the show is broadcast), chronicling the details for their readers while adding their own commentary and context.

This chapter describes the evolution of reality television from the days of radio and early television to the rise of modern reality programs. As blogging and reality programming intersected at the beginning of the 21st century, the result was the emergence of reality television blogs, which navigate the world of reality television for viewers. This chapter will also introduce a selection of reality television blogs. Finally, this chapter will describe the gratifications readers seek from a reality television blog and how these blogs foster fan fascination with reality television.

HISTORY OF REALITY TELEVISION

Although the term *reality television* became a part of our vernacular in 2000 with the premiere of the show *Survivor*, television has always included an element of unscripted drama or entertainment involving regular people. In recent years, our fascination with ordinary people has been exploited by reality television producers seeking to capitalize on this basic human desire to watch others compete, fall in love, or live their lives. Andy Dehnart, of the blog reality blurred, described reality television as the "human drama that results from the situation its cast members are in."[1] Producers have provided viewers with much human drama through a variety of permutations of the basic reality genres.

The earliest television programs and their radio ancestors included entertainment, talk, and game shows that displayed this human element. Allen Funt's *Candid Camera*, which set up uncomfortable situations for unsuspecting people, debuted in 1948 on television, but first started as *Candid Microphone* on radio a year earlier.[2] A version of the show appeared on the air for five more decades, and with the prank genre firmly entrenched in popular television, television audiences have seen the rise of other prank reality shows, such as *Punk'd, Girls Behaving Badly*, and *The Jamie Kennedy Experiment,* and even some prank dating shows, such as *Joe Millionaire* and *My Big Fat Obnoxious Fiancé*.[3]

Early talent search shows included *Ted Mack's Original Amateur Hour* and *Arthur Godfrey's Talent Scouts*, both introduced in 1948, to allow ordinary people to present their talents and audience members to vote for the winner. Based on a similar talent show concept, *The Gong Show* presented an often-quirky performer to a panel of three judges, who would either award the performer a score or a gong. The show ran from 1976 until 1978, and then continued in syndication into the 1980s. *Star Search*, hosted by Ed McMahon, soon followed, continuing in syndication until 1995. Winners in the various categories would continue to the semi-finals and then the finals, providing a serial nature that earlier programs lacked. These shows are considered the predecessors to the more contemporary *American Idol, Nashville Star, So You Think You Can Dance, America's Best Dance Crew, Last Comic Standing,* and *America's Got Talent*, which feature ordinary people in the context of competition and elimination, with a more modern emphasis on backstory, behind-the-scenes, and, as in the case of *American Idol*, auditions. The talent genre has also spawned celebrity talent shows, such *Dancing with the Stars, Celebrity Duets,* and *Skating with the Stars.*

In television game shows during the 1950s, such as *Beat the Clock* and *Truth or Consequences*, contestants performed stunts or competed in wacky competitions to win. Other popular reality game shows included *The Arthur Murray Party*, where viewers who correctly identified a mystery dance received two free lessons at a local dance studio, and *Let's Make a Deal*, where contestants decided which of the offered deals they would accept. Game show predecessors of the modern reality television program from the 1970s included *The Dating Game* and *The Newlywed Game*, two shows where contestants not only try to win, but also reveal personal information in the process.

The game show *Queen for a Day*, which first aired on the radio in 1947 and then on television until it was canceled in 1964, was described by television critics as "a horrible example of what hits the antennas when the breadwinners are away."[4] On the show, contestants were selected based on the nature of their wishes, with finalists competing for the grand prize of having those wishes granted. Initially, wishes were "whimsical or flippant" with contestants wanting to "meet Errol Flynn, direct traffic on 42nd Street in New York, sleep on the top of the Empire State Building, or ride a camel down Fifth Avenue."[5] The show eventually evolved into a competition of the most down-and-out, hard-luck stories, with contestants expressing needs for special bicycles for ill children or cars to visit disabled husbands in the veterans' hospitals.

As reality television found its place in the family room, some viewers also found a place for a camera crew in their lives. In 1973, PBS offered a 12-part program called *An American Family*, a documentary of the private life of the Loud family who, during the seven months of filming, experienced the divorce of parents Bill and Pat and the coming-out of son Lance. The show attracted nearly 10 million viewers an episode.[6] Portable cameras and wireless microphones—now standard fare for reality television—replaced stationary cameras to better follow the action and capture the story.[7] Writer Richard Keller states, "There's no doubt that *American Family* was the inspiration for the many relationship and family-oriented reality programs that emerged in the 1990s and in the 21st century."[8] Some recent reality programs also show regular people living fascinating or extraordinary lives. MTV's *The Real World* falls into this category as does TLC's *Jon and Kate Plus Eight* and *Little People Big World* and Bravo's *The Real Housewives of Orange County*.

The series *Real People*, which ran from 1979 to 1984, featured otherwise ordinary people with unusual hobbies or occupations, a concept later copied by the early 1980s series *That's Incredible*. Later reality programs involved viewers who submitted their own footage, as in the long-running series *America's Funniest Home Videos*, which started in 1989 as an hour-long special and was picked up as a series in early 1990.

As one of the first examples of truly tabloid television, the documentary *COPS*, which premiered in 1989, follows patrol officers in a variety of cities. Predating this television show was a radio serial in the 1950s that followed Culver City, Calif., police officers on patrol.[9] Similar to the manner in which paparazzi stalk celebrities, the police officers of *COPS* are in hot pursuit of assailants. This "copumentary" needs no narration to drive the story, as the actions of the police officers speak for themselves. As Walter Podrazik notes about the show, "The most excessive offerings represented the shorthand signature of an emerging new reality genre, embracing a lurid tone of scandalous, crude, and shocking behavior."[10] Following in the tradition of *COPS* are *Lockup*, a documentary series on MSNBC that shows the harsh realities of prison life, and *Dateline NBC*'s hour-long *To Catch a Predator* investigations. Other series with "shocking" behavior soon followed as reality television moved from being a television novelty to a staple with the introduction of *The Real World*.[11]

In 1992, MTV unveiled *The Real World*, most recently set in Washington, D.C., for its 23rd season. The model for *The Real World* was a Dutch show called *Nummer 28*, which first aired in 1991. *Nummer 28* introduced many techniques that would become standard elements of reality programs, including confessionals where the cast members privately reflect on events directly to the camera and the heavy use of soundtrack music. The narration that had been prevalent in earlier shows, such as *An American Family*, is not present in *The Real World*, which instead uses cast member confessionals or the action itself to drive the story.[12]

The seven castmates, seven who live together in a house over a several-month period keep little, if anything, hidden from cameras, including arrests, public drunkenness, abortions, sexual relations, deaths of family members, pregnancy scares, and physical violence. MTV President of Programming Brian Graden described *The Real World* as "quite simply the undisputed granddaddy of modern, commercial reality television."[13] *The Real World* is just one of the 11 reality series either on the air or in production by Bunim/Murray Productions, the most in the history of the company.[14] Another popular Bunim/Murray reality program was *Road Rules*, which featured young people traveling around in an RV, solving clues, and completing missions. The reality travel genre spawned later shows including *The Amazing Race* and the one-season *Lost*.

Even home improvement programming has evolved by adopting an element of reality. Introduced in 1996, the British show *Changing Rooms*, the model for the American program *Trading Spaces*, follows two couples who trade houses so that each can remodel a room in the other couple's house. Other popular home improvement shows at the time, such as *Design on a Dime* and *Room for Change* began to introduce the actual family whose home was receiving the makeover, often shown at the beginning and during the big reveal at the end, an element of the shows that had not previously been there. On HGTV and beyond, home improvement shows have proliferated, including *Extreme Makeover: Home Edition* on ABC and *Flip this House* on A&E. This improvement reality genre more broadly includes more recent programs that feature makeovers for the body, such as *Extreme Makeover*, *Queer Eye for the Straight Guy*, *The Biggest Loser*, and *The Swan*, and makeovers for the family, such as *Supernanny* and *Nanny 911*.

According to James Poniewozik, when viewers demonstrated an interest in serial plots as well as shows about relationships, they were ready to embrace reality programming. In addition, time-shifting made possible by DVRs eliminated the demand for reruns. All those rerun time slots are now filled with reality programs. The genre particularly flourished during two Writers Guild of America strikes—one in 1988 and one from late 2007 to early 2008. After the 1988 strike, network television schedules were filled with remakes, news magazines, and reality programming, including NBC's *Unsolved Mysteries*; CBS's *High Risk*, featuring people with dangerous jobs; and ABC's *Super Model Search*.[15]

In 2000, when *Survivor* combined the concept of reality (regular people in a non-scripted drama) with the element of a game show (competing to win $1 million), the genre was completely redefined. During the summer when the networks usually dump their repeats, movies, and bad shows, CBS premiered *Survivor*, a reality show that quickly built a fan base, averaging 28 million viewers a week, and whose season finale, at 52 million viewers, drew one of the highest ratings for an original show aired in the summer.[16]

Also on the air during the summer of 2000 was *Big Brother*, a program structured somewhat like *The Real World* where contestants live in a house together, but with weekly eliminations of housemates. Like with *Survivor*, the last one standing receives a cash prize. The success of these shows launched countless other programs that copied the basic concept, including *The Mole*, where contestants attempt through challenges and observation to determine the identity of the mole with the contestant answering the fewest number of quiz questions correctly each week being eliminated; *Boot Camp*, where teams trained and competed in missions with the losing team voting out a member; and *The Amazing Race*, where pairs of contestants travel around the world and the first team to the finish line receives $1 million. *The Amazing Race*, while not a ratings heavyweight, has received numerous Emmy wins for the Best Reality-Competition Program and is the fifth longest-running reality show on the air behind *COPS*, *The Real World*, *Survivor*, and *Big Brother*.[17]

Although some reality shows are elimination contests, others are documentary-style dramas that feature the lives of celebrities. Included in the *celebreality* subgenre are *Hogan Knows Best*, *The Ozzy Osborne Show*, *Newlyweds: Nick and Jessica*, *The Anna Nicole Show*, and *The Girls Next Door*. Many of these programs air on E!, MTV, or VH1. Other reality documentaries portray people with interesting jobs, as in the programs *Miami Ink*, *The Janice Dickinson Modeling Agency*, and *Dr. 90210*. TLC and A&E are two cable networks that show programs of this type. Less glamorous job-focused reality programs include Discovery's *Deadliest Catch* and *Dirty Jobs* and the History Channel's *Ice Road Truckers*, which have been classified as "working man's reality television" by Eric Deggans.[18]

Another popular reality genre is a competition based on a talent other than singing, dancing, or skating. In *Design Star*, *The Apprentice*, *America's Next Top Model*, *Project Runway*, *Top Chef*, *Shear Genius*, *Top Design* and others, contestants showcase their talents and face a panel of judges for weekly eliminations. The winners of these shows often receive an opportunity to work in the industry that is the focus of the show, whether modeling, clothing design, or hair styling.

In the early days of television, "reality television" was a programming staple because it was live, simple, and inexpensive.[19] Viewers were intrigued because it gave them an opportunity to peer into the lives of others. Podrazik describes how reality television has remained an essential programming ingredient throughout the years. "Even as recording techniques grew more sophisticated, reality programming remained a part of the mix," Podrazik writes. "They were far less expensive to produce than heavily scripted programs with big name stars and elaborate sets. But they also remained because they featured people and activities that connected with the personal experiences of viewers."[20]

Michael Hirshorn argues that network primetime television lacks original programming concepts, "remain[ing] dominated by variants on the police procedural (*Law & Order*, *CSI*, *Criminal Minds*), in which a stock group of characters (ethnically, sexually, and generationally diverse) grapples with endless versions of the same dilemma."[21] As a counterpart, reality programs provide a commentary on race and class that is not touched by these scripted dramas and sitcoms.[22]

The criticism that is launched at many reality shows is that they celebrate exhibitionism, cruelty toward others, and self-destructive behavior, a formula that is easy to achieve because of the contestants chosen and the incessant prodding by the producers. Douglas Rushkoff describes how reality show drama is about so much more than the determination of the ultimate winner:

> *America's Next Top Model* is not really about who wins a modeling contract but rather about observing what young anorexics are willing to do to one another under the sanctioning authority of supermodel Tyra Banks. *Survivor* has never been about human ingenuity in the face of nature but about human scheming, betrayal, and selfishness in the course of competition. And *The Surreal Life*, which throws a bunch of has-beens and recovering alcoholic former child stars into a halfway house, has nothing to do with our desire to emulate celebrities. It's about watching sad people sacrifice any remaining vestige of self-respect to garner an extra few minutes of life on the tube.[23]

Despite the lack of a moral compass in some reality television programs, the genre is likely to continue as a mainstay of television programming because of its ability to attract significant ratings at little expense, as well as the possibilities for the integration of television and Web, which is discussed in the next section.

BLOGGING ABOUT REALITY TELEVISION

As reality television programming was exploding with new concepts and variations on old concepts, blogging was also on the rise. Many fans of reality television found themselves blogging about their favorite reality television programs and attracting an audience of readers interested in reading recaps, news, interviews, commentary, and other original content. This forum for expression provides both the blogger and the blog reader an opportunity to engage in a conversation about reality television. Blogs often utilize the comment feature on posts or message boards to allow readers and bloggers to interact.

The process of blogging often alters the way the blogger watches television. Instead of being a passive viewer, the blogger must actively attend to the nuances of the show. The use of DVRs or TiVo also allows the blogger to capture shows for later viewing or add visual elements, such as video and screenshots, to their blog posts.

A reality blogger becomes a critic, a reality guru, and a trusted source of information for his or her readers. But for all the rewards that come with being a reality television blogger, the job does have some drawbacks. Maintaining a successful blog requires a great deal of content and time, particularly with the writing of recaps, which are a reality blog standard. Even blog readers who watch the program will read the recap for the humorous commentary or the context provided by the blogger. Blogs will also often link to news stories about the shows or contestants. The best blogs will offer original content, including interviews with reality show contestants. For reality television bloggers, quick turnarounds are another necessity as readers expect blog entries about programs to be posted in a timely manner. As Dehnart of reality blurred explains, "Writing is a lot of work, and therefore so is blogging. But because blogging demands immediacy, there's always pressure to get to a story first, or to respond to a development on a show as immediately as possible. It's also increasingly difficult to find time to watch, follow, or even just keep track of all reality shows, because there are so many."[24] Bloggers need to be motivated and dedicated because blogging is rarely financially rewarding.

Reality television blogs fall into one of three categories. Some are run by independent bloggers, some are members of blog networks, and others are corporate-owned. Corporate ownership is a result of media organizations recognizing the value of dedicated fans who frequent reality blogs. As a result, some media organizations have created their own Web sites and blogs, and others have purchased reality blog start-ups.

Independent Reality Blogs

Independent reality bloggers are challenged by the continual need to provide fresh content to readers. For many, blogging will not be financially rewarding. Others have been able to launch a related career from their blogs.

reality blurred

The blog reality blurred (realityblurred.com), founded by self-described "writer/teacher/TV addict" Andy Dehnart in July 2000, was the first reality television blog. Dehnart discusses how the idea of the blog was conceived:

> In the summer of 2000, reality TV found its way to network TV, and as a fan of the genre, I was constantly searching for news and gossip about the new shows. Nearly every blog that existed then was more of a personal diary, but one that I read frequently, Jim Romenesko's Media News, covered a single topic: media. So, I borrowed his format and created reality blurred, primarily as a way to gather together everything I could find about reality TV. The life and audience it found because of that was definitely unexpected.[25]

Dehnart is solely responsible for the daily writing, producing, and editing of the blog's content, which includes news items about reality stars or reality shows and commentary about reality programming. Dehnart maintains that the site is not a comprehensive guide to reality television nor a recap site, although a few recaps are available. The site does not offer a message board or the comment function for additional conversation among participants. Dehnart discusses how his blog has evolved over the years:

> In the early days, I tended to link to a story and write a quick, witty (or not) response. As the site grew, I realized that part of its value was as historical record and also as a way for people to get a quick read of what was going on before they followed links to read more in-depth. So, the site became more of a digest as I started summarizing relevant parts of news stories or highlighting buried news in longer pieces. I also tried to find those stories from smaller papers, Web sites, or forums that not everyone knew about.
>
> As reality TV exploded over the following years, I had to become more selective with what I covered, and I think that's when it took on its current form as a more analytical, personality-driven column.[26]

Dehnart does not merely post links to news articles from other sources, but also adds insightful commentary from his own observations and knowledge or original content, such as interviews. The infamous *Amazing Race* couple of volatile Jonathan Baker and girlfriend-turned-wife Victoria Fuller are just one example of reality stars interviewed by Dehnart. Dehnart has also broken several reality television news stories, including the locations for two seasons of *The Real World*. For these reasons, his blog differentiates itself from the competition. As Dehnart explains:

> I don't know of any other reality TV blogs that really have a single voice, one person who drives the editorial content. reality blurred is primarily about my take on what I'm watching, reporting, or reading. A few sites or blogs do a great job of being witty and snarky constantly, but I just read those and admire them for being able to be so consistently funny. Unlike some other sites, I don't copy and paste press releases as posts, but rather, report on and discuss the contents of those press releases. I also don't watch and recap every second of every show, but rather high-light or mock the greatest and worst moments that come across my TV screen.[27]

Deemed "influential" by *Newsday*, "indispensable" by the *Chicago Tribune*, and "the most schooled blog on America's guiltiest pleasure" by the *New York Times*, reality blurred receives almost a million page views a month.[28] The audience is characterized as young (71% are 18–39) and female (66%). The blog is now part of Federated Media Publishing, which connects independent Web authors to marketers. Also part of Federated Media are the popular sites of Digg and Boing Boing.

Reality TV World

Reality TV World (realitytvworld.com) might be the most comprehensive online source of reality television news. Described on the site as having the largest reach of any independently-operated television Web site, the Massachusetts-based operation follows over 300 reality shows.[29] The home page, organized into news about people, shows, TV ratings, TV schedule, show applications, and spoilers, is full of one-line links to the rest of the story.

Not only is news provided about reality programs, but other sections also include links to other television stories and more broadly, other entertainment stories. Although the blog has the comment function disabled, it does offer message boards where almost 48,000 people are active users and thousands of messages are posted. Quantcast estimates this blog receives 358,000 readers a month. The site has been featured and cited on CBS News, MSNBC, MTV, ESPN, E!, *TV Guide*, *Entertainment Weekly*, the *New York Times*, *USA Today*, Associated Press, and Salon.[30]

Other Independents

On Vancouver-based dingoRUE (dingorue.com), Shane writes the recaps, news, and spoilers about *Survivor*, *The Amazing Race*, *The Apprentice*, *The Biggest Loser*, and more. The blog was founded in July 2006 with the purpose of covering entertainment news, but it quickly became more focused on a select group of both reality and scripted television programs.[31] Over 1,000 people subscribe to the dingoRUE RSS feed and users can leave comments on the blog posts. According to Quantcast, about 14,000 people per month visit the site.

Real Television (realtelevision.net), created by Matt Howell during the summer of 2003 to blog about *Paradise Hotel* and *Temptation Island*, relies extensively on content from other sources and provides readers a feed from Reality TV Magazine.[32] Quantcast calculates total readers per month to be approximately 4,700.

Reality Shack (realityshack.com) offers recaps, commentary, interviews, and other content for 45 reality shows. The site does not have the slick look of other reality television blogs and the site's statistics for blog post readers tend to number in the hundreds for blog posts. Carrie Grosvenor, the owner, editor, and a writer for Reality Shack, has recruited a team of volunteer writers to contribute to the site. Grosvenor is an Ontario-based freelance writer who has covered reality television and game shows for seven years.[33] Quantcast's estimate for monthly viewers is 3,900.

Reality Blogs in Blog Networks

Some reality television fans pursue blogging through an established network of blogs on a variety of topics. Just as television offers multiple channels of entertainment, so do these networks.

Reality TV Magazine

Founded by Joe Blackmon of Brentwood, Tenn., in June 2003, Reality TV Magazine (realitytvmagazine.com) provides news about reality shows, recaps, original content, and interviews. The original Web site was relaunched as a blog in late

2004, a change that caused a significant surge in readership as the blog began to reach tens of thousands of readers every day, according to a company press release.[34]

In 2008, Reality TV Magazine became part of the SheKnows network, which is a division of AtomicOnline, an online media company that connects and brands online communities.[35] SheKnows had previously added Soaps.com and LovingYou.com to their network in an attempt to expand to 100 sites from about 50 by the end of 2008.[36] The partnership may have helped grow the readership of the blog, with it now serving almost 90,000 people per month, according to Quantcast. Joe Blackmon still contributes to Reality TV Magazine under the alias of "Joe Reality."

Reality Exploits

Reality Exploits (realityexploits.com) is part of a conglomerate of more than 300 blogs on a variety of topics managed by b5media, a Toronto-based company. Lynn DeVries, who is solely responsible for the content on Reality Exploits, also writes blogs about Fergie of the Black Eyed Peas, VH1, *CSI*, *Bones*, *House*, and dancing programs, such as *Dancing with the Stars* and *Dance Wars*. Although DeVries produces a tremendous amount of content for her reality blog, she receives few comments.

The 70 entertainment blogs managed by b5media now produce feeds into the entertainment site Starked.com. Thirty bloggers create and contribute this content. The entire network of b5media blogs receives 10 million unique visitors a month, according to its Web site. Reality Exploits does not boast strong traffic, reaching only about 4,900 people per month, according to Quantcast.

Watching Reality TV

451 Press started in September 2006 with a group of 10 blogs; as of July 2007, the group maintained 329 entertainment and "edutainment" blogs, according to the company's Web site. Blogger Rachelle Thomas creates the content, consisting primarily of recaps and news, for the blog Watching Reality TV (watchingrealitytv.com). Although much content is produced, the blog generates few comments, ranging from zero to four comments per post. The site offers readers the chance to join a community and create a profile.

Bloggers are paid by 451 Press at a rate of 40% of advertising sales, and advertisers are actively sought and matched to the appropriate blog by the company. 451 Press promotes its blogs as a way to get exposure as a blogger, improve writing skills, and be a part of a community.

Corporate-Owned Reality Blogs

Some reality blogs are maintained by media conglomerates. AOL's television blog called TVSquad (tvsquad.com) also covers reality programming. MeeVee, a *TV*

Guide-like Web site, also has a reality television blog. Several blogs with independent starts are now owned by media corporations. BuddyTV is now owned by Comcast, and Bunim/Murray Productions purchased reality blog TVgasm. The advantage of these corporate-owned blogs is that they have the financial resources to hire enough writers to keep up with reality television recaps and news. They also offer original content and outstanding interviews. The shows' creators can also capitalize on the fandom they have energized through the television shows. They can also sell advertising on both television and online. For the independent bloggers who built the audience, they can walk away with the financial resources to start new projects.

TVgasm

TVgasm.com was the brainchild of Dartmouth graduates Ben Mandelker and Joe Fahs. Founded in 2004, Mandelker and Fahs produced the blog under the aliases of B-side and J-unit. Known for its snarky recaps of popular reality television shows, the blog captured the attention of *Entertainment Weekly*, dubbing TVgasm one of the top 25 Web sites. TVgasm has received mentions from just about every major media organization including the *New York Times, Los Angeles Times, USA Today, Washington Post, Details, Spin,* and *Us Weekly.*

A project in a non-majors computer science course in college prompted Mandelker and Fahs to express their shared fascination with pop culture through a Web site. The resulting project—a Web site dedicated to *Survivor: Australia*—generated both a fascination with and many opinions about the show, according to Fahs.

Fahs continued by explaining the birth of TVgasm. "Around 2004, I had lost a job and wanted to learn more about PHP and CSS, so I decided to start a blog. Ben and I had always thought about doing a TV Web site, but the ideas we had before were always very complicated. Blogging was just getting really popular, so it seemed like a good time. Ben was still trying to get his writing career started, so he had ample time to write. We had a few other friends we thought would be able to write for us, so we went with it."[37]

TVgasm's first foray into the world of reality show blogging began with recaps. Following every episode of a reality show such as *Big Brother, Survivor,* or *The Amazing Race,* the writers would post a snarky commentary that involved detailing the drama, critiquing the decisions of the contestants, or providing context from outside sources. The site eventually added recaps of non-reality shows, such as *24* and *Lost,* as well as message boards to allow members to continue the conversation away from the recaps.

The writers, being *Big Brother* fans, attracted a significant *Big Brother* following. The host of *Big Brother,* Julie Chen, was even given her own nickname by TVgasm. Dubbed "Chenbot" for her robotic movements and excessive use of the phrase "but first," her moniker garnered media attention.

Later, she admitted that she possessed a Chenbot coffee mug purchased from TVgasm.

The blog evolved from the recaps covering the favorite shows of Fahs and Mandelker without any consideration of schedule or writer assigned to the recap. "As the site got more popular and people liked our style of humor, they were always asking for our comments on plot events in shows," Fahs said. "This is when our writing really expanded and we started to perfect the TVgasm style. Eventually, we settled on our shows. This helped reduce our workload, and helped give every kind of recap a personality."[38] Later, a team of writers from the blog Tabloid Baby was hired to contribute television news and commentary. The style of Tabloid Baby was not compatible with the preferences of TVgasm readers and after 46 weeks, the team was fired.

In addition to the recaps, Mandelker and Fahs provided readers with photos of themselves with reality stars they met at an event or saw at an L.A. nightclub. In the beginning, Mandelker and Fahs blurred their own faces in these photos. As the site moved to include more video features, Mandelker and Fahs eventually revealed their physical identities to TVgasm readers. They covered *American Idol* auditions and the Big in '06 Awards; they live video-blogged television shows; they interviewed reality stars; and they investigated Laguna Beach hotspots.

The site gave Mandelker a great deal of visibility in the media. In addition to appearances on television shows such as *Today*, he was a regular panelist on *Reality Remix Weekend Round Table* on the Fox Reality Channel.

The difficulty of maintaining the TVgasm blog in terms of both content and technology eventually created an insurmountable burden for its creators. "I was doing all of the tech work and maintaining the site, but there was such demand for writing, something had to give," Fahs said. "I would have liked to have been able to hand off the tech side to people who did that for a living, but I never got to that point."[39]

Although TVgasm describes itself as the "premier independent television blog on the Internet," it was actually purchased in 2006 by Bunim/Murray Productions, producers of MTV's *The Real World* and other popular reality shows. Mandelker was hired in October 2006 by the Endeavor Agency and has set up his feature script, "Dead Girls Don't Bitch," at Wonderland Sound and Vision. Now working as a department technology analyst at UCLA, Fahs maintains his own blog at mokers.org and is a Los Angeles correspondent for gridskipper.com, which bills itself as an "urban travel guide." Several TVgasm writers, including EdHill, sg-dub, copygodd, and Umnata (now called BERJnata), jumped ship to create their own reality blog, Midseason Replacements (midseasonreplacements.com). The writer madeyoulaugh, who was involved in TVgasm when it was still managed by Mandelker and Fahs, now runs TVgasm. The Web site boasts a healthy readership, of 81,000 readers a month as estimated by Quantcast.

Television Without Pity

Television Without Pity's, with its slogan "spare the snark, spoil the networks," sought to provide snarky episode recaps with detailed analysis of the nuances for its devoted readers. The founders of the blog, Tara Ariano, Sarah D. Bunting, and David T. Cole, originally launched the blog Dawson's Wrap to blog about *Dawson's Creek*. In 2002, they broadened the coverage to more closely resemble the blog's current form and changed the name to Mighty Big TV before settling on Television Without Pity.

In 2007, the Bravo division of NBC Universal acquired TWoP, then attracting about 1 million unique visitors a month at the time, a move that doubled unique visitors to Bravo's Web properties.[40] Bravo also owns BrilliantButCancelled.com, OUTzoneTV.com, and BravoTV.com.

The founders remained as editors after the sale and at the time, plans included more recaps and the addition of audio and video.[41] The three eventually left the site in 2008 to pursue other opportunities.[42] The site is now seen by over 317,000 people a month who make approximately 8.5 million total monthly visits to the site, according to Quantcast.

BuddyTV

BuddyTV (buddytv.com) was founded in Seattle as an Internet start-up by Andy Liu and David Niu, two Wharton MBAs who had previously sold their company NetConversions to aQuantive. Perhaps best known for its extensive use of live blogging (i.e., blogging while watching a television program), the site uses an extensive group of celebrity "TVJs" who write commentaries about programs and moderate discussions using audio, video, and text. During the summer of 2007, the site was described as having 20 employees and 3 million unique visitors a month.[43]

After accepting a $250,000 loan from Charles River Ventures' Quick Start Seed Funding program in May 2007 and $2.8 million in Series A funding from Gemstar-TV Guide, BuddyTV was acquired in September 2007 by Comcast.[44] Because Comcast already owns similar site Fancast and acquired Fandango in 2007, BuddyTV is expected to be integrated into Fancast.[45]

The site covers popular reality shows, such as *American Idol*, *The Amazing Race*, and *Dancing with the Stars*, and has evolved into a television networking community. Users can create profiles and connect with other members who share favorite television programs. Quantcast estimated in 2008 that the site is visited by 1.2 million people a month for slightly more than 2 million visits.

Specialty Blogs

Other reality television blogs do an excellent job of chronicling a single series. For *Project Runway*, the blog Blogging Project Runway (bloggingprojectrunway .blogspot.com) remains the ultimate source of recaps, interviews, links, and news about the fashion designer competition show. *Laguna Beach* (lagunahookup.blogspot.com), *The Amazing Race* (tarflies.com), *American Idol* (rickey.org) written by Rickey Yaneza, and *America's Next Top Model* (community .livejournal.com/topmodel) all have specialized blogs created by fans who track each series in great detail.

GRATIFICATIONS OF REALITY BLOG READERS

Because reality show contestants have the ability to make their own decisions, the viewer may become more involved in this "real-life" drama, making reality television viewing a different experience than watching a scripted drama or sitcom. The very "real" nature of reality programs makes them all the more compelling and ripe for discussion. For every statement by Jeff Probst that the "the tribe has spoken," description by Chris Harrison of the "most dramatic rose ceremony ever," or command by Tim Gunn to "make it work," bloggers are frantically typing to re-create the scene for readers, and reality television viewers are desperate to share their opinions with other fans. As bloggers cheer on certain people, express indignation for others, or say what should have been done in the situation, readers congregate to read these opinions and share their responses. One could say that the blogs demonstrate "what happens when people stop being polite and start getting real."

Reality television allows the viewer to experience his or her fantasies vicariously through other people. These might be fantasies we wish to experience (e.g., a race around the world) or we enjoy watching others experience (e.g., a handsome bachelor whisking a girl away for a romantic date). As the viewer, we have the opportunity to become participants in the reality show, whether we become a member of the cast of *Survivor* or we vote for the next *American Idol*. We feel like we are part of the action, and we want to connect to others who are sharing this experience with us. Some blog readers may be able to achieve a kind of celebrity status within the realm of the blog through their active participation.

Tom Alderman argued on The Huffington Post blog that viewers enjoy the humiliation of reality contestants, dubbing a subsection of reality television Shame TV.[46] Alderman explained that modern viewers exhibit the notion of schadenfreude, or the ability to enjoy the misfortune of others. Much online conversation focuses on knocking down contestants. Perhaps, however, we are actually cheering for justice to prevail or integrity to be rewarded. For the best person to win, the untalented, unliked, or unnecessary must be removed.

Readers of the blog TVgasm provided feedback on how participating in the blog changed the way they watched television, how television blogs are used, and the benefits received from reading television blogs. Respondents cited a number of changes in their television viewing habits because of their participation in the TVgasm blog, including viewership of certain shows and the need to be more attuned to details while watching a show.

- Because of TVgasm I have started watching shows I would NEVER have watched before. When you read one of this site's recaps it makes you want to watch the show. I'm not sure how I watched TV without having a forum to go to afterward. Even if I don't post about a show I usually read what others thought about it so I can see a different viewpoint. —Cherie
- This blog totally dictates some of the shows I watch. There are shows that I would have never stopped at on my own and find myself watching just so I can get in on all the talk. —minda07
- It does change my viewing habits. I feel responsible to keep up with shows and I find myself jotting things down to remember later during shows like *Amazing Race* and *Big Brother* or *Survivor*. I will even get after a recapper if they ignore something I feel was vital or hilarious on the show. I also pick up shows I would never have watched on my own . . . I also TiVo shows so I can rewatch them after the recap posts. I miss stuff the first time around. I do not do this with everything . . . usually *Amazing Race* and *Top Chef* . . . I have started watching shows because of this forum . . . *Lost, Beauty and the Geek, America's Next Top Model, House*, and I am so sorry to admit, the stupid mom and daughter beauty queen show. —giffordsaz

The TVgasm blog and its message boards are used primarily by participants to first connect over the love of reality television, and then bond with others on a much more personal level.

- This site is a social gathering place as well as a place to talk TV. We all get to know each other and encourage others who stop in to join us in other threads. We have a lot of threads to read from. Some are just silly, some are serious, some are just a place to bitch or rejoice in some good news. We like to share. —chooch850
- Well, honestly people in my house don't want to discuss the programs in depth like we do here. We pull apart morals and motives and hotties and skanks. We talk about them in ways it might not be polite to in public, but you would say it with your best friend. So why do I feel the need to talk about these programs at all? Because I have found myself addicted to reality in a way I was never addicted to a sitcom or an hour drama . . . you tell me why? I have found people here I can relate to and would like to sit around and visit if we lived closer. As you can see, this forum branched away from televison and has run right up on our everyday lives. —giffordsaz
- I use this blog to talk about shows in a way that I could never talk about with colleagues and friends. I am much more honest in my opinions and brutal in my criticism, not because I feel safer behind my screen name, but because they never watch these shows or have the long, detailed conversations about them that we do. I also come here because I have made friends here; despite this primarily being a TV blog we have learned about each other. And like

most friends, we have bickered, fought, laughed, cried, and even gotten drunk with each other. Sure, we all came here originally to discuss our favorite television shows and read recaps, but we have found that the shows we loved were only a small amount of the large things we have in common. —lennonwhore

- I use this blog for many things. I am not a watcher of *Big Brother* but my computer illiterate mother is and I come on here and check the threads to tell her what other people are saying and what happened on the live feeds. I come here to vent about my parents splitting or informing everyone that I finally had a new job and that I love it. The people here are my friends and I love to hear the news about what is going on in their lives too. Chooch's adventures, Giff and her Crystal Light postings, Tink and her precious niece and nephew, Pek's love of math and toddler Pek, Jampony's love of Sci-Fi, Rach's amusing posts and how we might have been separated at birth by Gypsies, Julie's son's new chorus groupies, Peg's bluntness, LW's pantless drunken rants. That's just a few of the people here I have become invested in. I am curious what is going on with them, so much more than just sharing my views of a TV show that I watched, though that's important too. —minda07

Participants experience a range of gratifications from the blog, from access to great commentary to the opportunity to connect with others who share similar interests in television.

- The TVgasm site, or blog as you say, has the best recaps around. The writers are funny, snarky, and insightful. I enjoy reading all the recaps of my favorite shows. The Newsgasm is great. Nads does a great job of dishing us the dirt and giving us an inside look at some great events. Her news items are current and top-notch and she posts things you don't see on other sites. —chooch850
- I get a stress release from reading posts here I guess . . . (I don't read *People* magazine . . . or crap like that) . . . and sharing my crappy feelings when I have them. I find friendship . . . and I do have friends in real life . . . but who really can put up with the meanderings of my mind like they do here . . . no one. I also get a compass from others here. When I tend to rip too hard on real people, say in a reality kids show, Tink will bring it right back to me and remind me that I am talking about CHILDREN. I find in some ways over time she has made me a better person. Almost everyone here has, almost, and you know who you are. —giffordsaz
- I read the recaps of shows that I watch, because I feel the snark and insight provided bring a new depth to a favorite show. —lennonwhore
- The benefits are I feel a sense of community here. We all have a shared vested interest in something and it's nice to go somewhere where you feel like you belong and that there are people that have similar obsessions as you do. Yes,

everyone tends to watch TV, but not everyone gets in heated arguments or watches shows as intently or are as vested as the people do here. —minda07

THE ACTIVE VIEWER

Social media and reality television make good partners—both allow us to express our interest in others by becoming voyeurs. Reality television programs allow the viewer to observe, to live out fantasies, to vote for favorite contestants, or to apply to be on such a show. This perspective places the viewer in the center of the action. Through social media, we can connect to others to take the viewing experience to another level as we share opinions, observations, or insights.

Chapter 4

CELEBRITY HOT SPOTS: ENGAGING FANS THROUGH BLOGS

with Elle Galerman

Blogging has become such a part of mainstream culture that now even celebrities have blogs. The practice has changed the notion of celebrity, and the once untouchable actor or musician is now interacting with fans online, sharing his or her life in a more unfiltered manner. Celebrities from Moby to Alec Baldwin to Alyssa Milano maintain blogs. Although some celebrity blogs are undoubtedly written by ghostwriters, fans often read these blogs in the hopes of learning about the genuine person and not the identity constructed by tabloids, entertainment programs, or celebrity handlers. Celebrity blogs allow fans to see another side of celebrities and expertly play into the desires of fans who want an unfiltered peek into celebrity lives. Some of these blogs show us that celebrities are just regular people with problems, dreams, and thoughts not unlike our own. At the same time, blogs provide celebrities with a means of connecting with fans.

This chapter will first explore why celebrities blog and then examine the content of several key celebrity blogs. Blogs will also be discussed using the criteria of authenticity, consistency, and interaction with fans, three variables used informally in a *Fast Company* article by Aviva Yael.[1] Authenticity is described as the degree to which the celebrity is sharing life experiences instead of just posting press releases about career accomplishments. Consistency demonstrates the celebrity's commitment to posting on a regular basis, and interaction with fans is indicated by whether the celebrity responds to questions and offers a comments function or a message board.

Celebrity blogs are also used to extend the brand of a network, television show, or film. High-profile television journalists who write blogs for their network's sites (such as Meredith Vieira for *Today* and Katie Couric for *CBS Evening News*) will also be discussed in this chapter, as well as celebrities who are writing blogs for sports franchises. The chapter concludes with a mention of the rise of Twitter among celebrities.

WHY CELEBRITIES BLOG

An examination of celebrity blogs begins to reveal the reasons why celebrities blog. Some blog for personal gain and use their blogs as a way to plug their celebrity status or their products. Others revel in the opportunity to say something about politics or world issues. A review of celebrity blogs demonstrates a wide variety of perspectives and content, such as personal thoughts and feelings, political views, descriptions of experiences, attempts to repair a celebrity's public image, and announcements of upcoming events or projects. The comments from readers allow celebrity bloggers to receive feedback, which can be both supportive and critical.

Even though some celebrities use their blogs for publicizing themselves, not all may be motivated by the same reasons. It is sometimes easy to forget that celebrities are people, too—people with thoughts they want to share and creative energy to expend. Some of the creativity actors exude in their performances carries over into other pursuits, such as writing. As Stephanie Zacharek of Salon writes, "Is it possible that, just as people who hold down dreary jobs by day blog passionately about movies, knitting, or fish keeping by night, some celebrities feel that even their seemingly exciting, creative jobs don't use every muscle they've got?"[2] For the many actors who blog, this social medium is perfectly suited for these creative people who enjoy being the center of attention and need an outlet for personal expression.

Dr. Kaye Sweetser of the University of Georgia, in researching the content of celebrity blogs for her dissertation, found that the highest percentage of posts (41%) discussed personal thoughts or feelings, more than one-third of posts discussed experiences, and about one-fourth provided commentary on recent news events.[3] Also of interest was that 18% of posts expressed political messages. Celebrities have for years used their clout to demonstrate support for candidates and raise money for their campaigns. Blogs now allow celebrities a direct communication medium for disseminating their political attitudes.

A-LIST CELEBRITY BLOGS

The granddaddy of all celebrity bloggers is **Wil Wheaton**, whose current blog "WWdN: In Exile" (wilwheaton.typepad.com) and previous blog "WIL WHEATON dot NET: 1.5" (wilwheaton.net) include posts dating back to July 2001. Wheaton has likely surpassed other celebrities in terms of computer expertise. Although he acquired coding expertise by hand-coding his original Web site, he is now currently using Typepad.

Wheaton, probably best known for his roles in the movie *Stand by Me* and the television series *Star Trek: The Next Generation*, launched a new career from his blog and now has three books to his credit as well as a number of regular writing jobs. He blogs about poker on the Web site CardSquad.com, writes about classic gaming for AVClub.com, and writes the monthly "Geek in Review" column as a Geek Editor at SuicideGirls.com, described on the site as a "vibrant, sex positive community of women (and men)." He also contributes to the collaborative blog Blogging.la as "Wil."

As Wheaton describes on his blog, the idea for a Web presence came about when a Hooters waitress asked if he "used to be" an actor.[4] The Web site that followed and the blog it evolved into was a way for Wheaton to promote that he was still a working actor.[5] He writes from the perspective of an actor who is not necessarily living a celebrity life. The content of his blog comprises his own musings, which contribute significantly to the blog's authenticity. Wheaton averages about one post a day, with sometimes as much as five days passing between entries and sometimes several entries posted on a single day. His blog demonstrates a consistent effort over a long-term period, and the posts are difficult to classify. He writes about his professional life, including his books, movies, and writing jobs. He touches on political issues and offers a letter to Senator Chris Dodd. He recounts conversations with his wife about Dungeons and Dragons, a hangover, and allowing his teenage stepson to drive on the freeway at night.

Wheaton's posts do not generate considerable comments. In fact, most posts have fewer than 50. Wheaton contends in his FAQs that although he does read everything sent to him, he does not have time to reply. Readers interact with Wheaton by expressing concern for his cold, offering encouragement as he experiences a "logjam" while working on a script, and debating whether actual guitar skills can be acquired from a video game.

Wheaton's blog provides a much-needed forum for personal expression. He discusses in a post dated October 23, 2007, how he once considered himself an actor/writer and then a writer/actor (because he didn't want to be a "slash writer"), but now he describes himself as a writer. He notes that his family is supported by the money he earns writing and that a writer is what he wants to be when he "grows up." Wheaton still acts, most recently earning a guest role on the television program *Numb3rs* (an announcement that generated 239 comments from fans), and regularly performs improv comedy. He remains a unique example of a blogger who transcended the celebrity of his earlier television and movie roles to become a celebrity in blogging, technology, and Web writing circles.

Since October 2000, musician **Moby** has blogged about politics, issues, and music (moby.com/journal). In 2003, Forbes.com acknowledged Moby's blog as one of the top five best celebrity blogs (second only to Wil Wheaton's). Zacharek describes Moby's blog as portraying the "glamourous life of a musician in a way that's stripped of artifice—and that may be artifice right there, but no matter."[6] Yael notes that Moby's blog "is a bit preachy, but his musings about living in New York can be endearing."[7] After 9/11, in particular, he blogged extensively about life in New York.

Moby uses his blog entries to promote his interviews, guest hosting gigs, and limited edition single releases, as well as an organization that helps prevent injury to African children (amend.org). Moby never shies away from political issues in his blog. He expressed congratulations to Australians for voting out Iraq War supporter Prime Minister John Howard; condemnation for the Bush administration; disappointment with Arkansas Governor Mike Huckabee, who lobbied the state Parole Board for the release of a prisoner who then molested and killed a woman; and applause for Ron Paul's debate performance. He also shares behind-the-scenes concert information with fans, his punk rock playlist, his favorite David Lynch movies, and changes to his MySpace profile. He tells fans of his personal adventures, such as attending a Duran Duran concert in New York City and seeing the movie *Control.* His musings are, as Yael confirmed, "written 100% by Moby."[8]

Moby is a consistent blogger, posting several entries a week. His blog does allow comments, although prior to March 20, 2008, the comments function was disabled. On March 20, 2008, a post acknowledging the five-year anniversary of the Iraq War allowed for comments, generating just one response. Since then, most entries receive about 10 comments. Users must register in order to post responses, which may discourage some.

Singer/songwriter **John Mayer** may maintain one of the most authentic blogs in the blogosphere (johnmayer.com/blog). Launched in June 2006, his posts display a wide range of topics from concerts and his other projects to the promotion of other artists. *Entertainment Weekly* noted Mayer's blog on a list of 20 of the best and worst celebrity blogs, assigning it a grade of "B" and calling it "brainy, albeit a little ponderous."[9] Others have included it in lists of the best celebrity blogs.[10]

Mayer's blog includes photos of his meals, guitars, songwriting sessions, a passport forgery complete with a tan cover and hand-drawn design (so he can still travel if he loses the "blue one"), and a birthday party for his sound engineer. Another photo post reveals the results of site called myheritage.com that uses facial recognition software to indicate the similarities between the user and celebrities. For Mayer, the results revealed a 72% facial resemblance to Jessica Lange and a 68% resemblance to John Mayer.

Video posts are predominantly comedy sketches. In a sketch from 1999, Mayer, with his face completely covered with shaving cream, demonstrates the odd places on his face that require shaving. Mayer has also spoofed news programs like *60 Minutes* with his *The Paul Reddy Show,* where he addressed such offbeat questions as "What about putting cliffhangers in songs so people listen to the next one?"

Mayer's blog reveals his combination of intelligence and wit in a tone that is conversational and unassuming. Mayer writes to his San Francisco showgoers in September 2006: "I hereby promise that at no time during my set will I make any reference to the movie *Anchorman: The Legend of Ron Burgundy.* This includes, but is not limited to, the pronunciation of the area as 'sahn-dee-ah-go,' usage of the phrase 'stay classy,' and any reference to a whale's vagina." Mayer's blog demonstrates that he enjoys using this medium. His blog, however, with the comments function disabled, does not allow for much interaction with fans. In November 2008, Mayer asked fans to submit photos of "Interfaith Cakes" to celebrate the holiday season, awarding the winner an autographed signature series Fender Stratocaster guitar. The contest concluded with a tie between a Santa cake and *A Christmas Story* tribute leg lamp cake. Mayer is not a prolific blogger, and his only post in the first few months of 2009 was the winning cake announcement.

Actress **Alyssa Milano** is an avid fan of baseball, particularly the Los Angeles Dodgers, and she has blogged about her love of baseball since April 2007 (alyssa.mlblogs.com). Major League Baseball's Web site, mlb.com, is an official affiliate of Milano's blog. Although the majority of the entries are about the Dodgers or baseball in general, she occasionally talks politics and other sports, such as hockey and football. She occasionally plugs her clothing line, TOUCH, which is also promoted through the name of the blog: Touch 'Em All.

Milano's female perspective on sports is a refreshing one. She demonstrates an incredible level of knowledge about baseball and her passion for the Dodgers is apparent. Milano's blog is particularly unique, not only because of the specific subject matter, but because of her use of photographs. Many of the photos show Milano at games posing with fans or at baseball events with the players. She goofs around and has been photographed wearing Manny Ramirez dreadlocks or a soft drink cooler on her head, which shows a more natural side to herself.

The blog offers readers the opportunity to see another dimension of this actress. Milano obviously has other interests outside her own career, and her blog gives her an outlet to express these passions. Her posts do not just report baseball scores and play-by-plays, but are reflective. She talks about her excitement for the sport, the history of the teams, particular players, and the overall experience ("What is the smell of the ballpark?" she asks). When Milano does discuss her career and personal life outside of baseball, she is brief, but informative and often witty. She mentions that she is in Toronto filming the Lifetime movie *Wisegal* and that her ABC pilot *Single with Parents* has been picked up. She addresses sports journalists by telling them to stop reporting that she is in a romantic relationship with someone she never dated. She chides them with statements such as, "You are journalists, not bloggers." She also posts photos of her new puppy and talks about her love for her dog. The overall tone of the blog is very personal and informal. It almost reads like she is talking directly to the reader.

Milano posts frequently—sometimes weekly and sometimes even daily. Some posts receive comments ranging from 50 to over 100, but some entries do not receive any comments. Milano appears to address her fans and fellow baseball fans in her posts by asking questions like, "Who watched that game?" and signing every post with "Peace, Love, and Baseball."

Mathew Ingram, writing for Canada's *The Globe and Mail*, notes that "the blog and Web site of actor, director, painter, author, musician, and all-around Renaissance man **Jeff Bridges** stands out."[11] No standard templates here; the design and text of the site incorporate the personal sketches and handwriting of Bridges himself (jeffbridges.com). His expression is mostly through drawings, rather than words, adding to the authenticity of the site. Posts are not dated, so it is difficult to determine the posting consistency of Bridges. He offers a message board for conversation, but it does not seem to be used as a way to interact with fans. The site is mainly a place for Bridges to showcase his talents and career news, but he also provides links to sites that might interest his readers.

Comedian **Margaret Cho** has been blogging since August 2003, far longer than many other celebrity bloggers (margaretcho.com/blog/). Her blog is similar to a journal in that it is very personal. She talks about her past, her personal life, her struggles, and her opinions. Her comedic side shows in many of the entries, even when the subject matter is sad or serious. Cho occasionally uses her blog for promotional purposes, but appears to write the posts herself and addresses her fans, inviting them to watch her show or participate in various activities.

One of Cho's main topics of discussion is beauty, a platform about which she is very passionate. Cho tells a story in which a male DJ asked her, "What if you woke up tomorrow and you were beautiful?" She was shocked because he was alleging that she was not beautiful. He said, "I mean, what if you were tall and blonde with blue eyes?" She said she felt terrible—not for herself, but for him. She said, "If that's all he thinks is beautiful, he must not see very much beauty in the world." For someone who is funny, she is also very contemplative and touches on many important issues affecting her fans and the average American, such as body image. Cho calls herself chubby and admits that she has struggled with body image issues, which makes her a celebrity to which ordinary people can relate. Cho is very encouraging to her fans and addresses them in her posts, often telling them how beautiful they are.

Her posts occasionally discuss political issues, and she frequently gives her opinion, particularly on topics that relate to equal rights for gay and lesbian citizens. She expresses her outrage regarding Egyptian men being jailed for their homosexuality. She also describes her frustration with California voters for passing Proposition 8, writing, "These 'yes on 8' idiots really think they have God on their side, but they don't. Trust me, Jesus is totally bummed right now because He is not registered to vote in California because he is technically dead, although he has everlasting life." Some of Cho's posts are a bit random, simply posing questions to readers about pets or talking about experiences at the airport. Some posts end with a call-to-action, such as suggesting that readers get involved with animal rescue organizations.

Cho makes her blog interactive by posting photos and providing links to other Web sites and blogs she enjoys and supports. Her categorization of her entries into such groups as politics, religion, sex, tattoos, beauty and body image, and women's issues facilitates the ability of readers to navigate the blog and find Cho's interests that align with their own.

Cho posts often, usually daily. Most of her entries receive a modest number of comments, normally about 10. Cho does not appear to regularly respond to readers' comments, but it seems as if she reads them because she often encourages comments and asks questions of readers. Most comments address the topic of the post, though many fans take the opportunity to tell Cho how much they love her.

Although American celebrities have dominated the previous discussion of celebrity bloggers, an actress/director from a country that ranks second to the United States in the number of Internet users received more hits on her blog in 2006 than any other Web site in the world, according to Technorati.[12] Beautiful **Xu Jinglei** writes not about her fabulous celebrity life, but about her ordinary experiences, fawning over her cats Weibo and Weiqun, discussing the difficulty of learning English, or describing her reaction to an episode of *Prison Break* (blog.sina.com.cn/xujinglei with the English translation available at: sinoangle .blogspot.com). The posts are intimate, but not too personal as she avoids any discussion of her family (outside of her cats) and love life. Posts can generate hundreds or even thousands of comments.

Xu started blogging in October 2005, earlier than many of her fellow Chinese actors. She describes spending about 20 minutes a day chronicling her life. The writing results in a daily post; sometimes several posts are displayed in one day. The actress remains surprised at the popularity of her blog. As she told London's *The Times*, "Maybe readers are curious to know about the everyday life of an actress." Jane Macartney, writing about Xu in *The Australian*, notes that Xu's girl-next-door in jeans and a T-shirt image makes her accessible to her fans, further boosting her appeal. Xu was awarded the Technorati 100 top spot for blogs, ousting Boing Boing on May 4, 2006. On July 12, 2007, she reached 100 million hits.[13]

B-LIST CELEBRITY BLOGS

Actor **Zach Braff** (zachbraff.com) is another notable blogger. His posts, dating back to June 2006, generate anywhere from several hundred to over a thousand comments. Braff is not a prolific blogger, posting about once a month, although he had only two posts in 2008. Although Braff devotes a lot of space to promoting his projects, including the HBO movie *The Last Kiss*, the movie *The Ex*, and the new season of *Scrubs*, and announcing appearances on *Late Night with Conan O'Brien* and radio station Indie 103.1, the blog exudes authenticity and appears to be the thoughts of the actor himself. Braff discusses his love of Avril Lavigne's "Girlfriend" and asks if it's bad that he likes to "bop" his head to the song. He is buying a bike, has someone mending his fence, and is going shark fishing. He thinks one of his Sims characters might be gay. Braff even gave a "phat" donation to the "Idol Gives Back" program. He recommends movies and plays, such as *Romeo and Juliet* in Central Park, the musical *Wicked*, the movie *Knocked Up*, and the television program *The Sarah Silverman Show*. Braff also addresses tabloid fodder, such as whether he plans on leaving *Scrubs* (he's not) and whether he is a cad (he's just a single 32-year-old who enjoys dating).

Braff's fans are an enthusiastic bunch, many expressing appreciation that he maintains a blog. He does maintain a dialogue by responding to comments. He thanks fans for the nice comments about his Leno appearance (he was nervous) and *The Last Kiss* movie (it's apparently "no *Garden State*"). To the supposed fan question "Will you marry me?" he answers, "Yes, send pics."

Since October 2005, actor **Alec Baldwin** has written a blog as a member of The Huffington Post cadre of bloggers (huffingtonpost.com/alec-baldwin). He writes about his personal reflections, such as the loss of a friend, or comments on news events, such as potential running mates for Obama, Clinton, and McCain, or the Eliot Spitzer controversy. His posts tend to be serious, though he is witty at times. He offers his own opinion on many issues but also looks at both sides. With respect to Spitzer, Baldwin reveals that he literally danced in the street when Spitzer was elected governor of New York. Although he says that prostitution should remain illegal and he does not condone what the former governor did, he makes the potentially controversial remark that most women he knows exhibit the same sex drive as men and that men do not go to prostitutes as men but as human beings.

Baldwin's posts are not particularly insightful. Instead, he discusses a lot of public issues and offers a watered-down version of the analysis that could be found in newspapers and on news talk programs. He makes his support for the Democratic Party clear and challenges McCain's intelligence and experience. Baldwin voices support for both Clinton and Obama, but thinks that Obama has a better chance because he can bring a hope to American people that Clinton cannot match. He tends to draw parallels between more light-hearted matters and political perspectives, as in a post where he described the movie *No Country for Old Men* as a metaphor for 9/11 and the Iraq War. A lot of Baldwin's posts are personal responses to various statements printed about him in the media; in this way, his blog functions as a public relations tool allowing him to attempt to control his public persona.

Baldwin tends to post weekly, though he may write more than one entry a week. Comments on the posts vary from 20 to 40, although some posts receive over 700. It appears that the entries with fewer comments tend to be more personal while posts about politics and controversies get the most attention—and Baldwin has certainly experienced his share of professional successes and personal setbacks during this time. Baldwin mentions browsing through comments, but does not appear to read all of them or personally respond to them. Instead, he occasionally acknowledges particular comments by thanking the person for posting on a particular topic or by challenging someone who commented.

X-Files actress **Gillian Anderson** has a blog on her Web site (gilliananderson .ws) with posts dating back to March 2002. Anderson uses the blog to interact with fans who submit questions to her via the form on the "Ask Gillian" page. The site explains how her webmasters select various questions to submit to her and she answers when she can. The posts come and go in spurts; sometimes they are just a few days apart and sometimes a year apart. Recent posts state that the contents of the blog cannot be published on- or offline and are only for the enjoyment of fans. She expresses frustration about not being able to talk about politics, her feelings, or the truth. Like other celebrities, she recommends movies to her fans. She uses the blog to raise awareness and funding for the Alinyiikira Junior School in Uganda. Her blog expresses the uncomfortable boundary between celebrity and privacy. She wants to share with her fans and feels compelled to talk about her personal life, yet does not want that side of her available to the public. She appears to refrain from posting when her personal life is not going well and deems the tabloids ridiculous.

D-LIST CELEBRITY BLOGGERS

Sometimes D-List celebrity bloggers are A-List celebrities and sometimes they are D-List in both blogging and their careers. Although the escapades of these celebrities may generate a lot of interest in the tabloid media, their fans are not always equally fascinated by their personal musings. Not every celebrity is all that smart, funny, or even mildly interesting in real life.

Notorious D-List bloggers include **Britney Spears**, who is not so much a blogger as someone who posts stream-of-consciousness ramblings on her Web site at britneyspears.com. For every fan who has wondered "What's the deal with Britney?", the blog fails to provide any rational explanation. She describes her dogs and her umbrella outburst at photographers. EW.com describes her blog as "a bad excuse for a blog, especially after she discontinued the über-juicy 'stream of consciousness' section and deleted the archives."[14] Her blog, now at britneyspears.com/blog.php, is managed by Team Britney, who write the posts for her.

Rosie O'Donnell, who used her blog at rosie.com/blog to post angry commentary during the infamous falling-out with Elisabeth Hasselbeck on the set of *The View*, often posts punctuation-free haiku, such as "lindsay lohan/dui again/relief i don't have 2 discuss it/on tuesday." O'Donnell undoubtedly writes the blog herself because nobody else would ghostwrite a blog in this manner. In 2008, O'Donnell launched an attack against Barbara Walters and *The View* from her blog. Walters retaliated, and O'Donnell responded with a video post on her blog that same day. She welcomes reader questions and often answers them using a webcam or the message boards. Earlier posts drew many comments, particularly a photo of her four-year-old daughter with a toy bullet bandoleer around her neck. The blog currently has the comments function disabled, although fans can respond to the question posted in the "Say What?" section every few days and send her a question through the "Ask Ro" page.

Victoria Beckham, a.k.a. "Posh Spice," maintains a blog that among other self-promoting entries, suggests David Beckham's cologne as a Valentine's Day gift (dvbstyle.com/blog). Between press releases, Posh discusses designer dresses worn to various events. Beckham writes on her blog, "As for the clothes—wow—there are some gorgeous dresses being worn by Hollywood's finest. I wore a Cavalli A-line shift dress. It had a detailed neckline and little pockets in the most gorgeous plum colour with beautiful shoes covered in shimmering crystals by Le Silla. It was FABULOUS!"[15] Yael describes her blog as "about as interesting to read as an eye exam chart at the DMV."[16] For someone who continues to try to convince the public that there is more depth to her than portrayed by the sour looks she produces for paparazzi photos, her blog has failed her miserably. EW.com grades the blog a C-, describing it as reading "like it was dictated to an assistant."[17]

ANCHOR BLOGS

The news anchors who put a human face on the stories of the day are also blogging. One of the most heart-warming blogs is written by *Today* co-anchor **Meredith Vieira**, who has blogged on iVillage (meredithtoday.ivillage.com/) since October 2006. Vieira reflects touchingly on the stories she covers as well as the stories from her own life. In writing about the murder of Amish children in a Pennsylvania schoolroom, she fears for her own children in school. She writes of her husband's battle with colon cancer and her oldest child leaving for college. The blog provides a counterpoint for the stories covered on the show and tightens the connection between program and viewer. Vieira also responds to inane reader questions, such as whether she cooks a Thanksgiving turkey, her natural hair color, and the model of her first car.

On CBS, **Katie Couric's** Notebook video blog series on the collaborative Couric & Co. blog has been the subject of much derision since she did what is now termed "pulling a Katie." The video blog entries purported to be the personal thoughts of the anchor were found to be not only ghostwritten, but, in one example, also plagiarized from a the *Wall Street Journal* column by a CBS News Web producer. The plagiarized video post is no longer available on the site, but has been replaced by the following message:

> Correction: The April 4 Notebook was based on a "Moving On" column by Jeffrey Zaslow that ran in the *Wall Street Journal* on March 15 with the headline, "Of the Places You'll Go, Is the Library Still One of Them?" Much of the material in the Notebook came from Mr. Zaslow, and we should have acknowledged that at the top of our piece. We offer our sincere apologies for the omission.

Similar to the way a student might handle a plagiarism accusation, the network claimed that acknowledgement of the source was inadvertently omitted.

The video blog entries on inconsequential topics such as holiday giving and "geek speak" have the production qualities and writing style of low-budget video news releases. As she ends each piece with "That's a page from my notebook," the viewer must wonder exactly why these topics would be included in her notebook.

Also blogging is *NBC Nightly News* anchor **Brian Williams** (nightly .msnbc.com). As noted by Jacques Steinberg of the *New York Times*, Williams is unlike other news anchors in that he provides an unfiltered and informal voice from behind the scenes of the anchor desk, sometimes posting several times a day.[18] Since May 2005 on his blog titled "The Daily Nightly," Williams expresses frustrations about shortcomings in the news broadcast and chronicles editorial decisions. The blog offers an opportunity to entice younger viewers who have grown up understanding the concept of the fourth wall.

CELEBRITY SPORTS FAN BLOGS

The NHL is even incorporating celebrity blogs on NHL.com as a way to promote the league. The Eastern Conference boasted 10 bloggers for 2008, including David Boreanaz, Eddie Cahill, Thomas Cavanaugh, and Kevin Smith, while the Western Conference's 10 bloggers included model Willa Ford, George Stults, Dierks Bentley, and Lauren Conrad. Supermodel Christie Brinkley was among the first bloggers and quickly racked up 50,000 page views within the first few weeks.[19] Brinkley did not, however, compose her own posts. An article by Joe O'Connor of the *National Post* describes how "Brinkley, admits [Nirva] Milord (NHL senior manager of corporate communications), works with a ghost blogger at the league's New York offices. When she has the urge to talk hockey, she talks to them, and they transcribe her thoughts for public consumption."[20]

CELEBRITY TWEETS

The microblogging service Twitter might be a better fit for some celebrities who do not want to compose long blog posts, as Twitter posts, or "tweets," are limited to 140 characters. Fans can then follow a celebrity's tweets. Founders Evan Williams, Noah Glass, Biz Stone, and Jack Dorsey started Twitter as a side project while with podcasting company Odeo Corp.[21] In 2007, Twitter became a separate company and is one of the fastest-growing social media services, with more than 2.6 million users as of January 2009.[22] When Oprah Winfrey joined Twitter during a taping of her program, visits to Twitter increased 43% over the previous week, according to Hitwise.[23] Actor Ashton Kutcher and basketball star Shaquille O'Neal have also been credited with increasing public awareness of Twitter.[24] Kutcher (@aplusk) garnered much media attention in his race to beat CNN to 1 million Twitter followers. In 2009, he had almost 3 million followers; O'Neal (@the_real_shaq) had more than 1.7 million followers.

Jessica Guynn of the *Los Angeles Times* describes how many of the actors from *Heroes* are using Twitter, among them Greg Grunberg, Brea Grant, James Kyson Lee, and David H. Lawrence, as well as the show's makeup artist and prop master.[25] Grunberg, with over 20,000 followers, uses Twitter to not only share insights about life on the set, but also to promote fundraising for epilepsy research. Like Grunberg, Kutcher has also been tweeting from the set, most recently while shooting a film tentatively called *Five Killers* in the south of France in March 2009.[26] Director Robert Luketic is tweeting from the set as well, often sending dozens of tweets per day. Through Twitter, fans can get a glimpse of life on the movie set, a space that was formerly off-limits to the public.

REFLECTIONS ON CELEBRITY BLOGGING

Celebrities know that when they talk, people will listen. Therefore, if they build a blog, fans will come. Many celebrity bloggers use this forum to promote movies, television shows, music, books, or clothing lines. The challenge for these bloggers is to avoid overcommercialism by blending subtle promotional messages with authentic non-commercial thoughts. Political themes figure prominently on the blogs featured here, including Baldwin's left-wing rants, Moby's veganism and animal rights activism, and Cho's position on gay rights. Others, including Anderson, Moby, and Grunberg, promote personal causes for fundraising purposes. Wheaton is blogging to complement his work as a writer, and anchors Vieira and Williams tell the context of the stories on which they report. Others, like Mayer and Braff, are blogging to have a good time with fans.

Some celebrities are obviously more successful at engaging fans than others, which helps build their personal brands as well as their fan bases. Blogs allow fans to connect with celebrities on another level, but that relationship will always be controlled by the celebrity. Although some celebrities allow fans to read posts and not comment, others will be more creative in engaging fans, as Mayer did with his "Interfaith Cakes" photo contest. Some celebrities enjoy the feedback that sometimes evades television and film actors. In an interview with the *Los Angeles Times*, Grunberg compared using Twitter to performing on stage: "It's the same feeling I would get if we performed in a 99-seat theater. We may have 10 million people watching an episode, but I can't really feel that. I can feel the immediacy of the reaction on Twitter."[27]

With the advent of social media, celebrities now have so many more platforms for connecting with fans. Yet, on all these platforms, the persona of the celebrity must be maintained. Some are better at navigating social media, and others will need the help of publicists and other public relations professionals. Some celebrities may not even write their own posts, which makes the online relationship between these celebrities and their fans a disingenuous one. At the same time, celebrity coverage has exploded because of social media, which impacts the ownership a celebrity has over his or her image. By using blogs and other social media tools, celebrities can regain some control over their online personas.

Chapter 5

YOUTUBE STARS:
SHOOTING FOR FAME AND FORTUNE

What is this, amateur night?

—Julian Marsh, *42nd Street*, 1933

On video-sharing sites, the most ordinary of situations can become an
Internet sensation. Babies laughing, kids lip-syncing, teens describing
their heartaches, animals playing, and grown men dancing can all be
found in the vaults of video-sharing sites. The viewers who connect with these
characters spread the videos to others, further accelerating the rise to fame for
those featured in the videos.

The Internet democratizes the entertainment industry and lessens the
dominance of Hollywood in determining who can and cannot become a star. For
those seeking the limelight, the quickest way to fame might be the online distribution of a video clip through a popular video sharing site. These aspiring or semi-
professional entertainers, filmmakers, or comedians turn to YouTube and other
video sites to find a distribution channel and a more significant fan base for their
creative works without the involvement of a television network or film studio.
Standing out among the many videos being added at a rate of about one per second to the several million already available on YouTube requires a creative concept
and for some, a solid marketing strategy. A relative unknown with a popular concept, such as the Ask a Jew guy, Free Hugs sign holder Juan Mann, or the comedy
team Smosh, can become a YouTube sensation attracting a large number of visits
and subscribers.

Following a discussion of the rise of modern celebrity and the connectivity of
YouTube, this chapter will profile Internet celebrities from YouTube, other video-
sharing sites, and personal Web sites. This chapter will also discuss how these
celebrities have been able to parlay their fame into other opportunities, whether
those opportunities are on another video-sharing site or elsewhere.

ORIGINS OF MODERN CELEBRITY

Today we live in a culture of celebrity where people can rise to fame from either
ordinary or extraordinary circumstances. Daniel Boorstin in *The Image* writes
that a celebrity is a "person who is known for his well-knownness . . . a human

pseudo-event."[1] Celebrity differs from fame, and while all celebrities are famous, not all famous people are celebrities. In a Penguin Lives series biography of Charles Dickens, author Jane Smiley builds a case for proclaiming Dickens to be "a true celebrity (maybe the first true celebrity in the modern sense)."[2] Conditions were ripe for the creation of a modern celebrity, namely industrialization, which catapulted the success of Dickens and his contemporaries as their books could be quickly produced and widely circulated.

Celebrity status came early in Dickens's life, as he was already the most famous writer of his time by the age of 30.[3] "He had achieved not simply literary success, but something else, a separate status. His voice and his vision had become beloved; as Ackroyd puts it, he was 'public property,'" writes Smiley.[4] What distinguished Dickens from other successful and famous writers of the time was the unrelenting interest and adoration by the public. As David Lodge writes in a review of Smiley's book, "Celebrity entails a certain collaboration and complicity on the part of the subject. It can bring great material rewards and personal satisfactions, but at a cost: the transformation of one's 'self' into a kind of commodity."[5] The celebrity that Dickens had brought upon himself became something he both loved and despised. During a trip to America, he bemoaned the lack of privacy as attention was lavished on him from the adoring public and inquiring journalists. This concept of self as commodity continues to be viewed by contemporary hopefuls as the path to success.

Preceding Dickens were other famous authors, namely Jane Austen and Walter Scott, who both published anonymously, a rare concept in modern culture, but not so dissimilar to social media celebrities who often use aliases. However, "It is Dickens who stands symbolically on the threshold of the modern literary era, and whose career embodies the difference between being famous and being a celebrity."[6] Referring to people by using the noun version of the word *celebrity* did not enter the vernacular until the mid-19th century, first appearing in the *Oxford English Dictionary* in 1849, the same year Dickens published *David Copperfield*.

The mass media play an important role in the creation of celebrity. P. T. Barnum, master of hype, became a notable personality in American history as he created celebrity from oddity for his traveling circus. "Swedish Nightingale" Jenny Lind, Jumbo the Elephant, Zip the Pinhead, "161-year-old former slave" Joice Heth, and General Tom Thumb were among the many curiosities of the show. In fact, Barnum was able to generate so much hype for Swedish opera singer Lind that 30,000 people met her boat when she first arrived in New York Harbor.[7] Clive James in *Fame in the 20th Century* identified Charles Lindbergh, hailed for his solo trans-Atlantic flight and other aviation accomplishments and then pitied for the kidnapping and murder of his son, as the first true media celebrity.[8]

Guy Trebay, in writing about MySpace star Tila Tequila for the *New York Times*, pondered the notion of fame. "We've gone from dazed idolatry to another and more familiar form of identification. Fame, when not concocted by Hollywood and available to only the genetically gifted few, takes on softer contours. It becomes less an exalted state than a permeable one, available to those from classes and cohorts that, in the days of the studio monoliths, the gatekeepers of the star-making machine kept at bay."[9] Today's fluid culture, according to Trebay, does not require that its celebrities have talent. These stories of instant online fame may have strong influences on the youth culture. Jake Halpern cites studies in his book *Fame Junkies* that show that 31% of young people surveyed said they honestly believed they would be famous one day and 80% thought of themselves as truly important.[10]

CONNECTING ON YOUTUBE

Much of the appeal of watching user-generated videos can be traced to the popularity of reality television. The contrived nature of some "reality" shows with their writers and scripted storylines, however, leaves viewers wanting something that is somehow more organic, more natural, and more real. Even a simple statement such as "I like turtles," a cry of "Don't tase me, bro!," or a discussion of "the Iraq" can be the basis of YouTube stardom. As Mathew Ingram described in *The Globe and Mail*, "Almost anything can become popular—including an unsuspecting prairie dog whose five-second long glare at the camera became known as the Dramatic Chipmunk clip. Within a matter of days, it had been viewed more than three million times."[11] Adding to the appeal of watching user-generated videos is the possibility that a Web user might stumble upon the "next big thing" that can be shared with friends via e-mail or blog, enhancing the user's reputation as someone "in the know."

Video-sharing sites allow users to upload their own video clips to share with others. With millions of viewers and billions of videos viewed across the many video-sharing sites, several sites have emerged as market leaders. Purchased by Google for $1.65 billion of stock in October 2006, YouTube, capturing the largest share of visitors to all video-sharing sites, serves as a breeding ground for breakout video stars. A comScore Video Metrix report from October 2008 revealed that Google-owned video-sharing sites, which include YouTube and Google Video, had almost 5.5 billion videos streamed that month, more than ten times the number of video views of Fox Interactive Media, the next most popular site.[12] Other sites are differentiating themselves from the market leaders by the quality of the videos available.

YouTube's strength is not only its widespread use, but also the community features that allow users to connect with one another. Users can rate, tag, flag, and comment on a video. Other features allows users to designate a video as a favorite, create a playlist, subscribe to a member's uploads, or subscribe to a tag. Viewers find the subscribe function particularly useful, as they can follow a video series by their favorite producers. YouTube videos also integrate with blogging and social networking sites, including Blogger and MySpace.

A performer with impressive talents might compete for a spot on *American Idol*, *America's Got Talent*, or *So You Think You Can Dance*. Posting a performance on a video-sharing site such as YouTube might offer a better opportunity for exposure and feedback. Performers should be warned, however, that even on YouTube, they can face a Simon Cowell-esque firing squad. The viewers, cloaked in anonymity, are free to spout the harshest of judgments. Several standouts have won the praise of the YouTube community and skyrocketed to the top in terms of total views, ratings, and favorites.

The popularity of videos sometimes leads to inbreeding where users create videos to piggyback on the fame of other YouTube celebrities. Caitlin Hill's breakout video came when she rapped a response to fellow YouTubers lonely-girl15 and Lazydork. Andrew Meyer's "Don't tase me, bro!" was mashed into a remix with MC Hammer's "Can't Touch This" by bradlee92 and has been viewed almost 700,000 times on YouTube, the third highest views among all the videos of the incident. "Brookers" posted her own response to "Numa Numa," and others have posted responses to many of "Brookers's" videos.

Adding to the online notoriety of some YouTube celebrities is the attention they have received in offline media. Oprah Winfrey, for example, featured YouTube stars on a show taped in 2007. In addition to YouTube founders Chad Hurley and Steve Chen, she highlighted "Evolution of Dance" creator Judson Laipply; cell phone salesman Paul Potts, whose *Britain's Got Talent* performance was watched online by millions; singer Esmée Denters; newlyweds Julia and James, who danced the last scene from *Dirty Dancing* at their wedding; Sean "Diddy" Combs, who used his YouTube channel, Diddy TV, to find an assistant; and Tyson, the skateboarding bulldog. "JK Wedding Entrance Dance," a popular video on YouTube in July 2009, attracted the attention of *Today* show producers who invited Jill and Kevin Heinz and their wedding party to the show. The video featured the wedding party dancing down the church aisle to Chris Brown's "Forever." The couple and their wedding party recreated the dance on a stage outside the *Today* studio.

YouTube celebrities are often courted with offers of cash and home page placements by other video-sharing sites. In response, YouTube started a program called "YouTube Partners," which qualifies preferred producers for a share of the advertising revenues. Others receive compensation through product placement. The company does not disclose the terms of the arrangement. YouTube competitor Metacafe pays $5 for every 1,000 views after a clip has been viewed more than 20,000 times. In the first six months of the pay-for-content program, Metacafe paid out $500,000 to producers with 21 producers earning more than $5,000 and nine earning more than $10,000. Additionally, some YouTube celebrities have offline deals with production companies.

DANCERS

The champion of all YouTube videos, with over 123 million views, is comedian and motivational speaker Judson Laipply's "Evolution of Dance." Starting with Elvis Presley's "Hound Dog" and signing off with 'N Sync's "Bye Bye Bye,"

Laipply danced his way through the past 50 years of music and dance genres. "Evolution of Dance" has been holding firm as the most viewed video of all time on YouTube, the number one top favorited video, and the number one most discussed comedy video.

Laipply has an official Web site for "Evolution of Dance" that not only hosts the video, but also his bio, an online store, and booking information. He has been featured on *Today* and *Good Morning America*. Even cats apparently love the video, as evidenced by a viewer who captured his cat watching and pawing at the computer screen as the video streamed. His current speaking fees from the International Speakers Bureau are in the $10,000-$15,000 range. Some question whether his appeal can be extended from the original dancing moves and say that his online fame has not made him a "mainstream star or a mountain of money."[13] Laipply produced a second compilation of dance moves, which was uploaded to YouTube in January 2009.

Another Internet dancing star is Matt Harding, who is known for traveling the world dancing in every location he visits, an idea suggested by his travel buddy a few months into his first trip in 2003. Harding describes himself on his Web site wherethehellismatt.com as, "That guy who dances on the Internet. No, not that guy. The other one. No, not him either. I'll send you the link. It's funny." After gaining sponsorship from Stride gum, Harding left for his second trip around the world in late 2005 heading to 38 countries plus Antarctica. His second YouTube video has attracted more than 9 million views. Appearances followed on *Good Morning America*, *Inside Edition*, *The Ellen DeGeneres Show*, and *Countdown with Keith Olbermann*. His video from a third trip premiered in June 2008. Now back from his travels, Harding has a book deal.

The high school award for "Most *Unlikely* to be a Viral Video Star" might have gone to Canadian student Ghyslain Raza until a 2002 videotape of Raza demonstrating his golf ball retriever swinging skills set in motion one of the most popular viral videos of all time. Raza did not become a YouTube star by choice; classmates posted the video on the site Kazaa in 2003, prompting Raza to file a lawsuit for harassment and distribution without consent. The "Star Wars Kid," as he came to be known for his interpretation of Darth Maul's lightsaber movements, has racked up over 900 million views, according to viral marketing company The Viral Factory, with over 7 million views of the original footage on YouTube.[14]

Andy Baio, an independent journalist and programmer, reviewed server logs to track the rise to viral video fame of "Star Wars Kid." After the initial posting on Kazaa, the video spread through the offices of Madison, Wisc.-based Raven Software, where game developer Bryan Dube posted it on his personal Web site and created a second version adding lightsabers, music, and sound effects, further supporting the *Star Wars* theme. An online community called Sensible Erection then linked to Dube's Web site, with one Sensible Erection member cross-posting the video, now titled star_wars_guy.wmv, to a private file-sharing community, where it quickly became popular. A few days later, Baio found the video, posted it to his own Web site with the new name Star_Wars_Kid.wmv.[15]

As Baio writes, "From there, for the first week, it spread quickly through news sites, blogs, and message boards, mostly oriented around technology, gaming, and movies. Throughout the life of the meme, most of the referrers are blank, suggesting people were primarily sending the links by e-mail or instant message." Many major news organizations covered the phenomenon, starting with the *New York Times* on May 19, 2003, just one month after the initial posting on Kazaa. Other news organizations that covered the "Star Wars Kid" over the next six months included *Wired News*, the *Los Angeles Times*, BBC News, *The Mirror* UK, *USA Today*, *Today*, *CBS Evening News*, the *San Francisco Chronicle*, the *Seattle Post-Intelligencer*, the *Tavis Smiley Show*, *The Globe and Mail*, and *Variety*.[16]

MUSICIANS, SINGERS, AND LIP-SYNCERS

The mysterious "funtwo," who donned a baseball cap and never looked directly at the camera while expertly playing an intricate rock version of Pachelbel's "Canon in D," generated much speculation about his identity while his YouTube video soared toward the top of the all-time views list, currently sitting at number 23 (with over 61 million views). Funtwo's video is also the sixth most favorited video of all time and the most favorited video for music. In this video, blurred by the sunlight streaming through the large window in a non-descript bedroom, a young man executes the complicated technique of sweep-picking.

Funtwo's story begins with an arrangement of Pachelbel's Canon by Jerry Chang, also known as "JerryC," a Taiwanese guitarist. Like other musicians before him, Chang created a guitar rock arrangement of the canon. After publishing his version on the Web site for his band, his fans sought the tabs (written music) as well as the backing track. When Chang made both available on his site, funtwo was just one of the many musicians who literally tried his hand at making a better recording than Chang. *New York Times* reporter Virginia Heffernan, using clues on Chang's message board and other videos by funtwo, identified the anonymous guitarist as Jeong-Hyun Lim, a 23-year-old Korean guitarist. But for Lim, fame is not his goal, and he remains surprised that people are interested in his performance.[17] Although he has performed for live audiences at the KORUS festival and for the Korean ambassador in Washington, D.C., and has been featured on CNN, *20/20*, National Public Radio, the Korean MBC news, CBC Radio, and KBS News, he does not yet have a recording contract, nor does he claim that he is interested in pursuing one. Recently, he traveled around the world working mainly as a busker while performing in public spaces and on stage in 42 countries over 300 days.[18]

When an A&R representative from Atlantic Records decided to locate Esmée Denters, whose YouTube karaoke performances had attracted hundreds of thousands of fans, he started with a telephone call to a hotel in her Dutch village of

Oosterbeck. After a local hotel clerk gave the rep every Denters listing in the phone book, the rep called each number until reaching Denters's mother. It was not, however, the first call from an A&R rep about a recording contract. According to Antony Bruno, "The doe-eyed girl-next-door with a soulful voice and shy smile has become a bona fide Internet sensation."[19] Her videos have been streamed millions of times, and she boasts more than 200,000 fans on her YouTube channel. Denters's YouTube popularity resulted in a working relationship with manager/producer/songwriter Billy Mann and then a contract with Tennman/Interscope Records, as the first artist signed to Justin Timberlake's label. Denters achieved even greater fame when she was featured on *The Oprah Winfrey Show*. She is reportedly currently in the studio with former Destiny Child's singer Kelly Rowland and is considering television deals with Sony Pictures Entertainment.

The case of Marié Digby demonstrates what can happen to a career when YouTube's ability to generate organic buzz is combined with the power of a record label in a major media conglomerate. Her homemade-styled videos posted in early 2007 had attracted quite a following, generating airplay for her music both on radio stations and during the popular MTV program *The Hills*. A press release in August 2007 described how "Breakthrough YouTube Phenomenon Marié Digby Signs with Hollywood Records." Although the label positioned Digby as a YouTube break-out star who had only just been discovered and signed, a scandal erupted when it was revealed that she had actually been signed by Hollywood Records in late 2005, long before she became well-known on YouTube. Until a *Wall Street Journal* reporter started inquiring into the situation in 2007, Digby had even listed "none" for her record label on her MySpace page. She had written on her MySpace page, "I NEVER in a million years thought that doing my little video of 'Umbrella' in my living room would lead to this. TV shows, iTunes, etc!!!" The artist and her label both defended their efforts, describing the method as a way to build a following before the launch of her album.[20]

Controversy has also swirled around English/Portuguese singer/songwriter Mia Rose, who is the fourth most subscribed to musician of all time on YouTube. Within a few weeks of opening her YouTube account in December 2006, she acquired more than 200,000 friends. *Rolling Stone* writer Elizabeth Goodman called her "a disturbingly well-packaged 18-year-old singer/songwriter."[21] Michael Dwyer of Australia's *The Age* describes Rose as one of the "faux Internet indies," explaining the reason she seems polished is "because she was most likely signed, coached, and groomed by management and marketing experts well before posting her latest videos about (surprise!) flying around the world negotiating with record companies."[22] Her strategy appears to be similar to Digby's, where a record company builds support online before publicly launching a new artist.

The quirky song "Chocolate Rain," performed by Tay Zonday, a.k.a. graduate student Adam Bahner, became an Internet hit during the summer of 2007.

In the video, Bahner, who looks much younger than his age of 25, sings with a deep voice and odd mannerisms. Subtitles inform the viewer that "I move away from the mic to breathe in." The original video was streamed almost 40 million times and led to a follow-up video called "Cherry Chocolate Rain," a promotional spot for Cherry Chocolate Diet Dr Pepper. The Internet success landed Bahner appearances on VH1's *Best Week Ever* and the *Jimmy Kimmel Live* show. Kimmel's audience, however, could not relate to or understand the appeal of this performer.[23] Bahner earns thousands of dollars a month from advertising on his YouTube channel, with additional income from ringtone and music sales.[24]

Gary Brolsma sat in front of his webcam in what appeared to be his bedroom and lip-synced his way through a Romanian pop song. Known better as "Numa Numa," the 19-year-old Brolsma gave viewers an energetic interpretation of the song, flailing his arms, raising his eyebrow, and flicking his tongue to mouth the word *hello*. More than 2 million people viewed the video within the first two months of it being hosted on a video-sharing site in 2004. After the YouTube population hit critical mass and the video was posted there, millions more were able to watch Brolsma's enthusiastic performance.[25] His video, according to The Viral Factory, has been viewed approximately 700 million times.[26] Brolsma now focuses his energies on video site Numa Network (numanetwork.com), his Web design business, and his band Nonetheless.[27] In 2009, Brolsma was hired to star in a YouTube video for Geico.[28] The commercial puts Brolsma back in front of his computer where he sings "Somebody's Watching Me" while the Geico gecko dances in the background.

Two Chinese students, Wei Wei and Huang Yi Xin, caught the attention of video viewers with their passionate lip-synced performance of the Backstreet Boys's "I Want It That Way." Dubbed the "Back Dorm Boys," the duo recorded the video in the comfort of their dorm room on a cheap webcam. Adding to the amateur nature of the video, a third student in view of the camera in the background continues to play Counter Strike on his own computer, oblivious to the performance going on in the room. The popularity of the "Back Dorm Boys" attracted Motorola, who signed the duo as spokesmen for cell phones in China.[29] They also work as bloggers and podcasters for the Chinese Internet portal Sina.com and have a five-year contract with media company Taihe Rye, where they appear in commercials for major advertisers.[30]

ACTORS AND NEWSCASTERS

Brandon Hardesty's shtick is imitations of the actors in famous movie scenes. His collection of 91 videos on YouTube includes 41 recreated scenes from such movies as *Pan's Labyrinth* (his most popular with over 600,000 views), *The Dark Knight*, *Full Metal Jacket*, and *Jurassic Park*. His performances have landed him acting opportunities, including a role in the art-house film *Bart Got a Room* and videos that were featured on five episodes of *Jimmy Kimmel Live*, where he recreated scenes from the best film Oscar nominees. Hardesty recently signed a representation deal with Endeavor.[31]

Michael Buckley performs as a fast-talking newscaster for his YouTube entertainment program *What the Buck Show*. Buckley's rise of fame began when his cousin started posting clips to YouTube from Buckley's part-time gig as the host of a weekly entertainment show on a Connecticut public access channel. One of the original members of the YouTube Partnership Program, this former administrative assistant for a music promotion company quit his day job when his online earnings surpassed his offline salary. Averaging about 200,000 views with his more popular videos reaching several million views, Buckley is reportedly earning over $100,000 a year from advertising.[32] In 2008, he signed a development deal with HBO.[33]

Larger-than-life Philip DeFranco has been creating and posting *The Philip DeFranco Show* on YouTube since September 2006 when he was still a college student. Posting under the alias sXephil on YouTube, DeFranco ad-libs the content of his show, which features humorous and sarcastic commentary about current events. In an interview with SuicideGirls.com, DeFranco estimated his core audience to be 300,000 viewers and confirmed that his income classification on MySpace ($250,000 or more) was now accurate, although it had started out as a joke.[34] He earns money from YouTube and other sources on the Web, adding "there's a lot of money to be made there." In November 2008, DeFranco announced that he would be retiring. He will, however, continue to work on other projects.[35] In September 2008, HBO's offshoot HBOlab announced a Web series featuring DeFranco alongside other Web celebrities, including Jessica Rose, a.k.a. lonelygirl15, and Kevin Wu, a.k.a. KevJumba. The 10-part scripted series *Hooking Up* was delivered through major Internet social media portals, including MySpace and YouTube, as well as on the show's Web site at hookingupshow.com. The actors play college students who, although they spend a lot of time e-mailing, instant messaging, and tweeting, still manage to have communication issues.[36]

Formerly of the videoblog Rocketboom, which produces a daily report of top stories and Internet culture, Amanda Congdon has been described as ranking near the top of the list of "blogebrities who've turned blog fame and notoriety into real world notoriety."[37] Congdon now produces video blogs for ABC News, occasionally appears on ABC programs as an Internet correspondent, and is developing a comedy for HBO.[38]

COMEDIC PERFORMERS

The teenage duo of Anthony Padilla and Ian Hecox, dubbed Smosh, lip-synced their way to claim four places on the YouTube top 100 most-viewed video list. Considered YouTube innovators by popularizing the concept of lip-synced videos, their most noteworthy video was created for the Pokémon theme song. Prior to the fame generated from the Pokémon video, the teenagers set up the site Smosh.com as a meeting place for friends. Now that site is a virtual hub for Smosh fans with 30,000 registered users and 10,000 hits a day. Sales of Smosh T-shirts and hoodies (shown in many of their videos) as well as advertising revenues from the site provide the funds to allow these two filmmakers to attend American River College and continue making videos.

Smosh's channel on YouTube, with its 81 videos, is the third most subscribed to channel of all time with over 900,000 subscribers and the 16th most viewed channel of all time with over 260 million views. The comedy team has signed a deal to produce two videos a month for YouTube competitor LiveVideo and are also attracting other commercial offers.[39] Mainstream media, such as *Time* and the *Sacramento Bee,* have taken note of Smosh and featured them in stories.

Hyperactive, high-pitched "Fred" is YouTube's most popular character, having the most subscribed to channel on YouTube and receiving 3–5 million views for each of his videos.[40] Played by Lucas Cruikshank, Fred attracted the producers of Nickelodeon's *iCarly,* who featured him on an episode of the show. In a social media twist, *iCarly* co-star Jennette McCurdy recorded an ad-libbed announcement about Fred's appearance on the show that was posted on YouTube.

David Lehre, a college dropout who was living with his parents, created short films that poked fun of popular culture products, including *High School Musical,* the magic of David Blaine, and Harry Potter, and social media applications, such as Facebook, iPhone, and MySpace. His film *MySpace: The Movie,* which has been viewed on YouTube almost 550,000 times, attracted the attention of executives at MTV, Comedy Central, and Fox. Lehre eventually accepted Fox's production deal to produce a half-hour late-night comedy show, called *Sketchin'.* The deal included $300,000 for the pilot and a film project.[41]

Prior to the YouTube success of *Chad Vader: Day Shift Manager,* a series that explores the frustrations of Darth Vader's younger brother, producers Matt Sloan and Aaron Yonda were creating low-budget films for the local cable access channel. Following a friend's suggestion to create a *Star Wars* parody, the character of Chad Vader was born. After the video was uploaded to YouTube and then expanded to an eight-part series, *Chad Vader* became one of YouTube's top channels holding the #27 spot for most subscribed to comedy channel and the number 16 spot for all-time views for a comedy channel. One episode of *Chad Vader* even premiered on *Good Morning America.* These two creators also maintain their own Web site at blamesociety.net and are represented by the William Morris agency and managed by Generate agency. Sloan and Yonda were also among the first YouTube Partners.

Inspired by the "Lazy Sunday" sketch from *Saturday Night Live,* production assistant Kent Nichols and Disney paralegal Douglas Sarine created the video series *Ask a Ninja.* Sarine plays the role of the ninja, wearing a $6 ski mask, and Nichols records the action. The Q&A format involves a sarcastic ninja answering such obscure questions as "Do ninjas catch colds?" The first episodes were posted on a blog and on YouTube. After submitting the video to iTunes and creating a supporting Web site (askaninja.com) in early 2006, this unconventional video series was selected by iTunes editors as a "new and notable" podcast, granting it a preferred position on the podcasts page, which led to a placement among the top-subscribed podcasts and mentions in several blogs. Back in 2006, it was estimated that the series was watched by about 500,000 people each week.

The creators have been able to profit from their *Ask a Ninja* fame, selling T-shirts from their Web site, providing premium subscriptions for advance viewings of the videos for $1.50 a month, and selling advertising space at the end of each episode.[42] They have also released a Boy Scout parody book called *The Ninja Handbook*.[43] Sarine and Nichols attracted the attention of *MadTV* cast-member Crista Flanagan, who collaborated with the duo on a new online video series called *Hope is Emo*, featuring an emotional Emo-fashioned woman. The first episode of *Hope is Emo* quickly racked up over 1 million views and now has been viewed over 3.6 million times.[44]

Comedy writer Shmuel Tennenhaus positioned himself on YouTube as the "Ask a Jew" guy. His sketches in the Q&A format sometimes include his grandmother "Bubby." As a result of his YouTube prominence, he has been approached by YouTube competitors Metacafe and ManiaTV.[45]

Although he built his following on MySpace, stand-up comedian Dane Cook could easily have been a YouTube sensation. Cook used MySpace to amass friends, whom he encouraged to buy his 2005 CD *Retaliation* the day it was released. Over 89,000 did so, causing his CD to hit number four on the *Billboard* charts.[46] The CD eventually became one of the best-selling comedy CDs in history.[47] Now a big-name comic who has starred in movies, Cook's YouTube videos have had hundreds of thousands of views, and he has almost 2.5 million friends on MySpace.

GIRL TALK

Videos featuring a single young woman talking directly to the camera, often in the intimacy of her bedroom, have been catching the attention of YouTube viewers. Caitlin Hill, a.k.a. thehill88, is an Australian teenager who ascended to YouTube fame after posting three videos in six days. The video that caught the attention of YouTube viewers was a rap response to a video by Lazydork, the YouTube comedian Richard Stern, about lonelygirl15. Although this video attracted over 4 million views, many of her other 111 videos have less than 1.5 million views, with some having as low as tens of thousands of views. In May 2007, Hill joined the YouTube Partnership Program. Many other YouTube and film opportunities have come her way including an unpaid role in an independent horror film called *The Girl in the Red Dress*.[48] She has also appeared on the *Tom Green Show*, been featured at a YouTube convention, and auditioned for roles in big-budget films, eventually landing a part in the remake of *Plan 9 from Outer Space*.[49]

Brooke Brodack, who uses the name "Brookers," created quirky videos for YouTube, most notably "Crazed Numa Fan !!!!!" where she danced and lip-synced the lyrics to "Dragostea Din Tei." Other videos explain why kids eat glue or demonstrate her ability to play a violin like a guitar. Brodack is notable for being the first YouTube star to receive a talent/development deal. Signed by Carson Daly under the Carson Daly Prods. company, Brodack will create content for television, the Internet, and mobile services. Brodack and head of development Ruth Caruso have discussed comedy sketches for *Last Call* among other possibilities.[50]

LITTLE PERFORMERS

Even young YouTube stars are getting attention. The mother of five year old Nia Frazier has posted more than 30 video clips on YouTube of her daughter performing renditions of songs by Earth, Wind, and Fire, Mary J. Blige, and Alicia Keys. Noticed by Earth, Wind, and Fire, she performed with the band in March 2007. Blige also sought out the young performer to star in a commercial for the release of Blige's new album.

"Landlord," a video featuring Will Ferrell and his production partner's two-year-old daughter as a foul-mouthed landlord attracted attention for Funny or Die, a video-sharing site by Will Ferrell and Creative Artists Agency. This Funny or Die exclusive has been viewed almost 62 million times. Although the tot's show business career may not be impacted by her performance, it has certainly helped raise the profile of this fledging video site. Recognizing the talent of the Funny or Die team, HBO contracted them to produce 10 half-hours of programming for television.[51]

TALENT DEALS

As mentioned with respect to some of these YouTube stars, Hollywood talent agencies have recognized the revenue potential of these entertainers and are signing them to development deals. Some of these stars will not extend their fame to television or movies, but will be used for online promotions, a situation that is particularly attractive given the increasing advertising budgets directed toward online, spending that eMarketer expects to double to $50 billion by 2012.[52]

Some entertainment companies take a proactive approach and have a team of scouts searching the Web for the next breakout star. The four members of United Talent Agency's Web division, UTA Online, have already signed dozens of online entertainers.[53] Creative Artists Agency and Endeavor are other talent agencies pursuing these same tactics.[54] The difficulty in finding these stars among the millions of hopefuls is further complicated by the sheer number of content sites housing videos, estimated at 1,700 and counting by Chad Cooper of OVGuide.com.[55] According to Marco della Cava of *USA Today*, "The number of amateurs hoping to be discovered by Web talent scouts has mushroomed during the past year, making it increasingly difficult to catch an agent's eye."[56]

The industry is challenged to determine how to translate Internet success into offline value. At a time when the 30-second commercial is becoming less effective and more of a budget-buster in tough economic times, marketers are also exploring how to connect to their audiences on video sites. Young video stars, particularly males, help marketers gain admittance to a youth audience that is increasingly online.

ONLINE VIDEO OUTLOOK

Some question the long-term viability of concepts by amateurs. The Pew Institute reported that 62% of online video viewers would prefer to watch professional content, with another 11% saying they would enjoy watching both professional and amateur videos.[57] "Amateur" videos, however, sometimes approach the quality of "professional" videos, so those distinctions might not be so clear in reality.

Several video sites are eliminating or scaling back the emphasis on user-generated content. VideoEgg, Bebo, and ManiaTV all share this perspective, with ManiaTV even going so far as to eliminate all user-generated clips because such a high percentage of users were watching the professional content.[58] Additionally, advertisers do not always want to be associated with user-generated content, fearing that it might reflect negatively on their brand image, so this move is especially appealing for content sites that are advertiser-supported. This move could result in a situation where the antics of interesting, but ordinary people are replaced with content from already overexposed celebrities. Furthermore, people are becoming more comfortable watching television shows from the Internet, a shift that could also signal the end of our fascination with amateur videos.

The line between amateur and professional has already been blurred with acts like Marié Digby, who had professional backing. YouTube representatives are also in talks with the William Morris Agency to place agency clients in made-for-the-Web productions, which will provide serious competition for YouTube's popular amateur acts.[59] The deal would help to answer the question of how to make money by hosting videos. Although YouTube does not place advertising on or next to amateur videos, it does use this model for the videos hosted by its partners, which represent a fraction of the videos on the site.[60]

In February 2009, YouTube changed its default filter from "most viewed" to "popular," demoting "most viewed" from the default to the second tab. David

Sarno of the *Los Angeles Times* wrote that the company did not explain the change in a blog entry or press release, leaving open to interpretation what "popular" really means.[61] First called the "most popular" tab in December 2008, a company spokesperson at that time described popular as incorporating "more signals about video related to freshness and activity beyond just a view count." In an effort to respond to the needs of advertisers, perhaps "popular" suggests videos that advertisers would like the viewer to watch.

Chapter 6

FROM MEMES TO MASHUPS: CREATING CONTENT FROM CONTENT

Plus ça change, plus c'est la même chose.
(The more it changes, the more it's the same thing.)

—Jean-Baptiste Alphonse Karr

YouTube is awash in mashups that demonstrate fan loyalties to certain genres, television programs, movies, or musical artists by combining content from more than one source into a single integrated video. One of the more popular video mashups is "Brokeback to the Future" (viewed over 5 million times on YouTube). This video combines scenes from the *Back to the Future* movie series with the plot elements and soundtrack of *Brokeback Mountain*. Music provides another tool for mashups as demonstrated by the use of Dem Franchize Boyz's song "Lean Wit It" with clips from the Teletubbies program (viewed over 3.5 million times). The Teletubbies are a favorite performer for rap music mashups and appear in many other videos. This chapter will explore the variety of content used in mashups and the place of mashups in popular culture.

Mashups illustrate the concept of an active consumer who is re-presenting the content and adding an interpretation. No longer is music creation completely controlled by the recording industry or movie production dominated by Hollywood. As Sam Howard-Spink notes, "Maintaining a sharp division between producers and consumers of media and entertainment products is in the protectionist economic interests of those conglomerates."[1] Today's consumers have broken down the wall between production and consumption. The notion of creativity has changed from one where producers create content for consumers to enjoy to one where consumers are part of the creative process. As Catharine Taylor describes in a *Social Media Insider* article, "This practice views the original content creation as the mere starting point for what happens to it once it is embraced."[2]

Jeffrey Bardzell argues that amateur productions express a different kind of humor, one of juxtaposition, parody, and commentary. "It deflates the icons of the mass media and subjects them to puerile fun," he writes. "This discourse has become so powerful that it is making its way into the mass media."[3] This chapter will describe examples where the mashup has been elevated from an Internet phenomenon and integrated back into mainstream culture.

HISTORY OF THE MASHUP

The desire to remix blends our creative yearnings with our fondness for the familiar. Remixing predates the Internet and even the emergence of Western popular music;[4] some say it may even date back as long ago as the beginning of human existence. Peter Manuel describes in *Cassette Culture* how familiar texts in India were laid upon borrowed musical tunes for the purpose of parody.[5]

The roots of the musical mashup in the United States can be traced back to the 1910s when record companies remixed operas to fit onto 78-r.p.m. discs, which could hold only a few minutes per side.[6] In 1956, Bill Buchanan and Dickie Goodman released a recording of a skit about an alien invasion, similar to the *War of the Worlds* broadcast, that included samples of popular music breaking up the fictitious news broadcast with humorous commentary.[7] Lawyers later forced the musicians to replace some of the musical clips. In 1961, musician and composer James Tenney dissected and reassembled Elvis Presley recordings, particularly "Blue Suede Shoes" to create *Collage #1 (Blue Suede)*.[8] Even the Beatles sampled, using sound from 20 tape loops from the archives of EMI to piece together "Revolution #9" for *The White Album*.[9] In 1968, Alan Copeland created "Mission: Impossible Theme/Norwegian Wood" from the Beatles's vocals and the theme song instrumentals, winning a Grammy for "Best Contemporary Pop Performance by a Chorus," but failing to spark a trend.[10]

Modern mashups emerged in the early days of rap and hip hop, where the mixing of two or more songs was a commonly used practice in music production, often referred to in the music industry as music sampling or digital sampling. DJs Kool Herc and Grandmaster Flash sampled from vinyl records with rappers providing the lyrics. Chic's "Good Times" became the bassline for "Rappers' Delight" by Sugar Hill Gang, a song often considered the first rap hit.

Mashups evolved to sample music from different genres. Paul Morley describes this new formulation of a mashup: "The bootleg mix . . . where anonymous raiders of the twentieth century, or 'bastards,' armed with a decent hard drive, a lust for life, a love of music that borders on the diseased, and a warped sense of humor mash up tracks taken off the Internet, twist genres across themselves, and rewrite musical history in a way musicians would never think of."[11] The first true mashup of different genres is attributed to the Evolution Control Committee, who combined a Public Enemy rap titled "By the Time I Get to Arizona" with instrumentals from Herb Alpert and the Tijuana Brass.[12] The Evolution Control Committee has performed in recent years using the "Wheel of Mashup," which includes an outer wheel for the music and an inner wheel for the vocals.

The mashup emerged as a legitimate genre around 2000 as it took hold in clubs, first in Europe before emerging in the United States. In addition to being called a mashup, this genre is also referred to as "bootleg" or "bastard." In 2000, a small club in London's West End started offering mashup nights called "King of the Boots," orchestrated by Cartel Communique.[13] When a Belgian duo called 2 Many DJs released a mashup CD, the concept started receiving mainstream press attention, with this album being notable for the creators' unsuccessful attempt to be granted permission to legally use the music.

In large urban centers today, such as New York City, Munich, Paris, and Boston, "bootie" (short for bootleg) parties give mashup fans a unique music experience. San Francisco's Bootie, held since 2003, is the first and biggest mashup party in the United States and was honored as the "Best Mashup Party in the U.S." in the August 2005 issue of *Complex* magazine. Bootie DJ Adrian described San Francisco on bootiesf.com as the "epicenter of the American mashup scene."

Mashup music has thrived in the underground subculture of modern times, but has started to migrate toward popular culture, both online and offline. Today, user-friendly technology such as Acid and Pro Tools and distribution via the Internet allow many people to create mashups. As Howard-Spink writes:

> In fact, in a culture of disposability, the genre of the mashup might well have benefited from its underground status, which adds to its subversive cachet. The music is effectively contraband and is only permitted to exist to the extent that it remains below a commercial radar. It is also for this reason that to a large extent it has remained an Internet phenomenon, although there are signs that this is changing.[14]

Mashups can now be found in the commercial enterprises of television and radio. MTV Europe, for example, has a three-time-a-week program called *MTV Mash*, which mashes videos. New York City's WFMU offers a radio program called "Re:Mixology," and since 2000, London's XFM network has offered a radio show called "The Remix."

Through their creative products, musical mashup artists are often expressing dissatisfaction with the establishment of the music industry. As Bret Begun writes in *Newsweek*, "The London DJs spinning this stuff delight in coming up with goofy combinations—Missy Elliott with Nirvana, say—but their work is borne out of a serious discomfort with today's pop pap."[15] The creators take music that is "cheesy" and make it "listenable." Salon's Charles Taylor writes that mashups represent "the glorious return of format-free radio, the vindication of fandom, and an affirmation of the egalitarian spirit of rock."[16]

Mashup culture has many similarities to the youth punk culture in Britain studied by Dick Hebdige.[17] Both subcultures are formed around re-appropriation and subversion of the mainstream culture. While Hebdige's punk subjects re-appropriated safety pins, a common household item, by decorating their clothes or bodies with them, music mashup artists re-appropriate music to resist the dominant music industry, including professional DJs who once controlled professional remixing.

THE ROLE OF MEMES

To understand mashups, one must start with a meme, which is a unit of cultural information that replicates while still remaining whole. The concept of the meme was first described in Richard Dawkins's 1976 book *The Selfish Gene*, where he compared the development of ideas to biological evolution.[18] The best memes will continue to thrive through replication, thereby implanting themselves in our culture—stuck in our minds and documented in books and movies or on CDs. Memes not worthy of replication will die out, as has happened to the many songs, stories, and ideas of the past that are no longer familiar in modern times. Brent Silby tackles the issue of the memetic unit by referencing the well-known beginning of Beethoven's Fifth Symphony: "The best way to think of a memetic unit is to consider it to be the smallest idea that copies itself completely while remaining intact. So the first four notes of Beethoven's 5th is a meme, but the first three is not. The 4th note is always there making up the memetic unit. The entire symphony is a huge collection of small memetic units—a memeplex."[19] Memes are studied to deconstruct cultural products, such as music and art. Silby notes that the study of memes, called memetics, can demonstrate why certain memes are good replicators.[20]

INTERNET MEMES

Karl Hodge describes memes in the context of popular culture, adding the element of the Internet:

> These are much more than just whispers being passed down the line. Religion and ritual are memes, as are fashions, political ideas, and moral codes. They are copied from one person to the next, planting fundamental beliefs and values that gain more authority with each new host. Memes are the very building blocks of culture. Not every meme is a big idea, but any meme with the right stuff can go global once it hits the Internet.[21]

On the Internet, a meme often takes the form of a video, text, image, or musical phrase and spreads quickly through e-mail, blogs, message boards, social networking sites, or other online methods. Although memes can spread without the Internet, it is the Web that allows for rapid transmission around the world. The process of distribution can change the meme from its original form, as imitations and parodies flourish in response. Garry Marshall writes that on the Web, "infectiousness assumes an importance far greater than that of attributes that may well have greater long-term value such as utility or authority."[22]

Explaining why some content becomes an Internet meme while other content does not is complicated, if not impossible. Hodge suggests that "just about any daft idea will do."[23] Harvard University student Thomas Lotze found animated hamsters to be just that "daft idea." He captured the dancing hamsters from a

Web page that also included porn banners. By mashing the hamsters with a few musical notes (sung repeatedly), he created the Hampsterdance sensation. Web views racked up, hundreds imitated with their own hamster dances, and the UK group the Cuban Boys released a Hampsterdance single.[24] If animated dancing hamsters could be this popular, it is easy to imagine the range of other ideas that would become successful memes.

Some memes, such as several popular urban myths circulating on the Internet, are intended to be fiction, but are accepted as fact, even by the mainstream news media. A meme from Slashdot describing the use of potatoes to power Web servers was covered by *USA Today*, BBC Online, and *The Daily Mirror* (by their own IT columnist Matt Kelly).[25] Mainstream media validation certainly helps speed the replication of any noted meme. The "Save Big Bird" petition meme has been floating around cyberspace since 1995, when PBS was facing federal budget cuts. Although the financial troubles have long since been resolved, the petition still circulates.[26]

POLITICAL INTERNET MEMES

President Barack Obama's social media strategy played an important role in his successful bid for the presidency. As Matthew Fraser and Soumitra Dutta note in a *MediaPost* article, "He indeed will be the first occupant of the White House to have won a presidential election on the Web."[27] According to exit polls, Obama captured a higher percentage of the under-25 vote than any candidate since exit polling began in 1976.[28]

Gawker writer Nick Douglas reviewed popular Obama memes that were circulating before Obama earned his party's nomination.[29] The Progress Poster created by Shepard Fairey of the company Obey Giant is one such meme. Fairey, known for his distinctive street-artist style, mimicked the style of an earlier Andre the Giant poster in this poster of Obama. The poster sometimes declares "Progress;" others indicate "Hope" or "Change." Fairey has maintained in interviews that he was not contracted by the Obama campaign but did seek their approval.[30] He made the image downloadable from the Web, which has spawned countless reproductions. The movie *Henry Poole*, for example, used a similar image for its movie posters with actor Luke Wilson's visage. *Newsweek* has a version featuring baseball player Alex Rodriguez with the word "Dope," mocking his use of steroids earlier in his career.

"Barack Obama is your new bicycle" became the catchphrase for a Web site created by *Wired* magazine contributing editor Mathew Honan (barackobamaisyournewbicycle.com). His site greets each visitor with large block letters declaring one of 60 or so phrases. In addition to "Barack Obama is your new bicycle," users might read that "Barack Obama held your hand when you were frightened" or "Barack Obama favorited your photo." Imitators followed suit with similar sites for Steve Jobs ("Steve Jobs watches himself on YouTube"), Hillary Clinton ("Hillary Clinton is cheating at Scrabulous"), Michelle Obama ("Michelle Obama lets you eat carnival food on a stick"), and Ron Paul ("Ron Paul yelled at you to get off his lawn").

Building on the Indian culture Internet video "Tunak Tunak Tun," Obama's head is shown dancing to Punjabi music in the video "Barack OBollywood." Users have also created a mashup of Obama and *The Empire Strikes Back*, aptly titled "The Empire Strikes Barack." A Muppets mashup also compared candidates to various Muppet characters (with Obama as Kermit and Hillary as Miss Piggy).

VIDEO MASHUPS

Video mashups are remixed video clips using footage from television shows, movies, cartoons, commercials, or video games. The mashups might be recut trailers, mashups of two movies, or a bloopers mashups, also known as shreds. Australian college student Tom Johns created the Web site The Trailer Mash (thetrailermash.com) to index these videos, allowing users to watch trailer mashups, share their creations, and vote for their favorites. The Web site YouChewPoop.com started as a forum for sharing mashups, which the site calls YouTube Poop, although it has evolved over time to include other topic areas as well. The site defines YouTube Poop as "a video that has been made with appropriated footage and collage editing techniques for the purpose of either annoying or entertaining viewers in the increasingly indifferent world of YouTube."[31]

The lowest form of mashup involves the use of CD-i cutscenes, where words are often replaced and sentences mixed. CD-i refers to Compact Disc Interactive, which is an interactive multimedia CD player that attempted to gain market share in the games industry, releasing Hotel Mario and three Legend of Zelda games, and then eventually became insignificant with the launch of Nintendo 64 and Sony PlayStation. As stated on the YouChewPoop site, "The fact of the matter is that many poopers can still use CD-i footage to great effect, but it has largely become a tired and old source in an environment in which the fresh and creative is highly treasured. Be careful when choosing to use footage that has been frequently used in the past." Mashups are easily created using Windows Movie Maker, but more sophisticated effects can be found by using Sony Vegas or Adobe Premiere. The creators often find clips on YouTube and use vixy.net, idesktop.com, or mediaconverter.org to download clips.

Videos do not have to be high quality to have important cultural meanings, as indicated by a video created by UK-based "zichini." His video opens with video game images and a poorly translated line of video game dialogue—"All your base are belong to us." In the video, this message appears on the cover of *Time*, as the word puzzle in *Wheel of Fortune*, in a Budweiser ad, as a warning on a cigarette box, in Times Square, on a billboard for a news station, and on the Space Shuttle.

In the world of movie trailer recuts, "Shining" tells the heartwarming story of the relationship between a struggling writer and a boy who needs a dad. "Scary

Mary Poppins" is a witch who does all sorts of tricks to frighten young children. "Matrix" is a lost love romance where Neo searches for a lady in a red dress he spotted on a crowded sidewalk. *Jaws* has been recut with a love song track to produce the romantic film "Must Love Jaws." The horror version of *Sleepless in Seattle* has Meg Ryan's character stalking a nice single man and his young son, Jonah. All these recuts use video clips from the original movies while rewriting the voiceover and replacing the music.

Trailer mashups combine scenes from multiple movies, such as "Toy Story 2 Requiem," which tells the underworld story of toys with drug problems by combining scenes from *Toy Story 2* and *Requiem for a Dream*. Some mashup creators add subtitles, some change the trailer for a different result, and some tell a completely new story using multiple clips. Robert Blankenheim created a four-and-a-half minute mashup masterpiece as a purported sequel to *Titanic* called "Titanic: Two the Surface." This mashup combines movie scenes from 21 movies plus the soundtracks from two additional movies to tell the story of Jack Dawson being discovered embedded in a block of ice among the ship's wreckage. After scientists bring him back to life, he escapes into the streets of New York City and now has to live, as the voiceover describes, "in an unfamiliar town . . . and in the future." Others have created edited versions of popular movies, including *Star Wars Episode I: The Phantom Menace* and a "Kubrick Edit" of Spielberg's *A.I.*

Commercial footage is also incorporated into video mashups, with Celine Dion dancing to "Thriller" in a spoof iPod commercial. Another popular mashup (viewed over 3.7 million times) is the anti-Hillary Clinton political advertisement that features Clinton as the "Big Brother" of Apple's *1984* commercial.

RemixAmerica.org offers software for creating remixes and mashups, raw audio and video materials, and an opportunity to share creative products with other users. This non-partisan site is a project of Declare Yourself, an organization that encourages voting among youth. Users have access to political history through "America's Playlist," which includes classic footage such as John F. Kennedy's inaugural speech and Martin Luther King Jr.'s "I Have a Dream" speech, as well as more current footage from campaign speeches by Barack Obama and John McCain.

Studios are encouraging the engagement of fans with their movies, with Fox providing clips and tools on its Web site foxatomic.com. Lucasfilm offers over 250 video and audio clips from the six *Star Wars* films on StarWars.com, allowing fans to make their own mashups. A video editing platform, Eyespot, is also integrated into the site to make the mixing possible. On its Web site, cable station Nickelodeon provides scenes from *SpongeBob SquarePants* and *Avatar* for children to make mashups for distribution to their friends. Movie studios are also recognizing the cultural importance of mashups and are using them to promote new movies. New Line Cinema hired the British VJ duo Addictive TV to create a mashup of scenes from Antonio Banderas's 2006 movie *Take the Lead*.[32]

The description on YouTube calls the video the first sanctioned Hollywood studio remix.

MUSICAL MASHUPS

Technology has enhanced the ability of ordinary people to create and distribute mashups. User-friendly programs allow the composer to match the beats of two different tracks, and digital music simplifies the creative process. Additionally, file-trading networks such as Kazaa, Limewire, and Napster allow the mashups to circulate online.[33] One of the forefathers in the area of digital music mashups is Roy Kerr, a.k.a. Freelance Hellraiser, who, back in 2001, mixed the vocals of Christina Aguilera from "Genie in a Bottle" with the guitar of The Strokes's "Hard to Explain" to create a mashup called "A Stroke of Genie-us." *Newsweek* and the *New York Times* are among the mainstream news organizations that covered this unauthorized work. Freelance Hellraiser's talents attracted the attention of Aguilera, who commissioned additional remixes, and Paul McCartney, who hired the remix master to create an entire album of McCartney remixes.[34]

Jeremy Brown, a.k.a. DJ Reset, combined Beck's "Debra" with Jay-Z and Pharrell Williams's "Frontin'" to create the musical mashup "Frontin' on Debra," a creation which was supported by Beck and later sold on iTunes. As described by Sasha Frere-Jones of *The New Yorker*, "Brown's collage sounds not like two songs stitched together but one single theme song for inept Romeos everywhere."[35]

Other popular musical mashups include Soulwax's "Smells like Teen Booty," which combines Nirvana's "Smells like Teen Spirit" with Destiny Child's "Bootylicious." Kurtis Rush mixed the rapping of Missy Elliott with George Michael's "Faith." Eminem's music has been used to mashup his "Without Me" with "Come on Eileen" by one-hit wonder Dexy's Midnight Runners and "Slim Shady" with a ragtime instrumental to create "The Real Slim Shady." Kembrew McLeod writes of how this practice emasculates Eminem: "The humorless white rapper takes himself far too seriously, which at times reduces his image to self-parody. This is ironic because, at the same time that Eminem makes fun of 'boy bands' and other targets in his videos, Eminem doesn't like it when others satirize him."[36] Sometimes a commentary on the state of the music industry, songs like Party Ben's "Boulevard of Broken Songs," which mashes Green Day's "Boulevard of Broken Dreams" with songs by Oasis, Travis, Coldplay, and Aerosmith, demonstrate the similarity of the music produced by these artists.[37]

Musicians have also been providing fans with opportunities for remixing their music. Radiohead is one band that has been at the forefront of the social media revolution. On April 1, 2008, the band provided five "stems" of their song "Nude" on iTunes for 99 cents each. Each stem included one track of the song. The intention was to allow fans to remix the song and share it with others on Radioheadremix.com. Fans then voted for their favorite remix, with a creation by a professional group dominating the competition after a few weeks. A widget was made available to allow users to place their remixes on a Facebook or MySpace page, encouraging friends to play the remix and vote for it.[38]

Trent Reznor of Nine Inch Nails has for some time been allowing fans to download and remix multitracks of Nine Inch Nails songs on NIN.com. In an extension of this artist-fan relationship, Reznor broke from his label Universal Music Group to host his own site where fans could remix copyrighted material from other artists and labels.[39] The band also allowed free downloading of their 2008 album *The Slip*.

A service provided by Peter Gabriel's record company, Real World Records, is Real World Remixed (realworldremixed.com). The site allows for downloading of sample packs of tracks from Gabriel and other artists of Real World Records and then uploading of the remixed versions. In 2006, the site ran a contest for the best remix. The Coalition for Artists and Stakeholders (cashmusic.org), founded by Kristin Hersh of Throwing Muses and Donita Sparks of L7, along with their managers and other partners, gives artists a place to release music, videos, and other content and allows fans the opportunity to interact with that content or upload their own creations, including music videos, essays, or art.

A musical mashup of sorts was a collaborative song written by Weezer frontman Rivers Cuomo and his fans. Cuomo uploaded a self-made video series on YouTube called "Let's Write a Sawng" to encourage fans to help him do just that. Step 2, for example, encouraged fans to submit song titles. Step 14 sought help with the bridge, and fans responded by uploading videos of their suggestions.

Mashups are receiving attention in mainstream culture. Marketers, for example, are using musical mashups as the basis for consumer contests. In 2004, Audi ran a contest for the best David Bowie mashup after featuring a mashup of the songs "Rebel, Rebel" and "Never Grow Old" in an Audi commercial (calling the new version of the song "Rebel Never Gets Old"). The 47th Annual Grammy Awards opened with a live mashup, bringing the concept to the full attention of mainstream consumers. The Black Eyed Peas, Gwen Stefani and Eve, Los Lonely Boys, Maroon 5, and Franz Ferdinand performed five different songs at the same time, with the performance merging into a medley by the conclusion.

VIDEO AND AUDIO MASHUPS

Soulja Boy's "Crank Dat (Soulja Boy)" provides the perfect soundtrack for musical mashups. The 17-year-old Soulja Boy, a.k.a. DeAndre Way, quickly racked up over 37 million YouTube views for his music video and over 35 million views for the accompanying instructional dance video that demonstrates the combination of criss-cross feet, "Superman" breast stroke, and three hops to each side with arms pumping in the opposite direction. Remixes have Barney, SpongeBob, the Simpsons, Dora the Explorer, and the Lion King performing the dance or lip-syncing the lyrics.

The Kanye West song "Gold Digger" was used as the audio track for a collection of images of New Orleans and George Bush in the aftermath of Hurricane Katrina in a video titled similarly to West's now infamous line from NBC's Concert for Hurricane Relief: "George Bush doesn't care about black people." The audio is enhanced with rewritten lyrics as well as statements by West. The video slams the federal response to New Orleans, particularly with respect to Bush's delay in visiting the hurricane-ravaged city. The lyrics use the refrain "George Bush don't like black people" with verses describing how "News say the police shot a black man trying to loot" and "Forgetting folks who too broke to evacuate." Bush has also been attacked in a mashup by remixer RX, who combined segments of Bush's speeches with U2's "Sunday Bloody Sunday."[40]

Weezer's video for "Pork and Beans" is one of the greatest collaborations ever of YouTube celebrities, all of whom parodied their own original performances as they lip-synced along to the band's lyrics. "Numa Numa" guy Gary Brolsma, Jud Laipply, Chris Crocker, the Mentos and Diet Coke scientists, "Chocolate Rain" performer Tay Zonday, and Miss South Carolina Lauren Caitlin Upton are all featured here. Posted May 23, 2008, the video generated 1.2 million views during its first 24 hours on YouTube. The video included an "embed" link so that it could be shared on social networking sites, social news sites, or blogs, which amps up the viral power of the video. "Pork and Beans" director Matthew Cullen expressed an interest in having others create their own mashups. The Barenaked Ladies used a similar tactic for their 2007 video for "The Sound of Your Voice," but with much less success. A year later, the video had not even reached 500,000 views. Like the Weezer video, Gary Brolsma, Jud Laipply, and the Mentos guys are also here, along with such notables as Brooke Brodack ("Brookers") and dancing Matt Harding.

In 2009, Israeli musician and producer Ophir Kutiel, a.k.a. Kutiman, created a mashup from video and audio clips found entirely on YouTube. His seven-track creation *ThruYou* interweaves clips of a variety of artists demonstrating their musical talents. The Web site at Thru-You.com mimics YouTube's interface "if it had been left under a bus and run over a few times," as Catharine Taylor describes.[41] Roi Carthy of TechCrunch notes how social media made Kutiman's creation an Internet sensation:

> The entire snowball effect that resulted in over a million views, a crashed Web site, and a fair bit of buzz, was initiated by three people associated with the project. They e-mailed twenty people in total and it took a life of its own from there. From zero views to over a million in less than seven days with no marketing dollars, blackhatting, or SEO'ing involved. The team around Kutiman attribute much of this to word traveling across Twitter. If this is true, Kutiman may in fact be the first music star to be born on Twitter.[42]

Kutiman's project demonstrates the ability of a single person to make something culturally relevant and harness the power of social media to build an audience.

LEGAL ISSUES SURROUNDING MASHUPS

Digital products are easily copied, thus creating myriad questions related to digital copyright protection, particularly with respect to the legality of mashups. Although studios and record labels want fans to be able to engage with their films or recordings on a different level, they will also seek some copyright protection should fans attempt to profit from their remixed videos. A mashup combining the awkward dancing of Napolcon Dynamite with rapper Eminem's "Lose Yourself" from the movie *8 Mile* remained online, despite the fact Fox was not paid for the video clips.[43] With just over 1,400 views, the video is obviously not considered a significant violation.

DJ Brian Burton, known as Danger Mouse, created an entire album by mashing up the Beatles's *The White Album* with Jay-Z's *The Black Album*. The idea for this mashup came to Burton in 2003 after Jay-Z released an a capella version of his album for the purpose of remixing.[44] After creating *The Grey Album*, Burton then used a mashup video of the Beatles and Jay-Z, called the "Grey Video," to promote the release of his album and its single "Encore." Combining clips from The Beatles's movie *A Hard Day's Night* with Jay-Z's rapping of "Encore," the video is enhanced with a computer-generated Ringo Starr scratching the turntables and John Lennon break-dancing. A review in *Rolling Stone* called the album "the ultimate remix record" and a *Boston Globe* review described it as the year's "most creatively captivating" album.[45]

EMI Records and Capitol Records, holders of the copyright for the recordings on *The White Album*, were swift to threaten legal action against any sellers or distributors of this album, including Brian Burton. In response, music activist group Downhill Battle conceived and publicized "Grey Tuesday," the day the album was made available for free download on the Internet, described as a "day of digital civil disobedience." Downhill Battle called the cease-and-desist letters from EMI "a clear, simple, downloadable example of how the major record labels stifle creativity and try to manipulate the public's access to music, and it's the perfect way to explain to non-experts why the copyright system needs to be reformed." The download was positioned as a political act with the use of the material afforded by fair use rights. Downhill Battle reported that over 170 sites hosted the album and more than 400 demonstrated their support, with many sites going "grey" for the day. It is estimated that more than 100,000 copies of the album were downloaded.[46]

For Brian Burton, the cease-and-desist order garnered him mainstream media attention, further enhancing his reputation as a creative remixer. Burton found later success through his involvement with Gnarls Barkley, as one-half of the musical duo, and had a major hit in 2006 with the song "Crazy." He also produced

Gorillaz's second album. Burton, therefore, exists within the realm of the legitimate music industry as well as the subversive subculture of remix.

Jay-Z has continued at the forefront of mashup music, working with Mike Shinoda to produce *Collision Course*, a legally-sanctioned album using Jay-Z's music from *The Black Album* as well as some of his other albums mashed with the music of Linkin Park. The album became a *Billboard* number one album after its release in late 2004.[47]

Green Day's album *American Idiot* provided creative inspiration for a group from Perth, Australia with the Green Day spoof name of Dean Gray. Their remixed album, *America Edit*, mashed Green Day's album with recordings of The Bangles, The Sex Pistols, Mariah Carey, The Who, U2, and many other artists. The album was uploaded to the Internet in 2005, and within days they received a cease-and-desist letter from Warner Bros. and Green Day.[48] An online protest erupted in response, and magazines such as *Spin* and *New Musical Express* covered the legal battle.

Damien O'Brien and Brian Fitzgerald pose the following questions of Dean Gray: "Have they robbed the sound recording corporation of an opportunity in the derivative market? Have they 'ripped off' the reputation and notoriety of Green Day? Have they made money from their endeavour? Are non-substitutable, noncommercial derivatives such a bad thing for our culture? What value do we put on creative and transformative use?"[49] The legal question centered on whether Dean Gray violated copyright law or if their remixed version was protected under fair use.

John Shiga challenges the common assumption that remixers seek legal action: "The pattern of provocation through illegal remixing followed by legal orders and press coverage suggests that the logic of mashup culture can be reduced to a series of calculated moves on the part of amateur remixers to incite legal controversies that enable them to showcase their skills in the news media."[50] Although some remixers might view cease-and-desist orders as a badge of honor, Shiga suggests that the most notorious remixers are not always the ones singled out, nor do legal proceedings always result in media exposure and public acclaim for the remixer.

In the 2004 case *Bridgeport Music v. Westbound Records*, the landmark case in the area of digital sampling, the U.S. Sixth Circuit Court of Appeals ruled that samples must be paid for, including snippets of sounds or chords, even those made unidentifiable through distortion.[51] The case involved a sample of "Get Off your Ass and Jam" by George Clinton and the Funkadelic that was used in "100 Miles and Runnin'" by NWA.

Record companies have released several mashups, including Freelance Hellraiser's "A Stroke of Genie-us," as singles by licensing the music from the original copyright holders. The U.K. group Sugarbabes released a mashup of Adina Howard's "Freak Like Me" over an instrumental by Gary Numan after witnessing the online popularity of the mashup.[52] In an interesting legal twist, the mashup maker has no legal protection.

CULTURAL IMPLICATIONS

The mashup is a perfect example of postmodernist blending of styles from different genres. It also presents new ways of thinking about the nature of art. Instead of original works that are not derivated from other sources, mashup creators are bridging a new art form that combines cultural products in creative ways. Howard-Spink describes the relevance of mashups in modern culture in reference to *The Grey Album*: "It is also relevant that remixing and sampling are the currency of today's popular culture. Cultural appropriation takes place on our televisions and cinema screens, in the advertising that surrounds us, and in the music that is piped to us on radio—which is why the illegality of a project like *The Grey Album* strikes so many people as counter-intuitive."

Pete Rojas, writing for Salon, further echoes this sentiment: "Pop culture in general seems more and more remixed—samples and references are permeating more and more of mainstream music, film, and television, and remix culture appears to resonate strongly with consumers. We're at a point where it almost seems unnatural not to quote, reference, and sample the world around us."[53] Sampling has become a natural phenomenon in popular culture, allowing consumers to become producers who can express themselves using cultural touchpoints.

Mashups make music and movies relevant to new generations. Yet, although the practice seems like harmless fun, the mashups may change our cultural memory of those movies. When we think of *Brokeback Mountain*, do the humorous scenes of Michael J. Fox traipsing back in time come to mind? Studios and record labels lose control over the creative product when mashups flourish.

At a time when popular culture is being dictated by a small group of large media conglomerates, a distinction between consumer and producer helps to retain the relevance of the media organizations. Mashup creation breaks down the barriers between creators and consumers of art and the distinctions between low and high art. William Fisher in *Promises to Keep* describes digital technology as offering "semiotic democracy," which gives consumers power over cultural meaning-making. Fisher writes, "Reversing the concentration of semiotic power would benefit us all. People would be more engaged, less alienated, if they had more voice in the construction of their cultural environment. And the environment itself would be more variegated and stimulating."[54] The question is whether the voice of creative consumers can be heard over the din of the daft ideas.

Chapter 7

MUST-NOT-SEE TV:
MOVING TELEVISION VIEWERS ONLINE

Before the creation of video-sharing sites such as YouTube, if something news-worthy happened during the *Late Show with David Letterman*, the Academy Awards® live broadcast, or even the Olympic Games, those who were not tuned in would be lucky to catch the clip on a news program or watch a friend's VHS tape. With the advent of video-sharing sites and the extensive use of DVRs to capture clips from television, almost anything missed on television can be viewed later. Even prior to the airing of a television show or movie, videos from film sets and other plot details might be leaked on the Internet. In addition, programs cancelled from network television can find a home on video-sharing sites, much to the delight of the show's core group of fans.

Video-sharing sites lessen the need to watch television, or at least watch full versions of television programs. Anything noteworthy will be talked about on news, sports, or entertainment programs or written about in newspapers or on blogs. Interested viewers can then locate the clip on YouTube, a news organization's site, or another video-sharing site. The combined availability of widespread broadband access, DVRs, and social media significantly expand the possibilities for the viewing of programs from television.

This chapter will first discuss the replacement of television viewing by Internet surfing and then online video viewing, highlighting research and predictions since 1996 when the Internet made its way into mainstream culture. Next, this chapter will review dramatic television clips that exploded in popularity online, with some clips garnering more views online than the original broadcast. Next, this chapter will examine the use of the Internet for posting video clips prior to the release of a movie or airing of a television show and how the Internet can breathe new life into cancelled television programs. Also addressed will be Web-based shows and programming that migrated from the Internet to television. Finally, this chapter will address the response by television networks and the implications of online videos for the future of television.

From Television to the Internet

Since the World Wide Web became a household word, researchers have examined the impact of computer use, specifically Internet surfing, on television viewing. Researchers differ in their assessments of whether Internet browsing affects television viewing, with some suggesting that viewing decreases, others arguing that it increases, and some saying that it remains unchanged.[1] Several scholars have advocated a media substitution theory, whereby when a new medium is introduced that is more desirable, yet functionally similar to an older medium, the new medium will replace the older one.[2,3,4] Nicholas Negroponte was one such thinker who, in 1995, predicted the replacement of television viewing by online activities.[5] Some of these early predictions were mere speculation without data to back up claims.[6] The history of mass communication reveals people who predicted the downfall of newspapers in the face of radio, radio or film because of television, or network television because of cable. These predictions have been proven false, as those media still remain viable today.

The 1990s were characterized by excitement that the Internet would replace television, but that buzz soon faded.[7] As Barbara Kaye and Thomas Johnson describe, "Between 1996 and 2000, the Internet audience may have tired of waiting for television-like video and programming, so turned back to the broadcast medium, especially those Internet users who go online because it is convenient."[8] Using PC Meter data from 1996, Steve Coffey and Horst Stipp made some inferences about the relationship between television and personal computer use. The researchers suggested that Internet use does not cause a decline in television viewing. At the time of the study, computer use was not very high, with only 7% of PC owners aged 18–54 with a college education using their computers during an average minute, while 32% of the same demographic group were watching television.[9]

Coffey and Stipp also suggested that computer use may actually save time doing certain activities, thereby increasing available time for television viewing. Furthermore, many computer activities do not fulfill the same needs as television. For example, using computers for e-mail, bookkeeping, or information gathering is not the same as playing games or surfing the Web for pleasure. Finally, teens and children were not major users at this point, so it was difficult to quantify whether PC use was replacing television viewing in a significant way.[10]

Kaye and Johnson's research showed the impact of the Internet on traditional media use during the 2000 presidential election by comparing 2000 data to similar data from 1996. They found newsmagazine and radio usage to be most commonly negatively impacted by Internet use, but not television, the medium that had suffered the most in 1996. Overall, the highest percentage of users claimed that the time spent seeking information about the campaign in traditional media was unchanged.[11]

Deloitte & Touche's "State of the Media Democracy" study released in January 2008 revealed that almost 70% of respondents consider their computers to be a better entertainment device than their televisions.[12] Other studies have demonstrated that those with an Internet connection at home spend more time surfing than watching television, although much Internet-browsing may be attributable to non-entertainment activities, such as checking e-mail, online shopping, or information gathering.

A 2008 study conducted by Harris Interactive for blinkx showed that people enjoy watching television and surfing the Web at the same time. In fact, 78% of adults go online while watching television, and 35% do this always or often. About 25% of these "double-dippers" are seeking information related to the television program they are watching, including profiles of the actors (51%), products/services seen on the program or during commercials (40%), and related or upcoming events (39%).[13]

Until recent years, online video was not even a consideration, as the technology had not gained widespread usage nor was the bandwidth available. The popularity of online video and the Writers Guild of America strike of 2007–2008 may have dealt a double blow to the television industry, and it remains to be seen whether the industry will recover. In December 2007, during the strike, more than 10 billion online videos were viewed, at the time the heaviest viewing month since comScore had been tracking online videos viewing.[14] Two separate studies, one by Interpret LLC and another by Burst Media, focused on the impact of the strike on television and online video viewing. The Interpret LLC study found that 35% of adults said they changed television viewing habits because of the strike and the Burst Media study found that 26% of respondents said they would probably watch more online video.[15] No study has explored whether television viewing behavior reverted back to previous levels at the conclusion of the strike.

From February 2007 to February 2008, online video views increased 66% to 10 billion views (slightly less than December 2007), according to comScore data.[16] After a slight slump in January and February 2008, online video viewing continued to rise over December 2007 figures with 11.5 billion online video views in March 2008, according to comScore.[17] By October 2008, Internet users were viewing 13.5 billion online videos a month.[18] YouTube remains the video juggernaut with approximately one-third of all video views.[19]

A 2007 study by Horowitz Associates found that 61% of high speed Internet users watch or download online video content weekly and 86% do it monthly, both percentages up from 45% and 71%, respectively, from the year before.[20] In 2007, entire television shows and movies did not figure prominently in the type of content watched, with news segments, non-professional videos, movie trailers, music videos, and previews or segments of television shows the most popular content. Most who watched online did so because they missed the television program during its original airing (70%), came across the program on the Internet or someone told them about a program (20%), or wanted to watch a program a second time (18%). Only about 13% of Internet users said they intentionally choose to watch programs online instead of on a regular television.[21]

A 2007 study conducted by the Pew Internet & American Life Project found that 57% of online adults have ever watched or downloaded an online video and 19% do so on a given day, and of those with high-speed broadband, 74% have watched a video online.[22] Social media adds to the video fury, with 57% of online videos viewers sharing links with others and 75% having received a link to an online video from someone else. The most popular content formats include news (37%), comedy or humor (31%), and music videos (22%), followed by animation/cartoons, movies and television programs, political videos, commercials, and adult videos, with each category watched by less than 20% of respondents.

The 2008 study by blinkx and Harris Interactive found that Web users who go online to watch videos are more likely to watch full length television programs, movies, or sporting events (25%) than user-generated content (13%).[23] A Knowledge Networks study in 2009 found that 21% of Web users aged 13–54 stream long-form television programs on the Web. About 87% are watching a missed program, and 40% are watching an older or last season episode.[24]

Ipsos MediaCT found that a comparison of February 2008 "screen time" to the same month in 2007 demonstrated a decline in share of time devoted to consuming videos on television and watching movies in theaters, while PC video screen time almost doubled from 11% of screen time to 19%.[25] More than half of Americans report streaming or downloading a video and among that group, about 20% of the viewing time is spent watching content on a computer.

Nielsen's "Three Screen Report" for the fourth quarter of 2008 showed that the average person was watching about three hours of online video a month, with young adults watching about five hours of online video a month.[26] Leichtman Research Group's "Emerging Video Services III" found that 34% of adults are watching online video weekly, and 11% are daily online video viewers. The highest percentage are watching a news clip (24%), then a user-generated video (20%), sports news or highlights (15%), and a television show (8%). Most adults and teens who watch videos online disagree strongly that they watch television less often. Given that, just a small fraction (3%) of adults online strongly agreed that they would consider disconnecting their television service to watch television shows online, and there was no difference in agreement between those who watch recent television shows online weekly and those who do not.[27]

We are witnessing a demographic divide with respect to viewing preferences as younger consumers are less likely to say they prefer television for viewing as opposed to the Internet. A study by Frank N. Magid and Associates found that 23% of younger viewers as compared to 48% of 55–64-year-olds strongly agree that they prefer watching on television. About 36% of this younger demographic say that the PC is competing with the television for their entertainment time (compared with 27% of the older demographic). This younger demographic also believes that participation in social networking sites and Internet video viewing are the factors impacting their television viewing.[28]

The Pew Internet & American Life Project study also found that respondents aged 18–29 were more likely to have ever watched an online video (75%) than all adults (57%). Similarly, while just 8% of all Internet users have uploaded a video, 15% of those aged 18–29 have done so.[29] Younger adults are also more likely to say they watch comedy videos (56% of younger viewers), rather than the news that is more popular with older groups (43% of younger viewers).[30]

The Ipsos MediaCT study from February 2008 also shows a demographic divide, with 18–24-year-olds, 12–17-year-olds, and 25–34-year-olds spending 27%, 24%, and 21% of their screen time watching videos, compared with 16% of time spent by 35–54 year-olds and 18% by those age 55 and older.[31] A 2009 survey by LiveRail of 18–24-year-olds found they were more likely to watch Web-distributed video than television, which the researchers attribute to the increased availability of long-form television programs.[32]

TELEVISION MOMENTS ON THE WEB

YouTube's slogan "Broadcast Yourself" is a rallying cry for all consumers to be broadcasters, whether of their own content or television content. In this sense, YouTube becomes "Your Television Tube" and consumers may question whether broadcast television is even necessary. This section will discuss some of the most popular Web clips that originally aired on television. For some clips, online views are surpassing television ratings.

Although 7 million viewers who tuned into *Saturday Night Live* on December 16, 2007, saw the premiere of "Dick in a Box" featuring guest host Justin Timberlake and *SNL* cast member Andy Samberg, the YouTube clip had generated more than 7.5 million views by the end of 2007.[33] Connie Chung's over-the-top swan song "Thanks for the Memories" on her final appearance on *Weekends with Maury & Connie* in June 2006 garnered twice as many viewers on YouTube as on MSNBC.[34] An appearance by Paris Hilton on the *Late Show with David Letterman*, posted by several YouTube contributors, was viewed more than 2.7 million times during its first weekend online, approximately half the number of viewers the show typically attracts.[35] The *New York Post* even covered the YouTube frenzy over this clip. In 2009, a performance by *Britain's Got Talent* contestant Susan Boyle, originally seen by 11.4 million people on television in England, made her a social media phenomenon.[36] The frumpy Boyle shocked judges and viewers with her beautiful rendition of "I Dreamed a Dream." One popular video of her musical performance attracted almost 2.5 million views within its first 72 hours on YouTube.[37] The day after that performance, the YouTube video was the most popular story on social news site Digg.[38] During its first week, the video had received more than 66 million views and after nine days it had reached 91.6 million views (103 million if earlier Boyle performances are included) across 20 Web sites, according to Visible Measures tracking.[39]

The innumerable blunders of personalities are also exacerbated when they can be watched over and over. The split-screen catfight between Rosie O'Donnell and Elisabeth Hasselbeck on *The View*, available to all who missed the original episode in May 2007, had over 3 million views on YouTube alone across several videos posted by different YouTube members. Tom Cruise's enthusiastic couch jumping incident on *The Oprah Winfrey Show* from May 2005 is available in several different versions on YouTube, with the one dubbed "original version" having received over 800,000 views and more than 3,000 comments. Cruise continued to make waves with his Scientology recruitment video, with one of the many versions being viewed more than 2 million times on YouTube.

Great moments in sports can be experienced through online video. NBC's broadcast of the 2008 Summer Olympic Games attracted an audience for its Web property, with 40% of online viewers using the Web to watch events they had first seen on television.[40] The head-butting of Marco Materazzi by Zinedine Zidane during the 2006 World Cup Finals was watched millions of times across several video posts on YouTube, with one clip by DAN5555 receiving over 4 million views alone. Underwear-clad Boston Red Sox pitcher Jonathan Papelbon performing an Irish jig during the 2007 American League East Championship celebration party has been watched more than 1.1 million times. Sports-related moments are also popular, including Don Imus's derogatory comments about the Rutgers women's basketball team (over 1.3 million views for one YouTube clip); the marriage proposal by Boise State running back Ian Johnson, who ran off the field to his cheerleader girlfriend after scoring a game-winning two-point conversion during overtime in the Fiesta Bowl (over 400,000 views for one YouTube clip); and the 2004 Super Bowl halftime performance by Janet Jackson and Justin Timberlake (almost 3.7 million views among four YouTube clips).

Among the top TV moments of 2006 according to a TiVo poll are several that were viewed millions of times on YouTube alone. Leading the pack are Faith Hill's reaction to Carrie Underwood's CMA award (8.5 million views over three YouTube clips) and Kirstie Alley's bikini reveal on *The Oprah Winfrey Show* (2.2 million views for one *Late Show with David Letterman* clip of the event). Some of the best television moments in 2007, according to AOL Video, included the surprise series finale ending of *The Sopranos*, which had over 1.1 million views for one clip on YouTube. Everyone, not just those with HBO, could see (or not see) how the notorious mob drama ended. Britney Spears's much-hailed opening act "comeback" at the 2007 Video Music Awards drove viewers to the Internet after the performance was widely panned for her lackluster movements and lip-syncing. An unauthorized clip on YouTube has racked up almost 1 million views. Other classics of 2007 include Marie Osmond's fainting spell on *Dancing with* the Stars (almost 800,000 views over three YouTube clips) and Paula Abdul's confusion during a live Fox News interview (almost 5.5 million views over three YouTube clips). *Access Hollywood*'s Top Ten Moments of 2008 includes Sarah Silverman's appearance on *Jimmy Kimmel Live* where she introduced her "Bleeping Matt Damon" video (over 8.1 million views for one YouTube clip) and former *SNL* castmember Tina Fey as Republican vice presidential candidate Sarah Palin (holding five of the top six spots for *SNL*'s political skits of all time on Hulu and receiving over 8.5 million views on NBC.com for the show opener skit with castmember Amy Poehler).

Video-sharing sites offer an opportunity for users to scrutinize the television clips, trying to notice whether Marie Osmond's faint was a publicity gimmick, whether Tom Cruise is a lunatic or just in love, or whether Rosie or Elisabeth walked away the winner. Social media applications allow users to add comments to the online discussion, place the video on their own MySpace page or blog, or send the video to a friend. The experiences once shared in real time in our own family rooms are now shared with strangers in different geographic locations at different times.

PREVIEWS ON YOUTUBE

Hundreds of fans of *Sex and the City* congregated in the streets of New York City beginning in September 2007 to observe the filming of *Sex and the City: The Movie*. The City, often referred to as the fifth character in the series, could not be replaced by a movie set, creating many challenges for the production crew as they shot on location.

The *Daily News* publicized shoot locations to make it easy for fans to find the production crews. Armed with digital and video cameras, fans attempted to capture a glimpse of the scenes, even going so far as writing down overheard dialogue. Many of the photos and videos taken by fans were posted to Flickr or YouTube. Tabloid television programs were also capturing their own footage to air on their nightly programs.[41] Generating possibly the most speculation was the sighting of lead actress Sarah Jessica Parker in a wedding dress outside St. Patrick's Cathedral. Would she finally marry longtime love Mr. Big? Also noticed was actress Kristin Davis, as character Charlotte, with a baby bump. Will she finally get the baby she has so desperately longed for? Producers were quick to tell fans these scenes were merely part of a dream sequence.

Some networks have intentionally released previews and pilots on the Internet to generate buzz before the television premiere. NBC and Warner Bros. Television used this strategy for *Studio 60 on the Sunset Strip* before it debuted in September 2006, teaming up with AOL for an online premiere one week before the program aired on television. The pilot was available for rental through Netflix before the premiere date and bootleg copies could be found on many bit torrent sites as well as on YouTube. NBC released the 2008 season premiere of *30 Rock* a week early on NBC.com and Hulu.[42]

MOVING PROGRAMMING FROM TELEVISION TO THE WEB

Some programming originally intended for broadcast television has found a home on the Internet. The sitcom *Nobody's Watching*, originally developed for The WB, became available on YouTube after the network decided not to include the show in its 2005 schedule. The pilot first leaked onto YouTube in June 2006, and the popularity of the show motivated its producers to continue the series as webisodes until January 2007. The show's reputation on YouTube then attracted NBC to consider the show as either a series or a live television special for its 2006–2007 season, but no deals were ever struck to bring the show to broadcast television.[43] Several low-rated programs that were canceled before all finished episodes premiered on television also migrated online. NBC's *Kidnapped*, CBS's *3 lbs.*, and ABC's *Day Break* all appeared on the Internet, with some of these programs available on network Web sites.

PROGRAMMING FOR THE WEB

Networks are tapping fan fever for certain programs by creating webisodes, which are Internet-only episodes. NBC used this strategy for *The Office* during the summer of 2006, and the SciFi channel generated publicity for the third season of *Battlestar Galactica* with a webisode series. ABC offers video and audio podcasts for the popular series *Lost*.

Rosario Dawson is starring in the sci-fi Web series *Gemini Division*, representing the first Web series featuring a major Hollywood actor.[44] The series of 50 5–7-minute episodes resides on the Web at GeminiDivision.com and on NBC.com, while bundles of episodes are available ON DEMAND to Verizon FIOS TV and Comcast digital cable subscribers. The producers, Electric Farm Entertainment, had a previous Web hit with *Afterworld*, a show that depicts life after an event destroys 99% of the world's population. The ongoing series has produced 130 episodes on a $3 million budget.

Other big names from Hollywood have been featured in Web-only programming. The love life of actor Brad Garrett played out in a 10-part online reality show called *Dating Brad Garrett* in the fall of 2008. Each episode, running just 3–5 minutes, followed a date with a different woman, all of whom had uploaded their video pitches to Crackle.com.[45] In 2008, Seth McFarlane, the creator of *Family Guy*, landed a deal with Google and its AdSense program to create 50 two-minute episodes of "Seth McFarlane's Cavalcade of Cartoon Comedy." Advertising is integrated with the clip as pre-rolls, post-rolls, and overlaps. When the viewer clicks on the video clip, the advertiser pays a fee.[46]

A video series that attracted a huge following and much media attention was lonelygirl15. The videos, which debuted in May 2006, originally purported to represent the real-life struggles of an average American teenager named Bree. After much speculation, Bree's identity was exposed to be New Zealand actress

Jessica Rose, who was working in collaboration with filmmakers Ramesh Flinders and Miles Beckett. Furthermore, it was discovered that Creative Artists Agency was behind the videos. The lonelygirl15 series is now available on Revver, which pays out half of the advertising revenues to producers.[47] Lonelygirl15 also attracted the attention of CBS, who signed Beckett and business manager Greg Goodfried to create extensions of CBS programs for the Internet. Their YouTube channel now hosts 395 videos, with the most popular video having almost 10 million views.

Entertainment companies are also creating exclusive video content to feature on social networking sites. The program offerings are an attempt by social networking sites to capture some of the growth in online video viewing while reclaiming some of their past dominance. From January 2007 to January 2008, MySpace users decreased their time spent on the site by 10%, according to com-Score, while YouTube viewing increased 57% during the same time period.[48]

Social networking site Bebo, popular in the U.K., offers the mystery serial *KateModern*. The first season of this program, promoted through alerts to members, drew an average of 1.5 million viewers per week.[49] Now in its second season, *KateModern* has spawned the creation of other exclusive programs including reality show *The Gap Year* and a drama called *Sophia's Diary*. MySpace has also established its own exclusive programming. Premiering late in 2007 and now in its second season, *Roommates* draws 200,000 views per episode.[50] *Special Delivery*, a hidden-camera show, launched in 2008. This exclusive programming keeps members from fleeing to sites better known for their video content, such as YouTube.[51] The biggest original-programming endeavor on MySpace so far has been a program called *Get Married on MySpace*, where users vote for the winning couple and then make the wedding planning decisions.[52] The series will culminate with the wedding. MySpace also offers *BFF*, a 3.5-minute game show where two best friends are tested on their knowledge of one another.[53]

Advertisers are recognizing distribution of online programming as a viable advertising venture. Procter & Gamble created original programming for the Web with the show *Crescent Heights*, which follows recent college grad Ashley as she navigates the world of public relations in Los Angeles. Tide is the sole sponsor of the program.[54]

As television viewers become more comfortable watching videos on the Internet, even watching full-length television shows or movies, creating original online content has become an attractive option for producers or writers who might feel confined by networks. Online video sites need to offer original programming to stand out from the competition, and many will rely on professionals to develop this programming. As Frank Rose states in a *Wired* magazine article, "Sure, the YouTube explosion was fueled by amateurs, but it will be show-biz professionals who cash in on Web video. That's because most big corporate advertisers want a safe, predictable environment—not the latest YouTube one-off, no matter how viral."[55]

The challenge for these online content creators is to build and keep an audience. A study of the 50 highest-profile Web series, including *LG15: The Resistance, Hot Hot Los Angeles*, and *Back on Topps*, conducted by TubeMogul for *Ad Age* found that audiences dropped off an average of 64% between the first and second episodes.[56] Portals often promote the first episode of a new series, but it is hard to maintain interest among viewers when so many videos are competing for their attention.

Contrary to popular belief, online program creators generally need the support of promotional budgets to launch a successful series (unless a social network is commissioning the program and handling the promotion itself). Although the promotional budget may outweigh the cost of program production, Web content is not necessarily cheap to produce, according to a report by London-based Futurescape. Network television dramas can run $61,360–$75,000 per minute of production; in comparison, several popular Web programs cost several to tens of thousands per minute. For example, *Dorm Life* costs $2,000 per minute, Michael Eisner's *Foreign Body* costs $5,000, and *In the Motherhood* with big-name stars costs $40,000.[57]

MOVING PROGRAMMING FROM THE WEB TO TELEVISION

Television programs have been created from YouTube clips or inspired by successful online series. One video that successfully made the leap from YouTube to television was "Battle of Kruger." Featuring eight minutes of an African safari shot by Texan David Budzinski in 2004, the video has attracted more than 30 million online views. The footage captures the attack of a cape buffalo calf by a pride of lions and a crocodile. In a dramatic contrast to similar footage, the herd of buffalos fight the predators, saving the life of the buffalo calf. Budzinski attempted to sell the footage to *National Geographic* and Animal Planet to no avail.

Yet, the popularity of the video on YouTube eventually drew the attention of the National Geographic Channel, which purchased the video rights and then created an hour-long documentary called "Caught on Safari: Battle at Kruger," which aired in May 2008, possibly the first show of this nature to be derived solely from a YouTube video.[58] The show focused on the story of the video, including the initial spotting of the lions and the nearby buffalo herd by the tour guide, Budzinski's unflinching ability to capture the event on video, fellow tour member Jason Schlosberg's request of a copy of the video, Budzinski's unsuccessful attempt to sell the footage to networks, and then Schlosberg's use of YouTube to share the video with a friend in 2007. After that, the video vaulted to YouTube stardom, finally attracting the attention of the National Geographic Channel.

Popular video series from social media have also entered the realm of mainstream media to become a television series. In 2007, twice-weekly, eight-minute clips of a series called *Quarterlife* were released on MySpace video and YouTube and streamed on Quarterlife.com. The drama, with its television-quality production values and scripts by Emmy award-winning writer and producer Marshall Herskovitz, featured attractive 20-somethings navigating relationships and careers.[59]

A YouTube home page link gave *Quarterlife* more than 700,000 views for its first episode, but without that prominent reminder, the show's audience dropped significantly. The series found renewed success for the last 12 episodes, which averaged 105,000 views.[60] Although the series "ratings" were miniscule by television standards, the 36-part online series was granted new life on television in early 2008 with a contract from NBC for six episodes of a one-hour show. In a way, the Web presence was used to test the waters as well as build an audience prior to the show's television debut on NBC. As a television program, *Quarterlife* represented a departure from the industry where media conglomerates predominantly own the networks, studios, and shows, and thus have complete creative control over the producers; in this case, *Quarterlife's* producers received full ownership and control.[61] After the premiere episode managed only dismal ratings at 3.1 million viewers, the remaining episodes were shown on Bravo.[62] All episodes are now housed on Hulu.

Some YouTube auteurs aspire to launch a full-scale television program from their concept. The creators of the online comedy *We Need Girlfriends*, Brian Amyot, Angel Accvedo, and Steven Tsapelas, promoted their series through blogs and MySpace profiles for the characters, three young college graduates living in New York City who have all been recently dumped by girlfriends. Front-page postings of their videos on MySpace and YouTube ramped up views to the hundreds of thousands for most of the episodes, peaking at over 700,000 views for episode four and then losing steam through the rest of the season until the series ended with just over 100,000 views for episode 11. A script commitment from CBS is giving the filmmakers the opportunity to work with Darren Star to create a pilot of the program for television.[63]

The founders of CollegeHumor.com, Ricky Van Veen and Josh Abramson, used the site to promote videos they started creating while still in college. Helped by cross-postings on YouTube, CollegeHumor.com attracted a following of more than 6 million monthly visitors. Those visitors can visit the CollegeHumor.com store, which sells T-shirts and two books penned by the writers of CollegeHumor.com. In 2006, Barry Diller's holding company IAC acquired a majority stake in the site for a reported $20 million.[64] Their online success also earned the team a comedy tour and the opportunity to write a comedy pilot for MTV, which shares the name of the site and premiered in February 2009.[65] A film project is also in the works at Paramount Pictures. Other online content attempting to make the leap to television is *Atomic Wedgie*, a series of raunchy video clips intended primarily for mobile devices. Found on MySpace and atomicwedgietv.com, these videos have been viewed more than 3 million times.[66]

In the Motherhood started as a webisode series starring Leah Remini, Chelsea Handler, and Jenny McCarthy. Created by brand entertainment firm Mindshare, the program was picked up by ABC who issued a 13-episode order for the program.[67] Actors Megan Mullaly, Cheryl Hines, and Jessica St. Clair play the three lead roles in the television version.

NETWORK RESPONSE

The proliferation of online video clips would not have been possible if the copyright issues of online video had not been resolved through agreements between video-sharing sites and the major networks. Although uploading and viewing copyright-protected works is a violation of copyright laws, the networks and film studios also view it as an opportunity to further promote their content. A concept called "tolerated use" has become the standard, and media companies determine the extent to which the use is harmful before citing copyright violation.[68] YouTube polices unauthorized content and gives the networks an opportunity to place advertising on bootleg videos.[69] For a while, other video-sharing sites, like Paris-based DailyMotion.com, did not regulate copyrighted content and became the dumping ground of many YouTube videos.[70] DailyMotion.com now polices copyright infringement and notifies users of the illegal posting of copyrighted videos.

In 2007, Viacom sent over 100,000 Digital Millennium Copyright Act notices ordering the removal of copyrighted content from video-sharing sites, including many clips of *The Daily Show with Jon Stewart* on Comedy Central. The Digital Millennium Copyright Act of 1998 allows for a "safe harbor" provision for sites that host copyrighted content as long as they are not aware of the violations, do not profit from the content, and remove infringing content at the request of the copyright holder.[71] After filing a $1 billion lawsuit against Google and YouTube, an arrangement was made to allow Viacom content as long as revenues are shared with the company. Comedy Central now offers a searchable database of 13,000 video clips of *The Daily Show with Jon Stewart*, representing every moment of the program since its 1999 premiere.

A statement by Viacom reads, "Like our peers in the media industry, we are focused on finding the right business model for professionally created content to be legally distributed on the Internet. We want our audiences to be able to access our programming on every platform and we're interested in having it live on all forms of distribution in ways that protect our talented artists, our loyal customers, and our passionate audiences."[72]

After the *Saturday Night Live* sketch "Lazy Sunday" became a cult hit on YouTube, NBC cited copyright violation and policed the site for unauthorized videos.[73] When an *SNL* sketch surfaced on YouTube the next year (Justin Timberlake and Andy Samberg's "Dick in a Box"), the network realized that working with YouTube beats working against it. NBC allowed the network-bleeped

YouTube versions to remain online but drove fans to its own Web site for the uncensored version of the video. NBC has been criticized for circumventing the Federal Communications Commission in this manner, as the organization does not have any jurisdiction over Web content. The conservative watchdog group Parents Television Council particularly admonished NBC for making an uncensored version available on the Internet.[74]

The network also posted the video on YouTube's NBC channel, garnering over 2 million views during the first week at a time when *SNL* was averaging about 6.5 million viewers each week, according to Nielsen Media Research.[75] The video quickly become a top 20 most viewed video and was cited by Scott Button of ViralVideoChart.com as being one of the quickest and most ubiquitous viral videos on the Web.[76] NBC then made an agreement with YouTube to promote shows on the Web site and through its own YouTube channel.[77,78] The benefits to cooperating with video-sharing sites include the ability to share advertising revenue and protect against piracy.

Network executives at the National Association of Broadcasters meeting in 2008 questioned how to attract viewers to their television programs and to their network Web sites. One strategy was to stay ahead of consumers, who post unauthorized content on video-sharing sites.[79] Many of the networks are playing the online video game by gaining control of their own content through branded YouTube channels or their own video-sharing sites. The networks, not wanting to lose complete control over their content, provide incentives to drive viewers to the networks' own Web sites. Full versions of current and canceled shows are often found here.

NBC Universal and News Corp debuted Hulu in March 2008, as a one-stop shop for their proprietary clips that had once proliferated on YouTube and file-sharing sites like BitTorrent. Hulu uses embedded ads in programs, allows users to e-mail or post clips on another Web site, and tracks viewership even when the videos are e-mailed or posted on other Web sites.[80] The free site contains more than 3,000 full-length television programs and 100 movies.[81] Current and classic shows are both available, but not user-generated videos, and the site aggregates content from more than 130 partners.[82] Also available on Hulu are original webisodes of *Heroes*, *Chuck*, and *The Office*, which launched during the summer of 2008, weave stories from the television series with additional insight only available in the online experience.[83] In 2009, Disney announced that it would purchase a 30% stake in Hulu, which means content from Disney properties ABC and ESPN will follow.[84]

Hulu is attracting major advertisers, including Bank of America, Best Buy, and McDonald's among its more than 100 advertisers, and its inventory appears to be sold out.[85] Ad revenue for 2009 is expected to reach $120 million.[86] Users can engage with the site's social media features, including video rating, where 25% of visitors participate, and Facebook Connect, where Hulu users can interact with friends who also use the site.[87] In February 2009, Hulu surpassed

MySpace and Yahoo! to become the third-largest video site in terms of video views. With 309 million views in February 2009, Hulu is still dwarfed by YouTube's views of 5.2 billion a month.[88] By May 2009, Hulu was closing in on second-place Fox Interactive Media, with 380 million video views as compared to Fox's 437 million.[89]

During the summer of 2008, NBC.com also launched a *Saturday Night Live* site focused solely on political clips. Users also interact with the site by voting for the best clips and playing games. NBC.com also offers "Jay's Garage," based on Jay Leno's car fanaticism, which allows users to interact with other enthusiasts by sharing video and photos of their own cars.[90]

Video-sharing site Joost relaunched several months after the introduction of Hulu as a Flash video site with free, ad-supported television shows, replacing the software application that users were previously required to download to watch programs.[91] The site's library includes full-length programs from CBS, Viacom, and Warner Bros. Television. Television programs, such as *Friends*, *The Hills*, and *Diff'rent Strokes*, and movies, such as *Jerry Maguire* and *Men in Black* are all available here. Like Hulu, Joost also uses Facebook Connect and is the most popular client for this service with 27,000 Joost users.[92]

CBS had uploaded over 300 videos to the CBS Brand Channel on YouTube by late 2006, realizing 29.2 million views in the first month, 20,000 subscribers, and 857,000 views a day. In addition to the drama *NCIS*, the most popular CBS shows on the Web include the news and late show programs *The Early Show*, *Late Show with David Letterman*, and *The Late Late Show with Craig Ferguson*.[93] CBS made a deal with Google in 2008 to run full-length programs from its television archive, including *Star Trek*, *Beverly Hills 90210*, and *The Young and the Restless*.[94] Google and CBS share the advertising revenue that is generated by the ads sold around the shows. CBS then acquired TV.com in May 2008. Although the site offers more than 1,000 programs, they are not exclusive to the site. Traffic has actually declined between May 2008 and November 2008, dropping from 355,000 monthly unique viewers to 155,000, with many of these viewers assumed to be leaving for Hulu.

In May 2008, Warner Bros. Television launched TheWB.com, offering shows such as *Friends*, *The O.C.*, and *Gilmore Girls* as well as new content.[95] Warner Bros. will also eventually offer a similar site with animated programming for children. Now renamed The CW, the network ended the posting of new episodes of *Gossip Girl* on its Web site. The hope was to drive the hundreds of thousands of viewers from the Internet back to television. The experiment succeeded in improving ratings and making *Gossip Girl* the number one most downloaded program on iTunes at $1.99 a download.[96]

Although much has been noted about the broadcast networks' treatment of online video, many cable networks are offering the same services. iTunes is a primary distribution method of fee-based downloadable programs from a wide variety of networks and suppliers, including The History Channel,

MTV, Nickelodeon, and the Travel Channel, as well as all the major networks. Several sources have claimed that iTunes downloads resulted in a bump in ratings for several key shows. Even social networking sites are getting involved in the video revolution, with MySpace offering branded channels for TMZ.com, the networks of BBC and National Geographic, and advertiser Sony, who sponsors a "minisode" channel offering 3–5 minute segments of classic shows.[97]

CULTURAL IMPLICATIONS

The big question for the television industry is whether consumers will dump television for their newfound love of online video? The greatest implications of any possible shifting from television viewing to Internet video viewing is the potential loss of advertising and sponsorship dollars. How can the model that has sustained television for more than 50 years be viable when commercial-free programs can be distributed via the Internet? Even if a brief commercial is tacked to the beginning of a clip or rolled across the bottom during viewing, will the television industry be able to charge advertisers enough to continue to produce original content?

On the other hand, maybe viewers will continue to choose the experience of large-screen high-definition television in a comfortable family room over that of a smaller computer screen sitting on a desk—at least for now. Online video still lacks the high-quality and consistent picture of television, something that many consumers have demonstrated demand for in their frenetic rush to purchase high-definition televisions. The future might give rise to an integrated television and broadband access computer, but we are not there yet.[98] DVRs, however, combine the best of best worlds, giving consumers the ability to time-shift television programs and skip commercials while enjoying a comfortable viewing experience.

Consumers expect to have content when they want it. Content can be streamed or downloaded, with streaming popular for broadband viewing of clips or user generated content on YouTube and downloadable content useful for watching full-length programs at a convenient time, even when no Internet connection is available. Internet father Vint Cerf stated in an interview that in the future, broadcasters would use a model called Internet Protocol TV, whereby programs would be delivered over private Internet networks where they would be watched on computer-outfitted televisions that translate the data and display it on a monitor.[99] A Deloitte & Touche study demonstrated that 71% of consumers surveyed were interested in having their television connected to the Internet. At the Consumer Electronics Show in Las Vegas in 2009, Yahoo! unveiled an initiative with partners Samsung, LG, Sony, and Vizio to create a high-definition television that offers Yahoo!'s online services.[100] Online widgets will run alongside television content and allow users to watch videos from YouTube, connect on MySpace, message using Twitter, or share photos using Flickr.

The availability of online video changes the interpersonal experience of television. At one time, we all watched the same primetime shows and talked about them with friends the next day. Online videos fracture the shared experience of television. Instead, we now watch television programs on our own time, sharing the experience with others online through the use of social media.

Chapter 8

MUSICIANS ON MYSPACE:
BRINGING MUSIC TO THE MASSES

All the world is not, of course, a stage, but the crucial ways in which it isn't are not easy to specify.

—Erving Goffman

In 2002, MySpace was just another e-commerce site. The product—a $99 motor scooter made in China—was peddled by marketer Chris DeWolfe. In 2003, the repurposed MySpace began its quick ascent to become the largest online social network in the world, changing the way people connect with friends, brands connect with consumers, and musicians connect with fans. Music is very much a part of the culture of MySpace, making the story of MySpace a chapter in the history of music.

For the "new" MySpace, DeWolfe teamed with musician Tom Anderson to create a network that could compete with the popular social networking sites of Friendster and Xanga and provide a haven for Friendsters disillusioned with the site, which was rumored to be switching to a fee-based model. Musicians on Friendster, who were particularly disgruntled for being targeted for not complying with profile regulations, found a more hospitable community in MySpace and were able to persuade their fans to follow them from Friendster to this start up social network. As danah boyd and Nicole Ellison described in a 2007 article, the early growth of MySpace was not due solely to the influx of musicians and their fans, but that this relationship had a significant impact during the initial expansion of MySpace.[1] Some of the first MySpace profiles were created by indie-rock musicians from the Los Angeles area.

Just two years later after its launch, MySpace along with parent company Intermix were purchased by Rupert Murdoch's News Corporation for $649 million in cash and stock. Since its inception, MySpace has exploded to 172 million members, including actors, politicians, brands, television shows, and just regular people. Many established and new artists still use a MySpace profile to connect with fans. In 2005, more than 240,000 musicians maintained MySpace profiles.[2] That number is undoubtedly much higher today. Musicians are in good company with the millions of MySpace users, many of them young music fans.

We are seeing a cultural shift in music as a result of social media, and in turn, a shift in social media because of music. This chapter describes the relationship between the music industry and MySpace, and how established and unsigned artists as well as music labels are negotiating the opportunities of social networking sites.

MEASURING POPULARITY ON MYSPACE

Not only was MySpace founded with a concern for musicians in mind, but this social networking site also offers features that make it a particularly friendly and useful place for musicians to promote their music. Hosting a profile is not only free of charge, but also free from the many regulations of Friendster and other sites. The free profile allows a musician to host four uploaded MP3s; more features are available for a fee in an enhanced profile. Musicians use their profiles to host music tracks and videos for listening and downloading, photos, and links to their official Web sites. MySpace also offers the opportunity for musicians to interact with fans. The key difference between MySpace and other social networking sites is the ability of users to create pages that are uniquely their own.

At the end of 2008, MySpace released a list of its most popular musicians for the year; topping the list was the animated group Gorillaz with 682,875 friends.[3] These bands or artists were considered to be the most watched and listened to throughout the year. Also included on the list were Bullet for My Valentine (596,885 friends), Amy Winehouse (542,268 friends), Coldplay (525,110 friends), Lily Allen (462,159 friends), MIA (399,858 friends), Oasis (353,484 friends), and Imogen Heap (351,484 friends).

Several academic studies have explored the relationship between MySpace activity and music sales. Vasant Dhar and Elaine Chang, both of New York University, examined the impact of several independent variables, including the number of MySpace friends and blog chatter, on album sales.[4] This 2007 study found that the higher percentage change week over week of MySpace friends and increased blog post volume correlated with increased weekly sales of an album, with blog chatter having a larger impact than friend increases. In fact, higher percentage increases in friends actually begins to produce diminishing returns on album sales, possibly a result of the minimal effort it takes on the part of a MySpace member to "friend" an artist. Additional analysis showed that, unlike blog chatter, having MySpace friends may have no predictive value prior to the release of an album and is only important after the release.

Four researchers from IBM Almaden Research along with two university professors developed a way to measure popularity of an artist, album, or track based on the comments by users of social networking services such as MySpace.[5] They contend that traditional methods for determining popularity, such as album sales or radio plays, are not relevant in today's digital world. After generating a list of popular artists based on a comment crawl on MySpace, the researchers presented this list as well as a list of *Billboard* Top Artists to three samples composed of either young people (aged 8–15) or college students (generally aged 17–22). In twice as many instances, the respondents believed the MySpace list contained the artists who had been popular during the previous week.[6]

GOING IT ALONE

MySpace represents a new paradigm for the music industry by lessening the need for musicians to sign with a record label to promote and distribute their music. Musicians who can command a following have the opportunity to stay independent and handle their own marketing and management. Combined with the exposure provided by MySpace, the demand for digital music on the consumer side and the rise of desktop music production tools on the producer side have increased the opportunities for independent musicians. Additionally, online distribution costs are minimal compared to the costs associated with distributing a CD.

A record label, however, does allow the artist to be freed from handling the non-music aspects of managing a career, including recording, production, distribution, marketing, and promotion. These costs, however, are on the decline. Recording and production can be handled with a good laptop and Pro Tools; digital distribution can be accomplished through Orchard or INgrooves, companies that take a flat percentage of sales; CD distribution can be handled with CD Baby for $4 a CD; and for promotion, sites like PureVolume and Sellaband.com can help manage promotional Web sites. One-stop shops like Musictoday can handle all aspects for the artist. Yet, no act has been successful completely on its own. Although Clap Your Hands Say Yeah is often cited as a band that has found success without a label, their first album sold 125,000 copies and their second album, released on January 30, 2009, has sold just 29,000 with the help of Alternative Distribution Alliance, a major label-affiliated distribution company. The challenge for do-it-yourselfers is mass retail and radio promotion.

In 2006, MySpace began providing artists with Snocap, an online music service. Founded by Napster creator Shawn Fanning, this service allows an artist to sell music downloads directly from his or her profile page, assuming the artist owns the song's copyright. Particularly useful for unsigned artists, the downloads allow musicians an opportunity to benefit from their online popularity through direct compensation. MySpace receives a hefty fee of 45% of the sales price from each transaction. MySpace members, however, did not initially embrace the model and by October 2007, Snocap had laid off half of its employees.[7]

LANDING A RECORD DEAL

Many musicians have used MySpace as a springboard to a recording contract. For some of these artists, contract decisions were based on the willingness of the label to allow a great deal of creative independence. With MySpace serving as a means for vetting the music, some artists believe that interference from the record company might alienate their fans.

The Internet buzz swirling around formerly-unsigned British band Arctic Monkeys boosted its recognition by several major labels who courted the band for a contract. An NPR story describes the band in this manner: "With obvious influences from bands like The Clash and The Smiths, Arctic Monkeys have a blistering, guitar-heavy sound with infectious melodies and lyrical swipes on small-town life, teen angst, and the music industry."[8] With almost 140,000 friends, the band has built a relatively small but loyal MySpace following. After citing popular phrases used to describe the band such as an "Internet phenome-nom" with a "DIY marketing campaign," Laura Barton of *The Guardian* describes the impact of MySpace and the Internet on the music industry: "The simple fact that the Internet allows a fledgling band's music to be heard without label assistance has heralded a joyous new musical socialism."[9] Changes in the UK Top 40, which counts legal downloads toward chart position, allowed Arctic Monkeys to have 15 songs in the top 40 during April 2007.[10] The band, considered by some to be the greatest British rock band ever, eventually signed with independent label UK Domino Records. The band's debut album, *Whatever People Say I Am, That's What I'm Not*, sold more than any other British predecessor, a feat that may be credited to the band's MySpace popularity, according to industry experts.[11]

As an unsigned artist, Colbie Caillat attracted a massive MySpace following, eventually leading to a recording contract with the major label Universal Music. As described in her MySpace biography, after Caillat had a collection of songs, she placed them on her MySpace profile with little fanfare. It wasn't until she posted the infectious song "Bubbly" that millions of fans started coming to her page, more than 35 million worldwide.[12] The popularity of the song resulted in her being the top unsigned artist on MySpace for four consecutive months with over 10 million plays. Universal Music allowed Caillat to have total creative freedom. As Caillat stated in her bio, "[T]he great thing about MySpace is that you can build up an army of fans and then when you go to a record company, there's no point in them trying to change what you do because it's already been tried and tested."[13]

We the Kings, a band from Bradenton, Fla., represents another MySpace success story. The combination of the fan base built on MySpace and a PureVolume.com Top 10 placement attracted a major label.[14] Now signed to independent label S-Curve Records, the band toured with the Vans Warped Tour in 2008. Another Floridian to be noticed on MySpace is Matt Hires. Home-schooled as a teenager, Hires learned to play the bass guitar at age 12. At 16, Hires's father passed down his own acoustic guitar to his son, which is the guitar Hires still uses today. For a while, he played in the punk band Brer with several childhood friends and released two albums with them before embarking as a solo artist.[15] Hires secured a recording contract when an Atlantic Records representative viewed his MySpace profile and liked his melodic, acoustic sound. Since then, he has released a four-song live acoustic EP, had his music used on *Grey's Anatomy* and *Private Practice*, and opened for Dave Matthews Band, Marc Broussard, and O.A.R. In 2009, Hires headlined a solo acoustic showcase at South by Southwest, toured with John Mayer's "Mayercraft Carrier," and debuted his solo album.[16]

Winning Best Rap Album at the 51st Annual Grammy Awards in 2009 was Lil Wayne, an artist who also had the top-selling album of 2008. Like many of the other artists profiled here, the rapper built his fan base by distributing tracks of his music online and using other online methods. He continues to release free music despite having a recording contract with Universal.[17] Another rapper who got his start online was DeAndre Way, a.k.a. Soulja Boy. After receiving positive feedback for his self-produced tracks on SoundClick, he created MySpace and YouTube profiles to promote his music.[18] In March 2007, he released his album *Unsigned & Still Major: Da Album Before Da Album* and then the single "Crank That (Soulja Boy)," accompanied by a video demonstrating the "Crank That Dance," which he uploaded to YouTube in April 2007. In May 2007, he met with Michael Grooms, a.k.a. Mr. Collipark, and signed a deal with Interscope Records.[19] Later in the year, his single went to number one on the *Billboard* Hot 100, where it was a number one song for seven nonconsecutive weeks.[20]

One of the more heartwarming MySpace success stories is that of 43-year-old Tommy DeCarlo, formerly a credit manager of a Home Depot in Charlotte, N.C., with lifelong dreams of becoming a rock star. A longtime fan of the band Boston, DeCarlo recorded karaoke versions of Boston's hits, which were then placed on a MySpace profile created for him by his teenage daughter. His versions were a tribute to lead singer Brad Delp, who had committed suicide in March 2007. When the wife of founder Tom Scholz ran across DeCarlo's track while surfing the Internet, she mistakenly thought the singer was Delp. In August 2007, DeCarlo was on stage with Boston—his first time ever singing with a band—at a tribute concert for Delp. DeCarlo started his new job as Boston's lead singer when the band toured in the summer of 2008.[21]

The band Journey also found a new lead singer using social media, this time on YouTube. Arnel Pineda had had a successful 25-year music career in the Philippines, most recently with his band The Zoo.[22] In 2007, videos of the band performing cover songs from American bands, such as Journey, Survivor, and Aerosmith started appearing on YouTube. Journey guitarist Neal Schon, impressed with the vocal talent of Pineda and his similarity in sound to former lead singer Steve Perry, contacted Noel Gomez, who was responsible for uploading many of the videos, to get Pineda's contact information. When reached, Schon asked Pineda to audition for the band. The audition successfully landed Pineda a role as Journey's frontman. Journey has since toured and released an album.

Dubbed the "queen" of MySpace by *Time* magazine, model/actress/singer Tila Tequila (real name: Thien Thanh Thi Nguyen) has held firm at or near the top of MySpace Music's daily list of top unsigned artists list for years. A MySpace member since 2003, her only claim to fame prior to acquiring more than 3.6 million friends and over 177 million page views on MySpace was as *Playboy's* Cyber Girl of the Week. Her MySpace fame translated into a reality dating show on MTV called *A Shot at Love with Tila Tequila.* Her music career got off the ground in 2006 with a record deal with Will.i.am Music Group, an imprint of A&M. In February 2007, however, Tequila released the single "I Love U" independently on iTunes. Her debut album, *Sex,* was later released by independent label The Saturday Team.

Other bands that launched careers on MySpace include Hollywood Undead, West Grand, and Fall Out Boy. The Canadian band Time is the Enemy was signed by INgrooves after establishing a presence on MySpace. Punk band Hawthorne Heights, with over 180,000 friends, attracted indie label Victory Records.

PROMOTING SIGNED ARTISTS

Not just a community for unsigned or independent label artists, the credibility of MySpace is enhanced by the established musicians who have profile pages on the site. Beck, Nine Inch Nails, Weezer, the Black Eyed Peas, and Billy Corgan are a few of the hundreds of thousands of bands or artists who maintain MySpace profiles.[23] Bands are also creating profiles on Facebook, another popular social networking site. Of the top 25 most popular Facebook pages in 2008, musician pages comprised 40% of the list, with Coldplay, Avril Lavigne, Justin Timberlake, Chris Brown, and Dave Matthews Band all represented.[24] Facebook, however, has not been as aggressive as MySpace in courting the music labels.

Another British singing sensation is Lily Allen, who can attribute much of her early success to her MySpace profile. Although Allen had a recording contact with Regal, a division of Polygram, before she was a MySpace phenomenon, her label was not actively promoting her. With an album release planned for 16 months after her signing, her career was basically stalled while the company explored her sound. Meanwhile, Allen created a MySpace profile. In a 2006 interview with *Pitchfork's* Scott Plagenhoef, Allen described how she built a following on MySpace:

> Over the past two years I had been doing demos and I probably had, like, seven or eight that I was confident enough to put on the page for people to hear. I started putting them up in November [2005], two months after I signed. I just kind of swapped them around. When we did "Nan, You're a Window Shopper," literally five minutes after we finished, it was on MySpace.
>
> By February or March it was obvious that something was going on, because there were so many subscribers to the blog and so many people listening to the music— the plays were just going up and up and up.[25]

Since then, Allen's music has been played more than 19 million times on MySpace. In 2008, she chose to release two demo tracks from her second album on MySpace.[26]

Some artists have used MySpace or other music networks as a place to launch an album before it is available in stores. R.E.M. debuted their studio album *Accelerate* on iLike on March 24, 2008, approximately one week before the North American release of the album.[27] Other content, such as interviews with the band about the making of the album, was also made available for Web distribution. The online release built excitement for the album, which could be pre-ordered from iTunes or Amazon. Madonna launched her album *Hard Candy* on MySpace on April 25, 2008. In addition to R.E.M. and Madonna, Nine Inch Nails, the Black Eyed Peas, Outkast, 50 Cent, Sean Kingston, and the Shins had all exclusively premiered albums on MySpace.[28] Musicians can also place video content on the site. Foo Fighters provided users with a videocast of the making of their album *In Your Honor*. Coldplay offered behind-the-scenes footage from their tour in Japan.[29]

Artists are exploring creative tactics to get their music into the iPods of consumers. The rock band Radiohead, without the backing of a label, chose to release an album for download from their Web site and have consumers pay what they wished. The Smashing Pumpkins allowed a free download of their new song *FOL* as part of a Hyundai promotion that featured the song in a commercial that ran during the 2009 Super Bowl.

MYSPACE FOR FANS

MySpace is a fan-friendly site. Fans can express their admiration for certain musicians on their own MySpace profile pages by embedding a musician's tracks, friending a musician, or placing badges or skins with a musician's logo on their MySpace profiles. Ringtones for mobile phones and downloads are also publicly available on MySpace. According to the company, approximately 65 percent of members embed music on their profile pages.[30] Fans can also join one of the almost 400,000 music groups to connect with others who share similar musical tastes. Some of these groups are fan clubs for a certain band or a musical genre; others provide resources for musicians.

The personal nature of music translates easily into the community of MySpace. MySpace profiles are often created to project an image the user would like others to perceive. Similarly, music fandom is used as a way to express a particular image to others. It follows that on MySpace, users will declare an appreciation of certain artists, bands, or musical genres that they believe would enhance their image in the eyes of others. For some MySpace members, being a fan of a relatively unknown brand may bring a certain amount of cachet, leading some members to possibly consider such users to be on the cutting edge of music.

MySpace profiles can be examined using impression management or self-presentation theories, most notably influenced by sociologist Erving Goffman and his 1959 book *The Presentation of Self in Everyday Life*.[31] He advocated impression management for its prosocial abilities of fostering friendship and avoiding conflicts. Goffman's work describes the ways people use impression management behaviors to both *give* traditional expressions and *give off* unintentional communications. Although his theory originated long before the creation of MySpace, Facebook, or even the World Wide Web, it remains applicable in modern times. The online environment allows participants greater control of their self-presentation, particularly with respect to the communications they give instead of those they give off. Goffman described self as "a dramatic effect arising diffusely from a scene that is presented, and the characteristic issue, the crucial concern is whether it will be credited or discredited."[32]

Self-presentation has been the theoretical foundation of studies of personal Web sites by several academicians, including Nicola Döring[33] and Anna Malin Karlsson.[34] Nicole Ellison, Rebecca Heino, and Jennifer Gibbs explored self-presentation on online dating sites.[35] More recent studies have examined presentation of self on MySpace, including State University of New York Institute of Technology graduate student Heather Perretta in her 2007 thesis.[36] Now this theory provides insight into self-presentation of music fans on social networking sites.

David Beer describes how social media allow for a shift in the relationships between a musician and his or her fans. He proposes "that popular music plays a complex and central role in the connections necessary to the participatory functioning of Web 2.0."[37] Although fans do not know whether they are actually communicating with a musician on MySpace, they are often under the perception that they are. Beer refers to this belief as the perception of proximity. Another upshot is that fans of an artist are connecting with one another and, in some cases, other musicians who associate their music with an established artist are networking with his or her fans in an effort to promote their own music.[38]

MORE THAN MYSPACE

In 2005, MySpace launched its own record label, MySpace Records, which is a partnership between MySpace and label Interscope. The label released the compilation album *MySpace Records: Volume 1* and sponsored a tour in late 2007 with headliners Say Anything and Hellogoodbye and opening acts Young Love and Polysics. Artists on the label also include Mickey Avalon, Sherwood, Burning Brides, Kate Voegele, and Hollywood Undead. With almost 1.5 million friends, the musicians on MySpace Records also get exceptional exposure through their association with the label. For some of these artists, it was their Internet following that attracted the attention of MySpace Records. In the case of Hollywood Undead, for example, after just one week on MySpace, the band went to number one on the MySpace Top Bands Chart. As a result of this pop-ularity, Hollywood Undead became the first band signed to MySpace Records.

MySpace Records attracted industry attention for releasing a free ad-supported album for the punk band Pennywise. To receive a copy of the band's ninth album, *Reason to Believe*, MySpace members were required to friend Textango, who then responded by sending the member downloading instructions on March 25, 2008, and giving the member two weeks to download the album.[39]

MySpace's first venture into the touring business was the Tankfarm Future Sounds Tour, which kicked off in October 2008 and had more than a dozen stops in North America. MySpace also connects to music fans through MySpace Secret Shows, which provide free shows to MySpace members who add the Secret Show profile to their Top 8 friends list and then follow the instructions to receive a wristband for admission. Franz Ferdinand, Gnarls Barkley, the Aus-tralian band Jet, and James Blunt have all promoted secret shows on MySpace. MySpace LIVE also provides fans with live concerts, which are exclusive invite-only private events. With co-sponsor T-Mobile, MySpace LIVE presented T.I. and Friends at the Riv in Chicago on June 20, 2007. MySpace's The List features a band at myspace.com/thelist and sponsors a concert for MySpace members. Finally, MySpace's Transmissions gives artists a platform for performing a set of songs at a venue of their choosing, a concept similar to MTV's *Unplugged*. A video with exclusive content is made available for viral distribution, and the tracks can be purchased via MySpace for a price of the distributor's choosing, rather than a set price as with iTunes.

Advertisers have demonstrated their support of new artists by highlighting music on their MySpace profiles and sponsoring tours. For example, Jeep hosted eight musicians on its MySpace page at myspace.com/jeepuncharted and show-cased their music during the 286 shows of the Jeep Compass Summer Tour.

MOVING FROM MYSPACE

The concept of MySpace has been so successful that some artists with MySpace profiles are leaving to create their own social networks and taking their MySpace friends with them. Rapper 50 Cent, with over 1.1 million friends on MySpace, also maintains a social networking site at Thisis50.com, using the site to showcase his music to his more than 285,000 friends. Ludacris uses his site at WeMix.com to allow members to upload their own music. Singer Sara Bareilles offers the Sara B Community for her more than 1,000 fans who are members. Kylie Minogue (KylieKonnect.com) and the Pussycat Dolls have also branched out from MySpace with their own social networking sites. Although artists have long maintained their own Web sites, the social net-working application allows fans to interact and return to the site for more interaction. The artists can sell advertisements and own the content, usage data, and database of user e-mails.[40]

Two popular create-your-own social networking sites are Ning.com and Flux.com, a company partly owned by MTV. Each has its own revenue model, with Ning charging $34 monthly for the site and hosting and Flux receiving a percentage of revenue from ad sales. The benefit of Flux to records labels is that they can use the same profile template for a variety of artists. Universal Music Group and Virgin both use this service.[41]

An even more sophisticated move was made by Ice Cube and DJ Pooh, who launched the broadband TV and social networking site UVNTV using Microsoft's Silverlight technology. Artists and brands can develop their own channels, and members can create profiles and then connect with these artists and brands. This venture allows the artists to have access to user data and control sales of advertisements, merchandise, downloads, and subscriptions to the channel. Although not yet officially launched, artists Ice Cube and Snoop Dogg have channels, as well as brands RockStar Games and Source.[42] Similar to television, UVNTV delivers programming on a variety of channels, which can be browsed using a channel guide.

ALTERNATIVES TO MYSPACE

Part of the challenge for consumers is how to navigate the massive amount of musical content available online. Just as you might search for a partner on Match.com, you can search for an artist on MySpace based on a certain geographic area and genre. MySpace does not, however, incorporate a music recommender system that would make selections based on music preferences. Pete Rojas, an online independent label owner, describes how social networks can perform an important service when consumers have so many options.

> The majors thrived in an era of artificial scarcity when they were able to control the production and distribution of music. Today, we have an infinite number of choices available to us, and when content is infinitely abundant, the only scarce commodities are convenience, taste, and trust. The music companies that are successfully shaping the Internet era are recognizing that the real value is in making it easier to buy music than to steal it, helping consumers find other people who share their music tastes, and serving as a trusted source for discovering new music.[43]

Other music networks, such as Pandora, utilize these systems to play music in the style of a favorite musician or band and can help channel preference, expose an artist to potential fans, and help an artist create a relationship with consumers. Pandora users can vote on musical selections with a "Thumbs Up" or "Thumbs Down," helping to refine the selection process. Lesser-known artists can achieve wide exposure through their association with Pandora.

Other recommender systems include MOG and Last.fm. MOG, with its slogan "Discover people through music and music through people," is a community for music lovers that was founded in June 2005 by CEO David Hyman.

Users can find music, watch videos, and read news about their favorite artists. A helpful feature is the ability to find people with similar tastes in music. On Last.fm, users build personal listening charts using software that tracks their listening habits. A profile page can be created, and users can then link to others with similar musical tastes. Users also have the capacity to join groups and build playlists. Last.fm is unique in its use of a collaborative filtering algorithm that can recommend music to users based on the music similar users have in their playlists.

Launched in 2003, PureVolume rivals MySpace as a social network for promoting new and emerging artists, but, unlike MySpace, is a destination that focuses solely on music, and specifically, the music of unsigned artists. On PureVolume, artists can make songs available for free download on their profiles, and fans can use their profiles to track and share music they like. The site reaches out to music fans in venues around the United States and has sponsored The Vans Warped Tour, Rockstar Energy Drink's Taste of Chaos, and the Take Action Tour. Jamendo, Unsigned, and Soundclick are three additional sites where music fans can locate unsigned artists.

MYSPACE AND THE MUSIC INDUSTRY

Although CDs still represent the highest percentage of all recorded music sales, digital music sales are on the rise, representing about 10% of the market, according to IFPI's 2007 Digital Music Report.[44] This percentage is expected to rise to 25% by 2010. In 2008, more than 1 billion songs were purchased online, reported Nielsen SoundScan, representing a 27% increase over 2007. CD sales fell further in 2008, down 20% from 2007 to 362.6 million.[45] Despite the increase in digital sales, overall album sales, both CD and digital, still declined 8.5% between 2007 and 2008. The market for digital music is huge and expected to grow, predicted by eMarketer to reach $5.7 billion domestically and $14.8 billion worldwide by 2011.[46]

In addition to digital music, demand is also moving toward singles, instead of albums. The Smashing Pumpkins is one band that ended the practice of releasing albums, making their 2007 comeback album *Zeitgeist* their last. As lead singer Billy Corgan announced in a *Chicago Tribune* interview, "We're done with that. There is no point. People don't even listen to it all. They put it on their iPod, they drag over the two singles, and skip over the rest. The listening patterns have changed, so why are we killing ourselves to do albums, to create balance, and do the arty track to set up the single? It's done."[47]

MySpace has attempted to serve the musical needs of its millions of users through a special section called MySpace Music. The site originally served as a hub for musician profiles, later evolving into offering album exclusives, online shows, and sponsored tours. In October 2007, MySpace Music was the third most popular music Web site after Yahoo! Music and ArtistDirect with 17.9 million unique visitors, an increase of 42% over the same month in 2006.[48] In January 2009, Courtney Holt, formerly of MTV, took over the helm at MySpace Music as the company's first CEO.

In 2008, MySpace re-launched MySpace Music with labels Sony BMG, Universal Music Group, and Warner Music Group. These three major record labels plus EMI Group comprise 82% of the music industry market, with independent labels representing the remaining market share. A press release from Warner described the venture as providing "the most comprehensive catalogue of music content available online."[49] The deal benefits MySpace in that the social networking site can use music licensed by the labels and the major labels, who receive licensing fees and a share of the advertising revenue. Without these partnerships in place, MySpace retains all the advertising dollars that are generated when a fan interacts with an artist's profile page by watching videos or listening to tracks. Within five months of launching MySpace Music, more than 5 million bands offered streaming music, more than 100 million playlists had been created, and more than a billion songs had been streamed, according to a CNET News interview of Holt.[50]

In 2008, MySpace started combining free ad-supported streaming of music with downloading that is free of digital rights management restrictions, while also adding sales of merchandise, ringtones, and concert tickets to the mix.[51] MySpace, however, was not the first music community to offer such a service. That honor goes to imeem, a social networking site with 28 million visitors a month.[52] imeem also streams music on ad-supported pages and through content agreements allows for downloading of tracks, sharing revenues with their music label partners. Many Facebook consumers are connected to iLike, a music discovery service, which updates consumers with information about favorite artists. Consumers are directed to Ticketmaster for concert ticket purchases or iTunes to purchase tracks.[53] Social networking site Buzznet rivals MySpace Music and is funded by a multi-million dollar investment by Universal Music Group's Interscope records. Also competing with MySpace is the online label created by Engadget founder Pete Rojas in collaboration with record label Downtown Records, where artists make tracks available for free downloading and are provided a share of ad revenues in return. The ad-supported models are obviously dependent on the willingness of advertisers to continue to pay for access to the users on these sites.

Instead of developing their own model that works in a digital world or creating their own online community, the record labels have had to cooperate with nonmusic platforms, such as MySpace. This situation is reminiscent of 2003 when the labels gave up complete control over distribution by signing deals with Apple's iTunes Music Store. As Scott Galupo of the *Washington Times* explains, "The increasing integration of legally sanctioned music and the Web is a sign that Big Music, which had been slow and grudging in adapting to the decline of traditional music retail, is finally reading the ones and zeroes on the wall. Now the labels are agreeing to become minority stakeholders in various multimedia enterprises; they are, effectively, being folded into the ad-supported fabric of online media."[54]

The evolution of digital music heralds other changes for these industry fore-runners. Antony Bruno, in a *Billboard* article, describes how the digital ware-house models of iTunes and Amazon will become less relevant as a distribution method, and subscription services like Napster and Rhapsody, failing to partner with a social networking site, will need to replace their monthly fees with an ad-supported model and switch to DRM-free music.[55] Rhapsody, however, is try-ing to make the subscription model work, being that it is dependent on interest in the music and not the whims of advertisers, something preferred by the labels, but not yet necessarily embraced by consumers.[56] Other social networks, such as Facebook, are already in talks with record labels in response to MySpace's move.

Independent digital distributors had been critical of the deal the major labels made with MySpace and without their own relationships, they feared a loss of the foothold they maintain in digital sales, which Nielsen SoundScan data reveals to be 30% of the digital market.[57] Greg Scholl, president of independent digital distributor Orchard, cited in a *Billboard* article, says that "if reports are true, the apparent MySpace licensing approach is troubling. It harkens back to a time none of us wants to revisit." Orchard has since solidified a relationship with MySpace. In another article, Charles Caldas, the chief executive of Merlin, which represents 12,000 independent labels and 9% of the digital market, criticized MySpace for launching this program without them on board.[58] Furthermore, he chastised MySpace for moving away from its historically organic culture, which supported independent artists.

In January 2009, MySpace partnered with the four larger independent labels and indie music distributors: Nettwerk Music Group, INgrooves, IRIS Distrib-ution, and Royalty Share.[59] In addition, Wind-Up Records joined MySpace as a result of its digital distribution deal with Sony Music Entertainment. Merlin, a group of 12,000 independent labels, still lacks a deal with MySpace, criticizing the social networking site for providing equity stakes for the major labels and nothing for the independent labels.

MySpace Music has made improvements in recent months to make the service more valuable. These changes include profiles dedicated to albums, which was a personal initiative by Holt to reemphasize the album as the "locus for musical conversation." Search lists are now playable from the search page, which assists in the process of creating a playlist. Users can now create as many playlists as they want and share them with others, making MySpace more open and social. MySpace is also looking for the best playlist creators and plans to promote these users as tastemakers. Another initiative is to allow users to follow the playlists of others, including these tastemakers, in the same way one would follow a Twitter feed.[60]

CULTURAL IMPLICATIONS

The question for the future of MySpace is what the corporate takeover of the social networking site, both by News Corp and the major record labels, will mean for artists and the future of music. One possible consequence is that unknown artists on MySpace will be drowned out by all the mainstream artists who are using MySpace as part of a sophisticated promotional plan coordinated by their labels.

Another outcome of corporate influence is that artists discovered on MySpace may be no different than those who rise to popularity through traditional methods, except that they are building a fan base online instead of in local venues. As Jonah Weiner of Slate.com explains:

> In these early days of MySpace, it's naive to think that the artists who benefit most from the site's buzz will differ markedly from those at the top of the pop charts. Despite the Internet's many decentralizing effects on musical authority, it's natural that the millions of kids whose tastes are still informed by MTV and commercial radio are going to click to bands similar to those they already like.[61]

The ad-based model supported by record companies could impact creativity, as predicted by the *Washington Times*'s Galupo. "As labels spend more money on artist development and beef up their ad-sales teams and business development divisions, all in an effort to drive content into increasingly diverse media platforms, it's hard not to see music, as an art form, being drained of exceptionality."[62] Record companies are always looking for the hottest new sound, often using it to market ringtones, which generally sell for $1.99, while singles are sold for 99 cents. The labels do not always have the patience to develop new artists, sometimes casting them aside for the latest sensation. At the same time, some artists strive to create a song that would make a popular ringtone, with a sound that is catchy, but lacking complexity and content.[63]

These recent developments in the music industry have provided opportunities for consumers, emerging artists, and established artists. Consumers can easily access artists and their music through social networking profiles and digital downloads. Through sites like MySpace, emerging artists are able to build a fan base, distribute their own music, and possibly attract the attention of a record label. Established artists can engage with their fans online, further building their fan bases. Most hurt by the changes in the industry are record companies, who are attempting to reclaim some of their dominance in the face of declining album sales. Partnering with sites like MySpace, although possibly not the preferred route, certainly provides opportunities to recoup some of their losses.

Chapter 9

FROM SILVER SCREENS TO COMPUTER SCREENS: MARKETING MOVIES ON MYSPACE

with Andi Kuhn

The social networking site MySpace, which allows users to create personalized profile pages and network with others, has caught on with remarkable speed since its introduction in 2003. Not ignoring an opportunity to connect with consumers, the entertainment industry has been negotiating how to create sponsored profiles for its television programs and films.

Television and film production companies are spending millions to connect with audiences on sites such as MySpace and Facebook and are using traditional banner advertising, promotional partnerships, event sponsorship, content promotion, and the creation of member profiles to do so.[1,2] Entertainment companies pay anywhere from $100,000 to more than $1 million for custom-designed profiles by Fox Interactive Media, the News Corp division that sells MySpace advertising.[3] Members of the social network can then "friend" a film or television program. This chapter analyzes the elements of MySpace profiles for 15 of the top grossing films of 2008 along the dimensions of online marketing, multimedia, interactivity, and brand affinity to determine how blockbuster movies are establishing a MySpace presence.

HISTORY OF FILM FORAYS ONTO MYSPACE

Movie studios, followed by carmakers, were one of the first industries to recognize the potential of social networking sites and build a presence there.[4] One of the early MySpace trends was to develop a character as a representation of the brand or use a character from traditional advertising and develop a profile for that character.[5] Wendy's used the square "Smart," Volkswagen used "Your Fast," and Travelocity used the "Roaming Gnome." Movies and television shows already have characters, and some promote their products by creating profiles for these characters while others generate awareness for the movie or television show itself.

Studios have been faced in recent years with declining box office sales, spurring a need to look for new ways to build excitement for film releases. Social networking profiles provide a way for entertainment companies to connect with potential fans for a new release and then keep in touch with those fans for an extended length of time. As stated in a 2008 *Advertising Age* article, "One of the keys to being successful within social networks is not to continually hit consumers over the head with a marketing message but rather to maintain a steady stream of contact with them."[6] MySpace provides a means for keeping that connection and can be particularly helpful for a film that will likely be followed by sequels.

The movie *X-Men: The Last Stand*, released in May 2006, attracted attention for being a social networking trailblazer and also acquiring more than 2 million MySpace friends.[7] Profiles can increase the likelihood that a movie will receive online attention if they offer special features to MySpace members. The *X-Men* profile may have attracted so many friends because it provided a "Top 16" feature to the friends of *X-Men*, a function not previously available.[8] Friends could feature their "Top 16" friends on the main page of their own profiles, instead of the "Top 8" friends function provided on the standard MySpace profile at the time.

The MySpace profile for *X-Men*, although an early film entrant to MySpace, displayed many sophisticated features. The profile offered movie trailers and other exclusive video content; a contest and a poll; mobile messaging; integration with other Web sites, including the official site for the movie, Marvel Comics, and Fox; ringtones; photos; many ways to express fandom for the movie including computer wallpaper, an "Xtreme" desktop, buddy icons, MySpace skins, badges, and video for the member's profile; and the standard friends, forum, and comment sections. One of the more innovative concepts is the ability to locate other *X-Men* friends using Google Maps. The movie is now available on DVD and can be purchased through a link on the MySpace profile.

Once MySpace users friend a movie profile, the site can be repurposed for sequels, DVD releases, or soundtrack sales. The MySpace profile for the 2006 Disney movie *Step Up*, with more than 156,000 friends at one time, has been cited for contributing to the strong DVD sales of the movie as well as box office success for the sequel, *Step Up 2 the Streets*.[9] Although the first movie earned $65 million while in theaters for two months in 2006, the sequel earned $53 million in its first four weeks in theaters. The sequel's opening weekend in 2008 drew $2 million more in ticket sales than the original. The *Step Up* profile offered the opportunity for MySpace members to interact with the movie's stars and director, enter contests to win a bit part in the movie, and attend a "Black Curtain" screening of the film.

Another MySpace success is the 2007 Warner Bros. film *300*. The profile offered a trailer that was viewed more than 8 million times. In addition, the profile built a following of more than 200,000 friends.[10] The popularity of this profile might be explained by a profile feature upgrade, compliments of the movie *300*. All MySpace users who were uploading photos were alerted that they could now store 300 photos, which likely generated buzz and interest in the film and drove users to its profile. In another example, the 2008 movie *Cloverfield* was promoted using a viral Internet campaign that included MySpace profiles of its main characters.[11]

Media distribution company Nabbr develops widgets to promote movies on profiles of social networking members. For the LionsGate release of *Good Luck Chuck*, the company created an online channel for the movie, resulting in 26 million views of the trailer and 30,000 embedded widgets on fan profile pages. The user could interact with the widget by watching videos, reading the plot synopsis, looking at photos, and chatting with other fans. The same company also created a widget for the 2008 Sony Pictures movie *21* that allowed users to play blackjack, as well as view trailers and enter a sweepstakes.

A promotional campaign for the 2008 release of *High School Musical 3* used MySpace to launch a contest among high schools students. To participate, students were required to perform a variety of online tasks, including uploading photos and videos, decorating their school's MySpace profile, and interacting with *HSM3*'s MySpace profile. The class determined to have the most "school spirit" won a trip to a Disney theme park, and the school won a pep rally featuring Natasha Bedingfield.[12]

MYSPACE RESEARCH

A Nielsen NRG survey found that *Step Up 2 the Streets* was noticed by consumers more than the original, with 49% of respondents indicating they had seen an ad or information for the sequel on MySpace while only 37% had seen ads or information for the original movie in a similar study conducted during the first film's opening weekend. Consumers with MySpace profiles were more likely to have seen ads or information for the sequel than those without a MySpace profile (58% vs. 26%), numbers which were even more differentiated for the original movie (50% vs. 13%).[13]

Another MySpace study conducted by Nielsen NRG found MySpace to be the favorite site for 30% of 15–24-year-olds who are looking for information about new movie releases, followed by Google and Yahoo! (both at 23%) and AOL at 14%.[14] Even among 15–34-year-olds, MySpace was still the top destination for 25% of those surveyed, with Google a close second at 24%. The study, based on information for 13 new releases, also found that 44% of the 15–34-year-olds and 46% of the 15–24-year-olds who had been exposed to advertising or other information about the movies found additional content on MySpace. In some cases, users are learning more about movies on the Web than through television. The study found that 15–24-year-old males were more likely to use the Internet than television to find out information about *The Dark Knight*.

The youth market is a difficult one to reach using traditional advertising. Although this generation accepts advertising—having been exposed to messages from a young age while watching television, surfing the Internet, and attending elementary schools—they are more accepting of relevant pitches. Research has demonstrated that social networking members are willing to view advertiser profiles, with particular interest among 18–26-year-old users (37%) followed by 27–40-year-old users (31%) and among daily users (as opposed to weekly or monthly visitors).[15] Furthermore, social networking members tend to tell friends about products (50% of adult users and 67% of youth users), and an even higher percentage of those expressing interest in advertiser profiles are likely to tell friends about products (61% of adult users and 77% of youth users).[16] A study by MySpace and Isobar found that 40% of social networkers surveyed said they use networking sites to learn more about brands or products that they like and 28% said a friend has recommended a brand or product to them.[17]

BENEFITS OF MYSPACE

Advertisers can create a higher level of intimacy on MySpace than with traditional media formats or even with interactive advertising formats, and MySpace offers marketing tools to help this process. Profiles are built with incentives in mind that will reward consumers for interacting with the brand. Successful, creative profiles attract the right consumers and convince these consumers to share the experience. Users can also incorporate brand networking into their own profiles, which can serve as a word-of-mouth endorsement of the brand to profile visitors and a way for members to do the marketing for the advertiser.[18] In addition, companies can extract information from their profile friends, such as their favorite movies, actors, musicians, and television shows to use in further product developments.

Buzz occurs more frequently, more naturally, and with greater influence with youth than any other age group, making this group a particularly attractive one to target online. However, young consumers are better equipped to screen advertising messages and are increasingly difficult to reach.[19,20] Companies know that too much commercialization will alienate MySpace users and hinder buzz, and it is not in their interest to drive away users.[21] Consequently, they have kept traditional, overt advertising to a minimum and instead work with MySpace developers to build profiles that are relevant and "cool."[22] When executed successfully, companies will attract friends who will refer the profile to their friends.

The beauty of blending social networking with the promotion of movies or television programs is that the communities within which to discuss or share the content are already somewhat established. As John Hagel III and Arthur Armstrong state in their book *Net Gain*, "Those businesses that capitalize on organizing virtual communities will be richly rewarded with both peerless customer loyalty and impressive economic returns."[23] MySpace provides such a community for the entertainment industry.

ONLINE BRANDING ON MYSPACE

Even prior to the advent of online social networking sites, marketers used branding to build social networks among consumers in an effort to create enthusiasm and loyalty for a brand.[24] Previous studies have examined how product and service providers use the Web to build brands, focusing on the specific elements of a brand's Web site.[25] MySpace is a particularly useful tool for branding entertainment products, allowing entertainment companies to showcase multimedia content; conduct online marketing activities; provide interactive content; and encourage expressions of affinity.

Multimedia Content. The success of YouTube and iTunes are indicators that consumers are interested in watching videos online and downloading music or podcasts. This review will examine how entertainment companies are utilizing the multimedia capabilities of MySpace, including video, which can be used for trailers or other promotional video content; audio; and photography.

Online Marketing. Social networking sites have been attracting entertainment companies who are creating profiles to support marketing efforts such as sales promotion or public relations and direct consumers to a Web site for sales transactions. Another area of interest is whether profiles are integrated with other Web sites for the film. This analysis will examine how entertainment companies use MySpace profiles for promotion, public relations, and electronic commerce, and to what extent MySpace profiles are connected via hyperlinks to other online content created by the entertainment company.

Interactivity. Researchers have attempted to define interactivity in an advertising context and have noted the lack of a consistent definition in the literature.[26,27] Chang-Hoan Cho and John Leckenby classified existing definitions in terms of user-machine interactions, user-user interactions, and user-message interactions.[28] Applying these definitions to the Internet, user-machine interactivity allows the user to change the look of the Web site or navigate the site through links; user-user interactivity refers to communication between two people mediated by the Internet; and user-message interactivity allows for control of advertising messages on the Internet.

The present study considers perceived user-user interactivity. This concept has been operationalized as first-person blogs and feedback buttons and as chat rooms, bulletin boards, and enhanced navigation bars.[29,30] This review will explore how social networks allow users to interact with profiles in a variety of ways, including posting comments, reading blogs, taking surveys, playing games, creating art, and participating in forums.

Brand Affinity. Social networks provide a framework for consumers to express and also share affinity by passing content along to friends, a process dubbed the "momentum effect."[31] The value of MySpace for entertainment companies is enhanced by the ability of consumers to display a favorite movie and other studio-sponsored content on their profiles and to friend a movie.[32] The momentum effect is dependent on consumers' desire to share information. Some individuals are more motivated than others to spread messages, and some have a circle of influence that is larger and more complex. Emanuel Rosen, author of *The Anatomy of Buzz*, used the term "network hub" to describe "individuals who communicate with more people about a certain product than the average person does."[33]

Social networking sites make it possible for consumers to express preferences and initiate the momentum effect by efficiently displaying movie content on their own profiles and distributing viral content to friends. This review will explore how entertainment companies are employing the tools of MySpace to allow users to share content with others, display movie affinity on their own profile pages for online friends to see, share user-generated content expressing affinity for the film, or exhibit their affinity on their own computer screens.

PROFILES OF THE HIGHEST GROSSING MOVIES OF 2008

MySpace profiles for the 15 of the 18 highest-grossing films of 2008 in the United States (according to The-Numbers.com) were analyzed to determine how well they exhibited the marketing, multimedia, interactivity, and brand affinity capabilities of MySpace. The movies were: *The Dark Knight* (#1), *Iron Man* (#2), *Indiana Jones and the Kingdom of the Crystal Skull* (#3), *Hancock* (#4), *WALL-E* (#5), *Twilight* (#8), *Quantum of Solace* (#9), *Sex and the City: The Movie* (#11), *Mamma Mia!* (#12), *Juno* (#13), *The Chronicles of Narnia: Prince Caspian* (#14), *The Incredible Hulk* (#15), *Wanted* (#16), *Get Smart* (#17), and *Four Christmases* (#18). Three children's movies—*Kung Fu Panda* (#6), *Madagascar: Escape 2 Africa* (#7), and *Horton Hears a Who* (#10)—either did not have MySpace profiles or did not have profiles that could be located.

The most prevalent form of **multimedia content** hosted on MySpace profiles was a video. All MySpace movie profiles examined allow visitors to watch trailers for the movie. Additionally, many profiles offered video content other than trailers. Some of this extra video content included behind-the-scenes clips and some featured fans of the movie. One profile with extensive offerings is *WALL-E*, which houses nine videos including the trailer, five vignettes of WALL-E interacting with household appliances, and a featurette with the creators. *The Incredible Hulk* profile included a clip of fans acting like the Hulk while wearing Hulk gloves. Photos were the next most popular form of multimedia, with 87% (all but two) of the profiles making movie photos available. Audio, such as music from the movie or ringtones, was offered on only three sites. *WALL-E* has sounds that play when the profile loads, *Mamma Mia!* has an audio player, and *Quantum of Solace* offers ringtones through a link on its widget. Although the *Twilight* profile offers playlists for the four main characters, no audio is available.

An important element of **online marketing** is whether the profile integrates with the movie's primary Web site or a microsite, either as an identifiable Web site link or by clicking on other elements of the profile. Almost 67% of profiles are integrated with other online marketing efforts through a link on the MySpace profile, with all of these linking at least to the movie Web site. Contests were the most popular form of promotion and were used by three profiles, often requiring that the entrant add the movie as a friend. The profile for *The Incredible Hulk*, for example, asks respondents to submit a photo of their best Hulk face to enter the "Show us your Hulk" sweepstakes. *Get Smart's* profile offers a chance to win a trip to the International Spy Museum. The *Indiana Jones* profile featured a sweepstakes to win an *Indiana Jones*-inspired trip to Venice. Public relations efforts are downplayed with only one movie (*Indiana Jones*) providing news updates through a widget that can be embedded on the user's profile. It is likely, however, that friends of certain movies are notified through MySpace of any developments. Most of these 2008 hit movies are now out on DVD and 6 of the 15 profiles offered a link to purchase the movie, and an additional three profiles advertised the DVD, but did not provide a link. An additional two profiles advertised the soundtrack, but did not provide a link.

Studios are using tools on MySpace profiles to encourage fan **interaction** with a movie. All profiles included an opportunity for users to leave comments for the profile sponsor, and all but one offered a forum. Games were a popular interactive feature of 47% of the profiles, followed by the ability to create "art" in 20% of the profiles, or take a quiz or poll (13%). On the profile for *WALL-E*, users could create their own "bot." Some quizzes allow the user to interact with the characters of the movie, often in an attempt to determine which character is most like the user. This feature, available on the *Twilight* profile, can then be placed on the user's own profile. The *Get Smart* profile tests users on their secret agent skills, and if they pass, they can place a special badge on their own profile. Just one profile (*Juno*) offered a blog. The profile for *The Dark Knight* allows those who purchase the DVD to participate in an online chat with the director.

The final content area to explore is how MySpace marketers are providing tools for users to demonstrate or share their **affinity** for the movie by communicating with other MySpace users. These tools allow the studio to create a virtual community of consumer evangelists. The easiest way for a fan to demonstrate support for a movie is to friend the movie's profile. Friend requests are provided by all movie profiles so that users can join the movie's friends and vice versa. The number of friends for the profiles examined ranged from a low of 832 and 860 for *Mamma Mia!* and *Four Christmases*, respectively, to friends in the tens of thousands for a number of movies to over 525,000 friends for *Twilight*. Many of these movie profiles, therefore, are attracting a significant number of friends.

Almost all profiles (87%) offered a widget for users to place on their own MySpace profiles. Some of these widgets are countdowns to the release of the movie. The widget for *Twilight* is extensive, providing the user with a plot synopsis, cast and crew information, videos, links, photos, and an e-card to send to friends. *Twilight* also offers a badge for fans' MySpace profiles that informs their friends they are seeing the movie again. *Sex and the City* provides a feature that allows users to classify four friends as being a fashionista, idealist, vixen, or professional, paralleling the lifestyles of the movie's four main characters. *Juno* also offers creative widgets in their hamburger phone and the Juno Jargon Jenerator. The profile also links to a social community of *Juno* fans.

Users can also customize their MySpace profiles with skins or themes provided by 40% of the movie profiles to serve as a background for a profile. Communicating with others can be enhanced with movie buddy icons available on 80% of the profiles. Fans of *The Dark Knight* are provided with a photo to be used as their profile picture. For a user's own computer, 93% of movie profiles provide wallpaper and 13% provide screensavers. Movies have also engaged with consumers through the solicitation of user-generated content, and 13% of profiles host this content. The profile for *Iron Man* features user-generated renderings of Iron Man, ranging from childlike drawings to sophisticated computer-generated art. *The Dark Knight* profile offers a unique peel-back feature that can be posted to a blog or Web site. Users who click on the top right-hand corner of sites with the peel-back will see the screen peel back to reveal content for the movie, including videos, downloads, and images. The profile for *Hancock* offers a theme for Playstation and iPhone wallpaper.

OUTLOOK FOR MYSPACE AND MOVIES

Movie studios have recognized the sheer number of consumers on social networking sites and are learning how to build profiles to engage these consumers and create virtual communities. To brand their profiles in MySpace, studios are creating profiles using multimedia content, online marketing, opportunities to interact with the brand, and tools for displaying affinity.

Interesting, these profiles can be difficult to locate. Although MySpace maintains a MySpace Film content area, only a handful of new releases are showcased here. For the user searching MySpace for the profile of a particular film, the search results yield many fan sites for the movies among the studio site. Sometimes it is difficult to differentiate between the two, although the number of friends provides a clue. Additionally, studios rarely promote the MySpace profiles for their movies on their Web sites or in traditional advertising.

More research is necessary to determine the extent to which the tools available on MySpace can accomplish the objective of building word-of-mouth buzz for movie releases and keeping the fans connected to the movie for the purpose of later selling the DVD, soundtrack, or sequels.

Chapter 10

FAN CHATTER MATTERS:
MEETING UP ON MESSAGE BOARDS

Online message boards serve as virtual meeting places for fans of television shows who are drawn online by the opportunity to engage with other fans. Whether maintained by the network on the official Web site for the program or created by viewers, message boards present a variety of topics for discussion, each with its own threads of related conversation.

This chapter will first discuss the history of television fan cultures with a focus on the production of fan fiction. Concepts such as culture, community, and activism as they relate to message boards will also be explored. Much research has already been done to understand the use of message boards and this chapter will summarize and extend the results of these studies.

This chapter will also seek to understand how and why fans of ABC's *Lost* interact on message boards. An intricate show like *Lost* generates much online discussion about characters, actors, and plot elements. The LOST-TV message board will be used as a case study to understand user gratifications, television viewing practices, and perceptions of influence over the show's writers and producers.

HISTORY OF TELEVISION FAN CULTURES

Studies of fandom have often distinguished between viewers and fans. While viewers internalize their enjoyment of a television program and declare their interests privately, fans extend that enjoyment beyond their personal realm to engage with others.[1] Fans also express an increased emotional involvement in a television program and tend to perform such behaviors as reading fan magazines, writing letters to actors, attending fan conventions, and participating in online message boards.[2,3] Scott Thorne and Gordon Bruner define fans as people with enduring involvement with a particular subject or object, which could be an actor or television show.[4] Their research showed that fans exhibit the characteristic of internal involvement (seeing oneself as a fan) and desire external involvement, items related to the object of fandom, and interaction with other fans.

Although qualitative studies of television viewers emerged in the 1980s, it was not until the early 1990s that scholars began to examine the phenomenon of television fandom.[5] Using ethnographic research, early fan studies focused on primetime dramas, particularly *Star Trek*.[6] Studies of fandom differ from the earlier studies of television viewers by expanding the notion of the variety of ways to consume a television program, applying a fan-industry model instead of an isolated-viewer model, and examining other media that are consumed as by-products of the fandom.[7]

Daytime soap operas have also been fertile ground for studies of fandom. Denise Bielby, Lee Harrington, and William Bielby discuss how viewer commitment to a soap opera is translated into fandom: "It is the dedicated fan who derives maximum value from the product, typically by developing an interest in the circumstances of the soap's production, the relationship between the fictional characters and the actors' off-screen lives, and secondary sites such as the soap press where ancillary narratives about the soaps are produced."[8] The fan will then often seek information either on- or offline, participate in electronic discussion boards, or attend conventions or meetings.

Fan communities predate the Internet, with one of the earliest expressions of fandom being fan clubs. Fan clubs are a traditional method to allow fans to connect with a program and its actors or just a single actor. The communication and community-building tactics of clubs include newsletters with information about the program and annual gatherings for fans. Magazines, such as *Soap Opera Digest* for the soap opera genre, also provide a way for fans to stay linked to the programs and provide feedback to producers.

Fans also display their fandom by producing fan fiction, which involves creating new episode plots involving the characters and settings from television shows or movies. Henry Jenkins describes fan fiction in *Textual Poachers* as "a way of the culture repairing the damage done in a system where contemporary myths are owned by corporations instead of owned by the folk."[9] Modern fan fiction is often linked to fans of *Star Trek*, who founded the first *Star Trek* fanzine, *Spockanalia*, in 1967, a magazine that included some fan fiction. After the cancellation of *Star Trek* in the 1970s, fan fiction writers continued to produce their own stories, which they copied and handed out at *Star Trek* conventions. The short-lived drama *Beauty and the Beast* also garnered a large number of "textual poachers," as fan fiction writers are sometimes called.[10] More recently, fans of Showtime's lesbian drama *The L Word* participated in a contest to contribute scene ideas, and the winning scenes were compiled into an ezine of the episode.[11] Fan fiction has flourished on sites such as fanfiction.net. Fiction about *Harry Potter*, for example, has reached more than 400,000 entries on fanfiction.net and more than 56,000 on harrypotterfanfiction.com, a site specifically dedicated to *Harry Potter* stories. Although fan fiction has created some controversy, as long as it is not created for profit, producers tend to look the other way.[12]

In the early 1990s, fans began to congregate on boards located on AOL, Prodigy, and CompuServe and in Usenet groups. These boards do not depend on the network or producers for their existence, which allows for relatively uncensored content and complete fan autonomy.[13] J. Michael Straczynski, creator of *Babylon 5*, has been communicating with fans on the rec.arts.sf.tv.babylon5 Usenet group since at least 1991. A regular poster, JMS (as he is known online) discusses his work, its meaning, and the development of the plot with fans.[14]

Message boards are increasingly being employed by television networks to support online communication about television programs. A survey of 2,233 television programs by Ad*VIZR in 2007 found that more than 50% of programs had an official message board, serving as "the most popular touchpoint available."[15] Message boards allow fans to participate in virtual conversations, and today, much fan activity occurs here. The participant can post a complete thought without interruption and can respond to earlier comments rather than the most recent post, creating a conversation that is not directly sequential. The boards also allow an unlimited number of people to come together to share many diverse perspectives in a discussion that is both interactive and immediate. Often, fans of a television show, for example, wait to post until after watching a television episode, allowing themselves time to fully digest the content of the program and provide insightful commentary. Sometimes, however, viewers are posting or participating in a conversation as the episode is airing.

FAN ACTIVISM AND FEEDBACK

Mark Andrejevic points out that online communities not only give fans an opportunity to make shows more interesting and engaging for themselves, but also provide producers with valuable feedback.[16] Therefore, online fan activity is generally not ignored by media producers. As Andrejevic describes, "Perhaps out of a desire to encourage the kind of participation that fosters loyalty to a show—even if it is a program that viewers love to hate—producers have publicly said that they find Web sites to be useful sources of feedback."[17] In the literary world, for example, fan communities rallied so fervently around the first printing of *Harry Potter and the Sorcerer's Stone* by Bloomsbury Publishing in England that when the American publishing rights were auctioned, Scholastic paid an almost unheard of price of $105,000.[18]

Bielby, Harrington, and Bielby discuss how fan interaction in the online communities can foster a heightened sense of ownership. As they describe, "The evolution of electronic sites for fan interaction has had a major impact on how fans make claims to ownership of the narrative, their sense of entitlement to make such claims, and how those claims are perceived and managed by the industry."[19] They discuss the process as starting when fans feel an obligation to voice their concerns, sometimes criticizing a soap opera plot that is not moving in a desired direction. Participants then can see that others share their discontent, possibly further frustrating viewers who want to see changes. Claims to narrative ownership may be further enhanced when outside parties, such as writers or producers, respond to fans in some way.

Creating an active fan culture is now regarded by producers as an important component in the production process. The interaction of fans means that producers do not have to do so much work to understand their audiences. In 2008, Fox created a private online community using the social networking service Passenger to allow 2,000 invited viewers to provide feedback on new shows, communicate with producers, participate in polls, provide input on marketing campaigns, and engage with each another.[20] ABC has also created a similar private community, as have a variety of consumer goods companies, using this same service.

Several producers have discussed their monitoring of online chatter to understand how viewers are reacting to their programs. J. J. Abrams, creator of *Lost* and *Alias*, describes television as a play. "Movies are a done deal—there's no give and take—but in a play, you listen to the applause, the missing laughs, the boos. It's the same with the Internet. If you ignore that sort of response, you probably shouldn't be working in TV right now," he said.[21] John Wells, the executive producer of *ER* and *The West Wing*, said in an interview, "I don't overreact to the boards, but I pay real attention to messages that are thoughtful. If you ignore your customer, you do so at your peril."[22] He added that negative online reactions to the downy facial hair of *ER*'s Noah Wyle prompted a shave.[23]

Grey's Anatomy writer Allan Heinberg expressed similar themes on the Grey Matters blog: "So, here's the thing: You people terrify me. You're passionate, you're insightful, you're bravely outspoken. You know '*Grey's Anatomy*' better than anyone, except maybe Shonda Rhimes [the creator]. And I don't know if you realize this, but the way you write about the show, debate it, love and/or hate it carries an enormous amount of weight in the writers' room."[24]

CBS spokesperson Chris Ender said of *Survivor*, "In the first season there was a groundswell of attention in there . . . We started monitoring the message boards to actually help guide us in what would resonate in our marketing. It's just the best market research you can get."[25] Ender continued by speaking more broadly of monitoring: "It is now standard Hollywood practice for executive producers (known in trade argot as 'show runners') to scurry into Web groups moments after an episode is shown on the East Coast. Sure, a good review in the print media is important, but the boards, by definition, are populated by a program's core audience—many thousands of viewers who care deeply about what direction their show takes."[26]

The X-Files is another example of a series with an active online fan community that was monitored by show staffers. Fan fiction flourished online during the run of the show, and veteran participants on fan fiction sites often warned new writers that producers did not solicit scripts from the site. In reality, however, *X-Files* staff members did scan the fan fiction sites for suggestions, sometimes using online fan names for bit characters and once dedicating an episode to a online fan.[27] The prevalence of certain characters also reflected fan interest; most notably, Skinner's role expanded as a result of positive feedback from the online community.

On the Web, passivity has been replaced by interactivity, as television viewers provide feedback to producers, vote for contestants, and play an online contest related to a program. Fans tend to feel ownership over the content, despite the fact they are not writers for the program. Critical fans will note problems with plotlines and production values.[28] Fans are also prone to protest changes to a favorite program. When CBS attempted to replace the lead actresses in *Cagney & Lacey*, fans complained and the network did not make any changes.[29]

Television fan groups often mobilize when a favorite program is on the brink of cancellation. Fans of *Star Trek*, *Hill Street Blues*, *Beauty and the Beast*, and *Cagney & Lacey* instigated campaigns to ward off cancellation.[30] Predating widespread use of the Internet, fans of these shows were limited to the use of letters, advertisements, or other "offline" methods. Offline campaigns still occur today, as fans sent nuts to the producers of *Jericho* in reference to the last word uttered on what would have been the final episode, but much of the mobilization for these efforts happened online.[31] Similarly, The WB may have extended the program *Roswell* because of online fan pressure.[32] Fans responded to rumors that the show would not be renewed for a second season by sending the network thousands of bottles of Tabasco, indicating their belief that *Roswell* was a hot show. The producers then thanked the online community by posting letters of appreciation online.

Message boards are an effective means for communicating with other fans about the campaign. A "Save Dr. Quinn" campaign was prompted by members of an online community who used a Web site, letter writing campaign, and rallies to save *Dr. Quinn, Medicine Woman* from cancellation. The virtual community even raised $13,000 to advertise their cause in *TV Guide* and *The Hollywood Reporter*. This campaign, however unsuccessful in the end, "demonstrated how effective the Internet can be in mobilizing people quickly and efficiently."[33]

Siddhartha Menon explored Internet bulletin board sites for the ABC drama *Once & Again* (*O&A*).[34] The program about two divorced parents finding love again attracted a small community of activist fans who attempted to keep the low-rated show on the air. As Menon states, "The passion exhibited by *O&A* fans to save their program facilitated a sense of human connection and solidarity that is rarely achieved in either virtual or real-world communities."[35] Activism was revealed in the ability of board members to raise $10,000 to pay for three ads in industry trade papers, such as *Variety* and *The Hollywood Reporter*, and a billboard in Los Angeles. Participants also used online petitions, sent old paperbacks to ABC, voted for *O&A* at "Save that Show" (savethatshow.com), and attempted to initiate a public relations campaign by contacting television stations, radio programs, and magazines. Producers recognized the efforts of the online fans by posting messages on the official Web site, even as the show was being canceled. In the end, the efforts of the community members did not prevent its eventual downfall.

Vic Costello and Barbara Moore's study of online "cultural outlaws" found that television message board participants expressed interest in influencing programs. When they provided feedback on the boards, they hoped that writers and producers would read and respond, either through the board or through changes in the program itself. Several respondents had also participated in campaigns to save programs.[36]

Although some fans may become activists to save a cultural product, other fans may try to block an adaptation of a cultural product. Fans of the *Lord of the Rings*, for example, reacted negatively when the first installment of the movie trilogy was being filmed, fearing it would differ significantly from the book. Universal Studios, wanting to control and stifle all negative commentary, attempted to remove Web-based fan discussion and creation of materials related to the movie. In the end, the value of the fan subculture was realized, and marketing efforts were directed toward fan opinion leaders, who were provided with promotional materials about the movie.[37]

Consumers can also push to have a television show removed from the air, as was the case for Dr. Laura Schlessinger's television show. Gay organizations resented her anti-gay stance and used the Web site StopDrLaura.com to garner support for this campaign. They pressured advertisers to withdraw support, and in doing so, the show went off the air in many markets.[38]

Producers often employ "shout-outs" to the participants on Internet fan sites and forums as a way to signal they are listening. A character on the show *Popular* was named after a Television Without Pity (TWoP) recapper. His television namesake was a druggie who was killed in a car wreck.[39] Another TWoP recapper's name was used by the writers of *Ed*, and the site's logo appeared on a bag shown during an episode of *Once & Again*.[40] TWoP received another shout-out, this time on the show *My Name Is Earl*. The background story of the shout-out starts with someone who registered on TWoP as whojackie in 2006, and then posted a comment about Murphy bed fears in November 2006 followed by a post on January 17, 2007, saying how he talked when he typed and did not think shows should do shout-outs to the audience. The January 18, 2007, episode of *My Name Is Earl* then featured a character who dies in a Murphy bed. While planning the character's funeral, Earl realizes the man's friends frequent a Web site that criticizes television where he posted as whojackie. The character is then shown typing and talking out loud, "No, I don't think shows should do more meta jokes that cater to the online bloggers and I'm sure everyone at Television Without Pity Dot Com agrees with me." Another TWoP recapper who disagreed with the way *American Idol* equated the number of votes cast with the total number of voters was successful in eventually changing the way results were reported, a fact he heard from a representative of Fox.[41]

Other questions about the power of online communities center on whether an Internet campaign is as effective as an offline campaign. Do producers see the opinions of an online community as representing a fringe group and not mass popular opinion? Is it easier to ignore a predominantly online campaign? Menon suggests that online campaigns make it harder for networks to quantify fan support and detract from the campaign's efficacy.[42] Andrejevic's research of Television Without Pity participants suggests the perception that online fans have an influence is purely a way to build fan loyalty and cross-promote the program on other platforms, and that online commentary does not significantly influence producers and writers.[43] For some participants in Andrejevic's study, however, just having their posts acknowledged within the online community was satisfying enough.

FAN COMMUNITIES AND CULTURE

Is an online community really a community at all? Does the community have the same degree of rules, social norms, or communal bonds that define an offline community? These two questions are common research streams in studies of online meeting places such as message boards, chat rooms, and e-mail discussion lists. Some scholars doubt the existence of an online community. Stephen Dohery-Farina proclaimed that chat rooms and Multi-User Domains cannot function as communities,[44] and Elizabeth Bird found e-mail discussion lists to "offer little sense of community."[45]

Yet other scholars contend community can be found online. Participation in online forums enhances the value of the show to the fans and creates a community of shared meaning. Maria Bakardjieva believes that scholars use too narrow a definition of community and encourages thinking about online exchanges as *virtual togetherness*.[46] Nancy Baym examined rec.arts.tv.soaps (r.a.t.s.), an electronic newsgroup about American daytime soap operas, to understand how users navigate the groups to find discussion topics.[47] In 2000, Baym further explored how connections and social bonds are maintained online.[48] June Deery suggested that online communities are important because the sheer number of television programs available can make it difficult for fans to find people offline who share their interests.[49] Costello and Moore's respondents indicated that participation in a message board provided an online and offline community for fans.[50]

For scholars who acknowledge the presence of communities online, some question whether these communities are socially beneficial or destructive. James DiGiovanna, who considers online community participants to be "pathetic" and "narcissistic," believes that online communities "erase the identity of those who claim to be part of it."[51] In contrast, E. Graham McKinley finds online community discourse creates "a community among viewers and characters which seemed to empower viewers."[52] Baym writes, "The Internet gives fans a platform on which to perform for one another, and their informal performances might please fans more than official ones do."[53] Online communities that focus on television programs, as opposed to communities revolving around other interests, may offer a heightened sense of perception of community. Because some of the online discussion centers on characters who seem like friends, that experience may translate into a surrogate notion of friendship with others online.

When the primary text of a television show moves into the online world of message boards, users sometimes create a new culture through their participation and engagement with one another. Menon concluded that a culture was formed around *O&A* on multiple message boards. His research examined the "extent to which participants have negotiated overt and unwritten rules and regimes that suggest a consensus on the ethics and etiquette of the communal forums."[54] The board's unwritten rules were exposed when one poster divulged that Sela Ward's mother was gravely ill, information he gleaned from a source on the set of *O&A*. Other members felt this information should have been held in confidence and not released to the board.

THE PROCESS OF WATCHING TELEVISION

The process of watching television often changes for those who engage online in a more participatory experience. Andrejevic's study of Television Without Pity users found participation on the site altered their television viewing experience by making them active viewers who often took notes as they watched.[55] Additionally, many users also visited other sites on the Web to gather more information that could be shared on the Television Without Pity site. Many of Andrejevic's respondents stated that this additional effort enhanced their viewing pleasure. Reading recaps increased their likelihood to watch television in general, but also a greater variety of shows than they would have watched if not for the recaps. Others followed certain shows just by reading the recaps. In contrast, other studies have found that some message boards participants are selective television viewers, who may be obsessed with a particular show, but not necessarily television in general.[56]

Deery described how fans of *The Mole*, who had speculated online as to the identity of the mole throughout the duration of the series, shared their reactions online as the final episode aired, with many comments simply expressing "Wow!"[57] Deery writes: "Evidently, these viewers felt part of a virtual communication; they had been through the series 'together,' they had competed and collaborated in their speculations, and at the show's climax, they were using the computer not to transfer information but to share an experience."[58] For these viewers, the process of watching television changes as they can express their reactions in a forum willing to listen.

THE STORY OF LOST

Lost follows the passengers of Oceanic flight 815, whose story seemingly begins on a flight bound for Los Angeles from Sydney. After their plane crashes on a remote island in the South Pacific, the passengers must find a way to survive in a land of many secrets. Premiering September 22, 2004, the show was not only a Nielsen ratings darling for ABC, averaging more than 16 million viewers in the first season, but also an Emmy award winner for Outstanding Drama Series in 2005.

With the premiere of the series, viewers quickly realized that the plot of *Lost* was more *Lord of the Flies* than deserted island stories in the tradition of *Robinson Crusoe*, *Cast Away*, or *Gilligan's Island*. *Lost* combines the drama of such events as a plane crash, abductions, and failed escape attempts with the complexity of its characters and an island mystery involving black smoke, polar bears, a monster, whispers in the jungle, apparitions, and island residents called "The Others."

This cerebral show fully engages the senses, and viewers must be keen to notice its many verbal and visual clues. Each episode weaves together a storyline involving the island with a secondary plot that reveals the backstory of a character through flashbacks, allowing viewers to glimpse not only the history of the characters, but also their chance encounters with other characters in the past and clues to the island mystery.

The show's cross-platform extensions include podcasts called mobisodes, a magazine, an alternate reality game, and an official Web site with message boards. Producers have even created individual Web sites for the fictitious Oceanic Air (oceanic-air.com), which mimics an airline Web site and offers hidden clues and a seating chart for flight 815; Fly Oceanic Air (flyoceanicair.com), which served as a promotional tool for Season 4; and the Hanso Foundation and its Dharma Initiative (thehansofoundation.org/dharma.html), which appeared when the underground bunker, or "hatch," was opened in Season 2 and a set of training films for hatch inhabitants was discovered. The official look of these sites allows the viewer to believe for a few moments that Oceanic Air and the Hanso Foundation are real and further engage in the world of *Lost*.

Lost has excelled in a cross-media platform, not only by creatively extending the brand through an integrated campaign but also by providing compelling and cryptic content for fans to use as fodder for online engagement and speculation. The subtext of the show spawns even more discussion as viewers note themes of dualities (i.e., science vs. faith); nods to literary works, such as *A Wrinkle in Time*, *Watership Down*, and *The Third Policeman*; and references to philosophy, with characters Rousseau and John Locke among others sharing the names of philosophers. Additionally, the numbers 4 8 15 16 23 42 seem to possess some unknown significance as they are provided to one character by a patient in a mental institution and then used by that character to play and subsequently win the lottery. The numbers appear throughout the show on and off the island, possibly most significantly used to reset the countdown clock in the underground bunker. Keen viewers will note that every time a number is seen or referenced, it is often some variation of these numbers, whether a sum (e.g., the countdown clock in the underground bunker counted down from 108 minutes), a single number, or a combination of two or more of the numbers (e.g., seats in the stadium numbered 15 and 16).

Lost was quick to capture a cult following in the tradition of *Star Trek*, *Buffy the Vampire Slayer*, and *The X-Files*. *Lost* may boast thousands of Web sites about the show from official ABC sites to unofficial fan sites as well as many message boards. On the boards, fans develop theories about the many mysteries of the show, lavish praise on the actors, produce episode transcripts, ship characters (i.e., discuss their romantic liaisons), and write fan fiction.

Lost viewers expressed much disapproval on the message boards of the extensive use of reruns in Seasons 1 and 2. As a result, Season 3 began with six weeks of uninterrupted episodes and after a winter hiatus, returned to finish the season with no reruns. The return of the show for the second half of Season 3 signaled the beginning of the lowest ratings in the show's history, dipping as low as 11 million viewers. Nielsen ratings for Season 3, however, revealed *Lost* to be one of the most recorded shows on television.[59] Season 4 ran in its entirety with no interruptions, yet did not premiere until January 31, 2008, approximately eight months after Season 3 concluded. The decision was made during Season 3 to offer three more seasons of *Lost*, each with 16 episodes and no reruns or interruptions, so the series will conclude after six seasons. Throughout the first three seasons, *Lost*'s Wednesday time slot was bounced from 8 p.m. to 9 p.m. to 10 p.m. For Season 4, Lost was moved to Thursdays at 9 p.m. so that it would not compete with the *American Idol* results show aired on Wednesdays.

In contrast to other dramas, *Lost* is unlikely to attract new viewers at this point. The plot is too intricate, the character stories too complicated. Ratings slipped from the promising first season. Although a fan favorite, *Lost* has not been without its detractors who complain that the show fails to resolve its many mysteries—or resolves mysteries in an agonizingly slow way—all the while layering on new questions to answer. Understanding *Lost* requires the viewer to apply theories from the realms of science, religion, music, art, and philosophy. This is a show for the cyber-elite.

LOST-TV FORUM

Founded in 2004 several months before the show's premiere by a fan using the alias Master Xander, the LOST-TV forum (losttv-forum.com) is the oldest and probably most active message board for discussion of *Lost*. LOST-TV boasts many active posters, some of whom have had tens of thousands of posts since joining. Started as part of the Web site LOST-TV.com, the *Lost* message board is now part of a greater community of forums at mymedia-forum.com, which offers boards on a variety of television shows, such as *Survivor* and *Heroes*, as well as forums for movies, music, and gaming. The message board for *Lost* is organized into transcripts, characters, episode discussion, spin-offs and Webmazes, theories, and general discussion of the show, which includes multimedia, speculation, polls, and couples.

A survey posted on LOST-TV in May 2008 sought to understand the gratifications received from participating in the message board, whether the message board feels like a community, and whether members have formed relationships with other members based on more than just discussion of the show. The survey also explored how participation in the forum has changed the way the program is watched and whether members believe the forum influences the writers or producers of the show. The survey generated 51 responses from LOST-TV members, many of whom provided a name or alias to be used for identification purposes.

Gratifications

In terms of gratifications, a common theme among respondents was that the LOST-TV forum serves as a place to discuss theories, insights, and ideas about the show.

- I really enjoy reading all the theories and seeing all the "Easter eggs." I like to compare my own thoughts to these. —PW
- I enjoy the knowledge and imagination of the other posters. There are many scenarios that I could not think up and many things I miss on my own. During the hiatus I posted more than usual; I guess it was slow on the board. I felt at one point I was addicted to the forum and would rather go online that participate in "real life." —MO
- Everyone on the LOST-TV forum is very helpful. Someone will find an answer to another person's question. It's nice when I can be that person to provide the answer. It's nice to help others understand, and through an open discussion learn more about the topic. —Thomas Hobbes

Another popular benefit of participation is the friendships and relationships made on the LOST-TV forum, a topic that is revived in later questions about relationships with other members and whether the board feels like a community.

- A great sense of community and friendships with the other people who post. —MrSocko54
- I have made numerous friends here, like to think I've inspired others to come out of their shells, enjoy dissecting ideas with others. —jacksgirlfriend
- I'm among my own people lol, I don't feel like a lone obsessed wacko. I feel welcome and respected even if I'm not liked by everyone. —Tashi/Roary
- I've met so many interesting, intelligent, witty, fun people. I have developed very good friendships with several people. Personally, it's a place where I hang out with friends. —Frecklestoo

Finally, others participate to contribute, read for fun, or relieve boredom.

- It keeps me from getting too bored during the work day. It allows me to exercise a little creativity that there's no real outlet for in the "real world." —Fancy Monkey
- I like the humor and characters on the board. —Vonne
- Knowledge and entertainment. It's like going to school and it's fun. —Softlips

From the 51 responses, an overwhelming theme was that the LOST-TV forum does feel like a community or family. Participants have gotten to know one another through the shared experience.

- In the on-season, yes, this is the best, greatest family I've ever been exposed to or part of. —Tashi/Roary
- Absolutely!!! The same people post day in and day out. We have fun together and we have the occasional spat. You really feel like you are a part of a community and that people care about you on some level. —Frecklestoo
- It has evolved into something even greater than a community—a family. It started out as a place to share ideas and explore what others had to say about an in-depth and complex show but has since become a place to share about our personal lives as well. —Crandyman
- Definitely, as proven by the fact that the forums stay alive even during the hiatus. The show brought us all together, but the community has kept us here. —Master Xander

A common subtheme in many of the responses addressed the hierarchy of power in the community of the LOST-TV forum. Participants will take sides over various issues, and some participants will see themselves as superior to others.

- Just like any other community, there are groups, clubs, cliques, competing interests, friendships, rules, and rules enforcement. —sgtdraino
- [During the off-season] everything splits off into factions and some parts of the board are like living in a war zone. —Tashi/Roary
- In a community this large, though, there are going to be those that consider themselves superior, and go out of their way to belittle a new member, an older member who doesn't participate in the "brainy" section, or just someone who has an opposing viewpoint. —SAM

One respondent issued a warning for those who consider LOST-TV to be a community. When communication is occurring in the mediated forum of the Web, participants can hide behind their screen name.

- It can be pretty dangerous—no matter how well you may think you "know" someone, even if you think you know their name, what they look like, what defines them, well, in the end, you're not interacting with people, you're reading. It may sound callous or harsh to say that, especially because I agree that the forum can FEEL very much like community in that it produces a certain set of emotional responses in us . . . but as soon as forums like this become people's primary community or source of relationships, I think it signals a social breakdown that is having and will continue to have dangerous and far-reaching ramifications. This is not to say that there are no benefits to LOST-TV; obviously there are many. But I hope I never come to a point where I think of it as a community. —Fancy Monkey

Relationships

Some members have formed relationships, romantic or otherwise, through the LOST-TV forum and have connected outside the message boards, and others are vehemently opposed to meeting anyone from the site.

- I would say I have become real friends with at least five people from L-TV. I have met two of them in real life. In one case, a friend was having emotional and marital problems and he showed up at my front door in the middle of the night, looking for a place to stay. —blue
- Yes, I've become friends with several people, talked on the phone with a few and some of us are planning to meet in NYC a year from this summer. —Frecklestoo
- Yes. There are several people that I speak with on the phone or daily through instant messages. We're friends and talk about our lives, not just *Lost*. In fact, we rarely speak about *Lost*. Last month, I met a fellow LTV member who had become a good friend. He has visited my hometown, and I've since visited his. It has turned into a romantic relationship, and we are planning on moving to the same city. —MD
- I have met several members in person. I travel a lot, so have met many while traveling. I met two in Florida, one in the Dominican Republic, two in North Carolina, one in Montreal, Quebec, and one in Tennessee. I'm sure I'll meet more. The purpose was, we just liked each other, and why not? —SAM
- I've met over a dozen people originally from here (some have since moved on but we are still real-life friends). I live with someone I met here. —jacksgirlfriend
- I have met a couple in the world, basically because they were in the area and we thought it would be fun to get together. So, we met for drinks, dinner, and conversation. There was some awkwardness, because the pace of communication, and thus the manner in which your relationship is sustained, is much different online than in the real world. It was a good time, nonetheless. —neillt006
- I've met three people from the board—one as an "I'm passing through your town on a trip, want to meet up and have a beer?", one who was flying in to

see family nearby and spent a day hanging out, and one who lives in my city. All three times, it was actually a lot of fun and felt very natural. But, of course, I'd talked to them and known them pretty well beforehand. —Vonne
- Yes, without a doubt. I consider people I've met here friends, even if they are virtual. And I have gotten together with a fellow LTVer in "real life" for coffee. —ozchick
- I have never met anyone from LOST-TV in person, nor do I intend to use LOST-TV to find a soulmate. —LR
- I regret having posted even as much about myself as I have. I've never posted my real first name, but I have included that in PM's to people, which was a mistake. But, no, I do not consider any of the people I cheerfully interact with here a friend. They know next to nothing about the most important things about who I am, and I have never met (nor do I plan to meet) any of them. —Fancy Monkey

Television Viewing and Web Practices

The main theme among the responses to the question about forum participation changing the way the television program is watched was that participation has made them pay more attention to the details and subtleties of the show. Others participate in live chat while watching the program, and others have become more of a fan because of the message board interaction.

- I watch with a more keen eye to details. —GoPanthers
- I scrutinize EVERYTHING twice now—looking for the tidbit of information that may not have been discovered/posted yet. —Garden Mom
- More attuned to the "mysterious" phenomena during an episode. —dfr
- I think about little details and go straight to the board to ask about them. I look for hints to things I have seen mentioned on the boards. —Mzsandeestart
- I think I've become a little more sensitive to the finer details of the show. — Master Xander
- I tend to look for more symbolism and it makes me really think and analyze what's going on. It's not just entertainment—it's brain stimulation, which is rare on TV. —Frecklestoo
- Yes, absolutely. I love doing East Coast live, it's like having 50 of your best friends over to watch a show everyone loves, but without the mess, constantly occupied bathroom, hosting fees (soda, food, etc.) or being distracted and missing dialogue/scenes by people talking/confused/thinking out loud. And yet it helps, because if you do need help/clarification on something, you got a room full of people just waiting to help you understand. This is the first forum/TV experience I've ever had. I wish I had known about the Internet back in the day, I'd've started doing this a lot sooner. —Tashi/Roary

- I'm not sure if it changed the way I watch, but it's made me into a bigger and better fan than ever. Now instead of just watching, I can watch, dissect, interpret, and rewatch over and over with a place to talk about everything I find. —MrSocko54

Another theme among the responses was that participating in the LOST-TV forum has increased the urge to visit spoiler Web sites or blogs.

- I can't stay away from spoilers now. I used to like being surprised. —mdd
- I tend to spoil myself with information before I see the episode. —sgtdraino
- Sometimes I do read spoiler forums, which is kind of bad in that it spoils the new episodes for me, but it also lets me have a more global perspective toward the entire series. —abcdxyz

Influence over Writers and Producers

Many respondents believe that the posts on LOST-TV and other *Lost* message boards influence the show's producers or writers in some way, particularly with nods or "shout-outs" to fans rather than major plot changes. Many cited the Nikki/Paulo storyline as an example. The respondents believed the outcry of fans on message boards about the introduction of a new storyline prompted the writers to kill the characters.

- Yes, they do read the message boards and killed Nikki and Paulo prematurely due to the fact that fans didn't like them. —TM
- I feel sure that they do! Most obviously, when they got rid of Nikki and Paulo when fans made it clear they disliked them. —abcdxyz
- It's obvious they're reading, although the basic story they have to tell won't change much. But when the "Hurley bird" shows up again, Nikki and Paulo are offed early, and Skaters and Jaters are mentioned, you know they are paying attention to the forums. —dvb
- Possibly. Sometimes I think this is silly but then sometimes I see/hear something that just SCREAMS: "They've been reading the posting boards!!!" —HopelesslyLOST
- Two things that come to mind, one positive, one negative: a little Easter Egg "shout-out" to the fans in Season 2 when Hurley and Libby were washing their clothes in the Swan station and they talked about how the machines seemed too new to be in this hatch. That was clever and well-done. On the other hand, I fear that there was too much accommodation to the negative fan reaction to the season 1 finale, which, in hindsight, was a fantastic way to end the season, but at the time, felt to many like a ripoff just because they didn't get to see what was in the hatch. —Fancy Monkey

- PTB [powers that be] have often mentioned in interviews that they read message boards and they have contacted our site founder via email telling him how happy they were that we're still out here. Probably one thing I remember seeing on the show that was on the boards was someone mentioned there being Twinkies in the hatch. Somewhere in S1, maybe S2, I think it was Hurley and/or Sawyer who made the same reference. Obviously we don't know for sure if it came from us, but I like to think so. —Brian
- I don't think so. It's a pipe dream. If they're reading the boards or even have people read them and give feedback, they should not be influenced. I want to see what the writers envision, not what someone on a message boards wants. —Scroot
- I'd say our posts might occasionally entertain the makers, and in the case of extremely negative reactions (Nikki/Paulo) might influence them, but generally not much effect. —sgtdraino

CULTURAL IMPLICATIONS

The results of the survey of LOST-TV participants indicates that the gratifications received include additional insights into this complicated show, relationships with other participants, and a sense of community, but one where there is a hierarchical structure of power. The forum has changed the way the program is watched, often either in the way the participant pays attention to details or uses the Internet at the same time. Finally, many respondents believe that their voices have been heard by producers and writers.

The technological advances of the Internet may signal a power shift in the culture industry from producers to consumers, or fans. One could, however, question whether fans are actually gaining power or just acquiescing to the power of culture producers.[60] The communities that fans create will generate and increase support for the show. When fans rally around a show on the brink of cancellation and force networks not to cancel it, it may seem that fans are exerting their power when they are actually just under the control of networks who have now been assured of demand. Possibly producers expect fans to demonstrate their commitment to a show to prove its value to advertisers. Although fan communities certainly help to build additional support and loyalty for a show, even critical online commentary may drive consumers to watch certain shows that are denigrated online, therefore giving more power to producers. Even "shout-outs" to fans, while seemingly a nod to their power, give producers an easy way to show fans that they are listening, but do not require major changes to the show's plot.

Chapter 11

MUSIC MESSAGE BOARDS: FUELING FANATICAL FANS

Ratings juggernaut *American Idol* has provided much fodder for discussion and expression of fandom on the Internet. After the contestants endure the barking of Randy Jackson, the frankness of Kara DioGuardi, the platitudes of Paula Abdul, and brutality of Simon Cowell, they face millions of fans who continue the discussion online. This chapter will first detail the history of online music fandom, describe the popular show, discuss how social media has made it possible for fans to support their favorite contestants, and finally, detail the rise to fame by Season 2 contestant Clay Aiken.

A HISTORY OF ONLINE MUSIC FANS

Music fans have long used the Internet to connect with one another. In the late 1970s and early 1980s, fans used Internet mailing lists and Usenet groups to communicate. By the mid-1990s, music fans congregrated on Web sites.[1] Nancy Baym used the band R.E.M. to illustrate applications of these online communication tools. R.E.M. fans first created an online mailing list in the late 1980s, and later the Usenet newsgroup rec.music.rem after the mailing list grew in size along with the band's popularity in the early 1990s. A small group of insiders remain on the now invitation-only mailing list. Excessive spam and the ability to easily create a Web site motivated then 16-year-old Ethan Kaplan to create the R.E.M. fan site murmurs.com. Interestingly, Kaplan was later hired by R.E.M.'s label, Warner Bros. Recordings, as their director of technology.[2]

Baym herself has explored the online music community of Swedish indie music fans. Her research demonstrated how fans do not congregate on a single site, but find community on a network of sites. Fans who interact on the Internet do so by creating their own fan sites; posting comments on fan sites; friending musicians, bands, or labels on MySpace or Last.fm; creating YouTube profiles that feature Swedish music videos; or creating playlists on MySpace or Last.fm. Other fans are involved in file-sharing sites such as Soulseek where they can also build a profile. Music fan groups also exist within social networking communities. According to Baym, active fans will encounter many of the same fans through these various social media tools, thereby creating a loose sense of community. She describes this kind of community in more detail:

> The Swedish indie fans practice what might be called "networked collectivism" in which loose collectives of associated individuals bind networks together. On the one hand, this means that groups can avail themselves of many mediated opportunities to share different sorts of materials, including text, music, video, and photographs in real time and asynchronously. On the other hand, this creates many problems, particularly with coordination, coherence, and efficiency (i.e. the same materials must be distributed in multiple places, and sometimes there is a great deal of replicated efforts).[3]

AMERICAN IDOL BEGINNINGS

Fox's *American Idol* has been a ratings powerhouse since it premiered June 11, 2002. Created by former Spice Girl manager Simon Fuller of 19 Entertainment in conjunction with FremantleMedia, the show was a spinoff of the British program *Pop Idol*, which premiered a year earlier with the finale episode garnering 14 million viewers and almost 9 million votes.[4] Egon Franck and Stephan Nüesch describe the program as relying on "manufactured" celebrities, who earn attention through fabricated fame and are lucrative platforms for media businesses.[5] The show, however, has launched the careers of numerous, now-successful artists, including winners Kelly Clarkson and Carrie Underwood and finalists Chris Daughtry, Clay Aiken, and Jennifer Hudson. In 2006, 19 Entertainment was sold to CKX, Inc., an entertainment company, for about $200 million.

The summer premiere of *American Idol* meant less competition for the new program, and consequently, it shattered several ratings records. In fact, the show was the highest-rated summer program on any network ever and the highest-rated Fox show in over a year at that time. The finale on September 4, 2002, was viewed by 22.8 million people and the performers received 15.5 million votes.[6]

During the show's second season in 2003, the show averaged 21.7 million viewers, almost double the average number of viewers during the first season.[7] The battle between Ruben Studdard and Clay Aiken culminated in a finale viewed by more than 38 million people, with only the Super Bowl and the finale of *Joe Millionaire* garnering higher ratings that year.[8] A *New York Times* article from 2003 quoted an executive with ties to the show who dubbed the program "ratings crack" for Fox, referring to the hard-to-resist inclusion of *American Idol* in programming schedules, despite the possible oversaturation of the program.[9] The competition calls the show the "Death Star," as a result of their challenge to pit programming against it.

SOCIAL MEDIA AND THE SHOW

American Idol brilliantly integrates media to better reach elusive consumers, energize the fan base, and deliver the greatest impact. The show was described by Web site Drama 2.0 as a concept that combines a television show, live events, an

Internet presence at americanidol.com, the use of the mobile platform for voting and content, distribution of music, licensing, and franchising of the concept throughout the world, and finally, merchandising.[10] Although the primary format of the program uses the traditional medium of television in a time of fascination with the possibilities of new media, traditional media still maintain several competitive advantages over new media, namely a solid understanding of content production and an ownership of distribution channels.

American Idol is credited with many successes, not least among them the integration of the show with text messaging, iTunes, and product placement. A deal with Cingular (now branded as AT&T) has allowed viewers to text their votes since 2003, a voting method that has increased in use 500% between its introduction and 2006.[11] *American Idol* voting is considered one of the driving forces in consumer acceptance of text messaging.[12] The show's Web site features sponsors in creative ways: Coca-Cola's backstage highlights, a Ford music video featuring the contestants, and Idol ring tones from AT&T. Music downloads have spiked for music featured on the show, with sponsor iTunes seeing much of this business. For example, when Daniel Powter's song "Bad Day" was used throughout Season 5 as the send-off song each week, over 700,000 copies of the song were downloaded.[13]

Social media are also being used by others to cash in on the success of the show. The Web site Vote for the Worst encourages voting for the worst contestant in an effort to derail the show's voting system. The concept began in 2003 when Dave Della Terza encouraged participants of a reality television message board to vote for the worst performers. Della Terza launched the Web site in the fourth season, and the site actually made a small profit from Google ad sales during the fifth season and then $40,000 in revenue during the sixth season.[14] "Vote for the Worst" differs from other *Idol* knock-offs not only because "it openly mocks the competition but also because it was formed spontaneously by an Internet-connected group of television viewers," writes Brian Stelter of the *New York Times*.[15] The site is reported to have had 2.7 million page views in 2008 when it was rumored that Season 7 contestant David Hernandez had worked as a stripper.[16]

It should come as no surprise that votes for *American Idol* contestants are cast on the basis of more than talent alone. Certain contestants engender a high level of fan fervor for their unique personalities or ability to connect to the audience. The contestants or their fans can launch campaigns on MySpace, blogs, or personal Web sites to help garner votes during the show. Fans of Season 7 contestant Syesha Mercado, for example, created the Web site Syesha's Faneshas (syeshasfaneshas.com) to help build support for her while she was competing.

Former contestants can stay in touch with fans through their MySpace pages, which provide leverage for a future recording career. Contestant Josiah Leming, the teenager whose backstory included living in a car, racked up 2 million hits on MySpace and over 40,000 friends, attracting the attention of Warner Bros. executives, who gave him a record deal.[17] Leming's album was released in January 2009 under the company's Reprise label.

Social media also speed the spread of juicy gossip or scandalous photos of contestants and likely has an impact on voting behavior. During Season 6, the beautiful, but vocally-challenged Antonella Barba came close to elimination. Afterward, the racy photos that circulated on the Internet may have helped keep her in the competition a little longer, as she was not voted out the following week. During this time, Barba became the top search on Technorati, a search engine for social media, as reported by Steve Cullen of the blog Media Relations and SEO PR.[18]

CLAY AIKEN ONLINE

In an interesting case study of a fan subculture, one could say that although the show *American Idol* provided the exposure, it was message boards that fueled the superstardom of Clay Aiken. Among Aiken's many fans is a large contingent of middle-aged women who are fanatically devoted to a singer about 20 years their junior. They have made friends online, formed fan clubs (e.g., the Claymates), and met in person to attend his concerts (sometimes wearing self-designed T-shirts). They share television clips of his appearances, produce cellcerts, buy his CDs, and read his book.

Hailing from Raleigh, N.C., Aiken was a student studying special education at UNC-Charlotte when he auditioned in Atlanta for the second season of *American Idol*. Although Simon Cowell declared that Aiken did not "look like a pop star," he was given the opportunity to advance in the competition to the Hollywood round. After making the Top 32, Aiken was sent packing during an early round, but, in a fortuitous twist of fate, was able to return during a Wild Card show, which was only used in the first three seasons and again in the eighth season. Selection by the fans as the "Viewer's Choice" returned Aiken to the pack of 12, and he would eventually remain until the finale where he would be pitted against Ruben Studdard for the title of American Idol.

Studdard, the "Velvet Teddy Bear" with a penchant for sporting jerseys featuring his Birmingham area code of 205, was an oversized R&B singer. Aiken, once red-headed and gangly, transformed during the season to more closely resemble host Ryan Seacrest with his spiky, blond-streaked hair and modern, striped shirts. In the end, just 135,000 votes of the more than 24 million cast separated the two contestants, with Studdard named the Season 2 winner.[19] (Seacrest mistakenly announced during the live broadcast that Studdard beat Aiken by just 1,335 votes.)

Finishing second was still considered a win for Aiken. The *American Idol* runner-up may enjoy a more illustrious career than the winner, not bound by the same contractual agreements. Signed to RCA after music executive Richard

Sanders noticed Aiken's "emotional connection" with the audience, his first single, "This Is the Night"/"Bridge over Troubled Water," went straight to number one on the *Billboard* chart.[20] Only Kelly Clarkson, Chris Daughtry, and Carrie Underwood have album sales that have surpassed Aiken's.

The fans found one another online long before the conclusion of Season 2 and even started dubbing themselves with various monikers. In addition to the well-known Claymates, Aiken also has AmerAikens (American fans), Claynadians (Canadian fans), and Claysians (Asian fans). Clayniacs and other fans pine for a Clay/December romance, a reference to the age difference between Aiken and his many older female fans. Aiken's second place finish may have cemented his fan base, as his fans supported him in an effort to continue his music career.

In a comparison between Aiken and other contestants in terms of Internet searches, at the time of the Season 2 finale, he had 10 times more searches than the finalists at the time of the Season 1 finale and four times more searches than the eventual winner of Season 2, Ruben Studdard.[21] The Lycos 50 proclaimed "Clay Aiken" the top male search of 2004, with searches increasing 151% over 2003, the year he competed in *American Idol*.

Aiken's official Web sites, clayaiken.com and clayonline.com, are complemented by countless message boards, fan sites, and blogs about the singer. ClaytonAiken.com bills itself as the "official unofficial" fan site and hosts the popular "Clay Board." ClayAikenTheIdealIdol.com and Claymaniacs are other popular forums. MSN hosts a group of "Clay Dream Believers." A group dubbed "Lecherous Broads for Clay Aiken" also maintains a site for Aiken. A search of "Clay Aiken" on YouTube reveals 11,900 videos and on MySpace, Aiken has almost 32,000 friends. Fans talk about OMC (our man Clay) on the message boards and meet to attend his concerts, concert pre-parties, or charity fundraisers. In television appearances on a variety of talk shows, fans watch only to see him and post the clips online to share with others.

Because of his fans, Aiken has had a number of awards bestowed upon him, including "Favorite Reality Star of 2003" by *TV Guide* and "most-loved reality star of all time" in a summer 2005 *TV Guide* poll.[22] Aiken was also voted "Favorite American Idol" in a *People* magazine poll in 2006.[23] In an unscientific *Us Weekly* poll from 2006, Aiken garnered 67% of the more than 15,000 votes cast for favorite past Idol—a poll that also included winners Carrie Underwood, Kelly Clarkson, and Taylor Hicks.

Aiken's 2003 debut album *Measure of a Man* was heralded with International CD Release parties organized by fans on the message boards.[24] According to red-hottopic.com, who originated the concept of release parties, approximately 12,242 people turned out for the parties, including 180 people in Clay's college town of Charlotte.[25] At the parties, name tags showcased the fans' message boards and their online aliases. The Web site Clay Aiken CD Parties notes that 84 parties were held for Aiken's last album.

CLAY AIKEN FAN EXPERIENCE

Clay Aiken fan Kylene agreed to be interviewed to explain the fan experience. She described herself as "a somewhat peripheral observer," but she offers keen insights into the online community of Aiken fans. Kylene first discussed the function of the message boards in her life.

> At the height of Clay's popularity (and my own "fandom"), the fan boards were my first stop for Clay news. Clay was a hobby for me, so of course I wanted to stay up to date with tour news, TV appearances, and any new music he was releasing. Claymates are a serious army of eyes and ears, reporting snippets back to their base camp anytime there was anything to be reported. The boards were always more informative than any official source at that time. That's changed to some degree since the official fan club came online and offered their own message board, but in those first couple of years, it was all about fan communication (and still is, even on the official board).
>
> I, personally, didn't get very involved with the relationships of the fans posting at the site because I never felt as though I had the time to invest myself the way they expected each other to be invested. I answered questions if I could, asked them when I couldn't find the answers anywhere else, and occasionally shared my experiences, but for the most part, unless there was major news breaking (like a tour), I spent maybe half an hour a day browsing through the threads.[26]

Other online fan activities of Kylene's included friending Aiken on social networking sites, joining his fan club, blogging about Aiken, and sharing videos from his concerts.

> I learned from several other artists I am a fan of that you can never guarantee where the news is going to break, which makes it necessary to be declared "a fan" everywhere you can! Because I'm not naive enough to believe Clay reads the majority of the messages left at MySpace or Facebook, "friending" him there, for me, is basically signing up for his mailing list. And I do it to be kept "in the loop."
>
> I was a member of his fan club for a period of time, and, at the beginning, blogged infrequently about Clay-related experiences in my life, particularly around tour or ticket time. The fact that Clay posted personal blogs to the site for members was a perk for most members (particularly because it was obvious he—and not a publicist—was writing them), and I think many of us were inspired to blog after reading his entries.
>
> When it comes to YouTube and downloading music—OF COURSE! I think a lot of artists underestimate the value of allowing fans to share live media with each other—some of my favorite songs on my Clay playlist were recorded at his shows. The videos—particularly from his live shows—were a great tool to keep fans excited about his performances when he wasn't releasing new music, especially for people who couldn't get to his shows.

One of the most interesting activities, I think, was "cellcerting." I'm not sure where the term originated, but I had never heard it before Clay. Claymates were "tweeting" before Twitter was around! Even now, though people are using Twitter in a similar way, it's difficult to find an actively updated report from concerts of my favorite touring artists. With Clay, that was never the case—even when he starred in *Spamalot*. Fans could always get an immediate update on where he was, what he was wearing, and what corny joke he told on any given evening, and it was all very well organized and easy to follow.[27]

Finally, Kylene discussed how she thought the online communities contributed to Aiken's initial success.

I think the communication—and, in some cases, competition—between fans in online communities played a huge role in Clay's initial success. Fans got each other excited and challenged one another to KEEP things exciting—for better or for worse, their commitment to Clay never wavered. Online communities allowed fans to mobilize and kept people informed about his projects. Even a casual fan who maybe checked the Web site once a week or so would be aware of a new album coming out or a television special to be aired, and I think that's vital to an artist's success, particularly in between projects. Out of sight, out of mind—the message boards and fan sites are what keeps Clay around when he's not getting radio play or walking the red carpet.

I also think that the boards are a safe haven for fans—not only for Clay, but artists in general. It's a support group, a place for people to throw around theories about rumors, discuss controversies, and make sense of gossip. It's comfortable to act in a way that completely contradicts how you normally act, be it screaming like a teenager or speaking up in his defense or playing the role of "mother hen" when your fellow fans need your advice (which no one in the real world ever asks for!). Within that community, I think it's easy to get caught up in our own hype and believe our favorite singers or actors or whatever are more popular than they may actually be in the mainstream, which isn't necessarily a bad thing. It's nice to be surrounded by the undeniable enthusiasm of people who have nothing but unconditional admiration for the things they love. The message boards didn't believe that Clay could ever fail or be bad at ANYTHING, so, of course, they made sure he wasn't. His shows were sold out, his TV appearances were well-attended by screaming fans, his book became a best seller. The online communities made it their responsibility to help him do well—they were invested, and his success was their success, not unlike a proud parent bragging about their Ivy-league bound graduate.

Things are quiet on the Clay front, and I'll admit I haven't even visited the Clayboard more than a handful of times in 2009. If and when there's news to be heard, though, it will undoubtedly be whispered first on the boards and many of the fans will return to see what all the fuss is about. If and when there's news, Clay will, in my opinion, be almost totally dependent on the online communities to get the word out. Because if and when there's news, his most loyal fans are the only ones who'll be listening for it, and their excitement is what will prompt attention from everyone else.[28]

REFLECTIONS ON ONLINE FANDOM

For an artist like Clay Aiken who did not emerge onto the music scene in the traditional way of building a local fan base, the online community was particularly critical for his initial and continued success. Fans had to know they were not alone. As Aiken's life has taken many turns since his debut on *American Idol*, including announcing his homosexuality and fathering a baby with friend Jaymes Foster, it remains to be seen whether the fans will continue to stay loyal.

Chapter 12

FROM MAINSTREAM TO SOCIAL MEDIA: GIVING POWER TO THE PEOPLE

The economic models of media today are based almost exclusively on "pushing" the information and entertainment out into the public. Tomorrow's will have as much or more to do with "pulling," where you and I reach into the network and check out something the way we do in a library or video-rental store today.

—Nicholas Negroponte, *Being Digital*

The concept of news is undergoing a revolution that involves the distribution, creation, and selection of news stories. At the same time, social media, particularly blogs, have begun to set the agenda for mainstream news organizations. When the media described memos from President Bush's National Guard service as forgeries, the source was the blogosphere. Social media exploits can also become the news. This chapter will highlight how people are consuming and distributing news online as well as how traditional media sources cover social media news and news stories that emerge in the blogosphere.

THE NEW NEWS

At one time, news was delivered via television at set times or printed in the daily newspaper. On June 1, 1980, CNN changed the concept of news by providing 24-hour coverage. At any time of the day, viewers could turn to CNN or its competitors who later followed this model to be informed of breaking news or watch more in-depth reports on current stories. For today's consumers, news can be accessed from many different sources, including traditional media such as television, print, and radio, as well as the new media of the Internet through a computer or mobile devices, such as cell phones or PDAs. Consumers now have instantaneous access to the news story of their choosing at any hour of the day.

The news industry is also facing the rise of news production by ordinary citizens. Today, many consumers, often called citizen journalists, use the Internet and other technological devices to report on and distribute the news themselves.

As the megapixels of mobile devices have improved and video and still images can be captured by the camera function, consumers are now equipped with the tools needed to produce and upload video and images. Some phones even provide basic editing functions, including transitions and the ability to add a voiceover. Web sites are available for these citizen journalists to post their news stories to be shared with others. Citizen journalists also commonly use their own Web sites or blogs for news reporting.

Finally, consumers are now able to control the selection of news stories, a process that had once been the domain of gatekeepers at media organizations. News aggregators and RSS feeds allow users to pull news from a variety of sources. Social news sites provide an outlet for consumers to share and showcase certain stories.

THE RISE OF CITIZEN JOURNALISM

Interest in expressing commentary and opinion is certainly not a new concept that sprung into life with the advent of blogging software. In *The Press in America: An Interpretive History of the Mass Media*, Michael Emery, Edwin Emery, and Nancy Roberts link the beginning of the expression of opinion with the formation of the alphabet; the publication of religious and philosophical texts, such as Plato's *The Republic*; and the invention of the printing press, which facilitated the Protestant Reformation through the rapid printing of Martin Luther's *95 Theses*.[1] Colonial America in the 18th century saw the printing of pamphlets and broadsheets of propaganda against authority figures.[2] These pamphleteers were later pulled into media organizations and the profession of journalism. Many years later, desktop publishing in the 1980s and 1990s sparked easy creation of materials, but distribution still remained a challenge. Civic journalism also came into fashion in the early 1990s, a concept that elicited feedback from community members and readers about news stories.[3]

In recent years, participatory journalism, or citizen journalism, has received much attention. In the report "We Media," authors Shayne Bowman and Chris Willis define participatory journalism as follows: "The act of a citizen, or group of citizens, playing an active role in the process of collecting, reporting, analyzing, and disseminating news and information. The intent of this participation is to provide independent, reliable, accurate, wide-ranging, and relevant information that a democracy requires."[4] Early forms of participatory journalism existed on the Internet in newsgroups and bulletin boards. Today, although much citizen journalism is reported on blogs, it also exists within other forms of social media, such as chat rooms, instant messages, newsgroups, forums, and microblogging sites such as Twitter. Citizens who wish to cooperate in their reporting can participate in collaborative publishing systems.

The rise of citizen journalism in the United States can be traced to several key events in recent history. In the wake of 9/11, the Web sites of mainstream news organizations were flooded with traffic from users actively seeking information. As a result, "everything from eyewitness accounts and photo galleries to commentary and personal storytelling emerged to help people collectively grasp the confusion, anger, and loss felt in the wake of the tragedy," write Bowman and Willis.[5] A 2002 report by the Pew Internet & American Life Project also highlights 9/11 as a key event that directed attention to the prevalence of "do-it-yourself journalism."[6] The personal accounts from ordinary citizens heralded an increased interest in citizen journalism.

When the space shuttle Columbia disintegrated over Texas upon re-entry on February 1, 2003, news agencies and NASA both requested eyewitness accounts, photos, and videos that might provide clues as to the reason for the tragedy.[7] But 11 minutes before the Associated Press issued a wire-service alert about the space shuttle, an online discussion was occurring in real time.[8] On the Free Republic Web site, shuttle enthusiasts were tracking re-entry via NASA TV's webcast from mission control in Houston and watching the skies from their various locations in the western United States, including Nevada and Texas. At 9:05 a.m., the online participants were observing communication problems at mission control while a participant shared that he heard a "sonic boom" over Fort Worth. Nineteen minutes later at 9:24 a.m., a participant described MSNBC as covering the story of the lost shuttle, followed by CNN coverage at 9:29 a.m.

In 2004, Americans used the Internet to locate Iraq War-related news stories, photos, or videos that were not made available by mainstream media. This timeframe was described by Pew Internet & American Life Project researchers Deborah Fallows and Lee Rainie as a "time of intense and dramatic news coverage that includes an unprecedented volume of references to disturbing images from the war in Iraq," including the murders of American contractors in Fallujah, prisoners and guards at the Abu Ghraib prison in Baghdad, and the beheading of civilian Nicolas Berg.[9] Their study found that 24% of survey respondents had seen war-related images that were not used in mainstream media, and 28% of those respondents had actively sought these images.[10]

Citizen journalists provide a first-hand look at what the audience does not see in traditional media. For example, countless U.S. soldiers serving in Iraq have posted videos on video-sharing sites or are blogging, revealing a side of war that would not be exposed during an evening news program. As citizen journalists, users can also apply their personal news values to set a personalized news agenda. Additionally, the practice also provides users with more than one point of view.

FORMS OF PARTICIPATORY JOURNALISM

The first form of participatory journalism is user-customized news sites whereby the user can customize content on the home page of a news organization's Web site. Sites offering this service include *The Wall Street Journal*, MSNBC.com, the

Washington Post, and CNN. Other sites like Yahoo! also allow users to customize the home page by selecting content of interest and using RSS feeds to import content from other sources. People are now getting their news through instant messaging services or Twitter feeds on their PDAs or cell phones, which also allow for customizable content.

The second form of participatory journalism is user feedback and commentary. Many media organizations provide a means for the audience to communicate their opinions. Stories posted to the Web can offer a comments function or a rating mechanism. In 2008, NPR, described by its digital editorial director as being "late to this game," added rankings for the most commented-on and recommended stories.[11] Bloggers also provide commentary and analysis of news stories, adding another perspective for readers. Similar discussions are taking place in forums, newsgroups, and chat rooms.

The third type of participatory journalism includes social news sites, such as Slashdot, Fark, Digg, and Reddit, which allow users to not only submit stories or other content from the Web, but also vote for stories that appeal to them. Mainstream news sites also employ similar functions to these social news sites, allowing readers to see the "most read" or "most e-mailed" stories and to post the story to Digg or Reddit.

The fourth and final type of participatory journalism involves user-created content. This content may be provided to mainstream news organizations, as some of these news organizations are embracing the citizen journalism movement. Many television stations now encourage the submission of viewer footage, often when a citizen has been on the scene with a video camera during a crisis or calamity. After 9/11, news stations showed countless videos taken by tourists and residents of New York City. Tornado footage is often provided by a resident who would rather shoot coverage than take cover. Blogs and wikis also fall into this category of participatory journalism.

A social news community often employs a collaborative publishing system to facilitate the process. The popular Slashdot (slogan: "News for Nerds. Stuff that Matters") is an example of such a system to which users can submit stories that are moderated by the multitude of fellow users. More than 10 million unique users visit the site each month, with about 5% of those users actively participating by writing articles, moderating, ranking, and posting comments.[12] Newsvine is another example of a social news site that uses a collaborative publishing system.

Another participatory venture is the cable/satellite network and Web site CurrentTV, chaired by former Vice President Al Gore. The CurrentTV Web site describes the company as having pioneered a model of interactive viewer-created content for television.[13] About one-third of the station's broadcast segments are viewer-created, often short-form, non-fiction videos. Included in these user-created videos are news segments. Viewers also create advertisements for the corporate partners of CurrentTV. The Web site provides a community for CurrentTV users to connect and share their videos.

On August 2, 2006, CNN launched iReport, its citizen journalism initiative, which was moved to ireport.com when the company purchased the domain name for $750,000 in 2008.[14] iReport allows users to upload news packages, which may be aired on CNN television networks, CNN.com, or other CNN platforms. A tally on the site keeps track of submission statistics, which include almost 300,000 submitted stories and almost 1,000 aired on CNN for February 2009. Vetted stories receive the "On CNN" distinction. The stories might become part of the CNN International weekly half-hour program *iReport for CNN* or CNN's *News to Me*, which airs on HLN (Headline News) and shows clips from iReport as well as from other online video-sharing sites.

THE CITIZEN NEWS AGENDA ON SOCIAL NEWS SITES

Researchers have explored how the news agenda looks when non-journalists have the power to set it. A 2007 study by Project for Excellence in Journalism (PEJ) found that 40% of content on social news sites is from blog posts, followed by 24% from mainstream news sources, and 5% from wire services.[15] The study also found that social news sites often focus on technology and science, with 40% of the content examined in the study devoted to these interests. Lifestyle stories commanded second place. The nature of the content should continue to evolve as the use of social news sites becomes more mainstream.

The PEJ study also examined topics covered in 48 mainstream media organizations for one week (June 24–29, 2007) and compared these topics to what was popular on the social news sites of Digg, Del.icio.us, and Reddit during the same timeframe. Also included in the study was Yahoo! News, which offers both editor-selected stories and user-ranked news. Overall, the researchers concluded that little correlation could be found between the mainstream news stories and the social news stories. For example, while traditional media focused on the Iraq War and immigration during this period, the social news sites were posting stories about the release of Apple's new iPhone and how Nintendo passed Sony in terms of net worth. They also found the three social news sites to vary in terms of top stories: Reddit favored political stories, Digg focused on technology, and Del.icio.us did not have a particular bent. The three social news sites tended to focus on domestic events, rather than the international stories featured in mainstream news. Overall, only 5% of the stories on social news sites overlapped with the top 10 news stories in mainstream media. Yahoo! News did not show a relationship between the stories selected by editors and those preferred by readers.

A related article about the study states, "In short, the user-news agenda. . .was more diverse, yet also more fragmented and transitory than that of the mainstream news media. This does not mean necessarily that users disapprove or reject the mainstream news agenda. These user sites may be supplemental for audiences. They may gravitate to them in addition to, rather than instead of, traditional venues. But the agenda they set is nonetheless quite different."[16]

In 2005, Brian Morley and Chris Roberts examined 20 popular blogs to understand patterns of linking and types of content in the posts. The researchers coded all content into one of six categories: commentary with link, commentary with extended excerpt, excerpt from media, original reporting, original reporting with commentary, and personal item. Almost half of all posts linked to a mainstream media source, and many of the topics lined up with topics of interest in mainstream media. About 13% of blogger posts focused on criticism of mainstream media reporting. The fact that mainstream media tends to revolve around news stories, rather than commentary, is reflected in the 72% of posts with links that were directed toward news stories. The researchers concluded that blogs, and particularly political blogs, were found to set second-level agendas, described as telling us "what to think about topics that others have told us to think about" by providing commentary on mainstream media articles.[17]

SCOOPING MAINSTREAM MEDIA

Several major news stories have either been scooped by bloggers or perpetuated by bloggers, with the latter leading to an outcome that might not have happened if bloggers had not been involved. Bloggers played a major role in a story involving former Senate Majority Leader Trent Lott, with much credit given to blogger Joshua Micah Marshall of the Talking Points Memo. Lott's pronouncement at Strom Thurmond's 100th birthday party received little immediate attention in the mainstream media in 2002, despite the fact the event was shown live on C-Span and was reported in the press. Lott had said: "When Strom Thurmond ran for president, we voted for him. We're proud of it. And if the rest of the country had followed our lead, we wouldn't have had all these problems over the years, either." Because Thurmond had campaigned for racial segregation, many considered the comment to be a racist attack on civil rights legislation.[18]

Marshall wrote 20 blog posts after the comment aired, attracting the attention of other bloggers and mainstream media outlets. Paul Krugman of the *New York Times*, after quoting from Marshall's blog, credits Marshall with being the person "who, more than anyone else, is responsible for making Trent Lott's offensive remarks the issue they deserve to be."[19] The outcome of this attention was the resignation of Lott.

In 2007, Talking Points Memo was also instrumental in covering and investigating the firing of eight U.S. attorneys. An investigation on the blog started when the team noticed a pattern of stories about the firings from around the country, first from a story in an Arkansas newspaper, then from the *San Diego Union-Tribune*. Talking Points Memo readers also began monitoring any developments reported in their local media outlets.[20] The online investigation eventually prompted reporting in mainstream media and a Justice Department investigation. Blog readers then indexed a 3,000-page report on the dismissal of the attorneys after it was released in March 2007, pointing out a critical lapse in the inclusion of e-mail communications. The investigation culminated in the resignation of Attorney General Alberto Gonzales. In 2008, Marshall won a George Polk Award for this coverage, the first employee of an Internet-only news organization to do so.[21]

Blogger Russ Kick's specialty is acquiring photos and documents for his blog TheMemoryHole.org by exercising his rights under the Freedom of Information Act. He also locates documents posted to government Web sites, especially those that have been posted and then removed. Kick's blog is probably best known for the photos he published of American military coffins returning from the Middle East. After displaying the photos on the blog, they were featured on the front pages of newspapers around the world.[22] Kick has also posted a digitally uncensored version of a Justice Department report on diversity and the uncut five-minute video of President Bush sitting in a Florida classroom after hearing that America was under attack, which was later used in Michael Moore's movie *Fahrenheit 9/11*.

Following the plagiarism scandal of the *New York Times* writer Jayson Blair and the seemingly first-person narratives of fellow writer Rick Bragg, who relied on the reports of stringers and interns instead of his own personal experiences, the criticism swirling in the blogosphere may have contributed to the resignation of the *New York Times* editor Howell Raines in June 2003. Andrew Sullivan of AndrewSullivan.com was one blogger among many who was particularly critical of Raines. On his blog, Sullivan quotes from journalism professor Jay Rosen's interview with *Newsday*: "For a long time journalists haven't had to explain very much how they do things. The Internet has created the expectation that news organizations can be interacted with, can be questioned." To which Sullivan responds: "Imagine that. News organizations *questioned*. Next up, we'll be demanding that Howell Raines actually talk to the press!"[23]

During the presidential campaign of 2004, a group of swift boat veterans, calling themselves the Swift Boat Veterans for Truth, united to question Democratic candidate John Kerry's version of his military service during the Vietnam War. The group is best known for the anti-Kerry television commercials run during the campaign. Although the men in the ads portrayed themselves as serving alongside Kerry, it was later revealed that only one of the men from the ads actually had. Mainstream media at first avoided challenging the claims of the veterans, but talk radio and blogs were actively discussing it, particularly blogger Glenn Reynolds of Instapundit.[24]

The blogosphere can also be credited with investigating what came to be known as "Memogate," a crisis that led to an attack on the credibility of CBS News and the eventual downfall of CBS anchor Dan Rather. The story of Memogate began with a report on *60 Minutes II* on September 8, 2004, detailing possible preferential treatment afforded George W. Bush while a member of the Texas Air National Guard. The evidence for this treatment was found in four memos seemingly written by now-deceased Lieutenant Colonel Jerry Killian,

Bush's supervisor in the Guard. The memos had been in the possession of former Guardsman Bill Burkett who passed them on to CBS. After the report, the debate surrounding the authenticity of the documents that heated up in the blogosphere and mainstream media centered on three elements: the typography, the military terminology, and the recollections of those involved.[25]

Nineteen minutes into the program, the first attacks on the memos surfaced on the Web, first by Air Force officer Paul Boley on the site FreeRepublic.com and several hours later by Republican lawyer Harry MacDougald. Also on September 8, the blog Little Green Footballs posted a challenge to prove the documents were created on a computer and not a typewriter. Joseph Newcomer, a typography expert with a Ph.D. in computer science, took the challenge, eventually proclaiming that the documents were generated on a computer. He posted the results on his own Web site, and Little Green Footballs provided a link to his site, calling Newcomer's results "authoritative and definitive" proof that the documents had been created on a computer. Newcomer received a great deal of attention in mainstream media. He was mentioned in a September 14 *Washington Post* story, which was later that night discussed on Fox, MSNBC, and CNN, and the next day, he was a guest on *Hannity & Colmes*.

Other blogs jumped on the Memogate bandwagon, including the Power Line blog, which started its conversation with a morning-after post by Scott Johnson titled "The 61st Minute" and links to FreeRepublic.com. Readers provided further evidence via e-mail to Johnson who posted many of the comments on the blog. The popular Drudge Report was also talking about the issue and linking to the Power Line blog story. An additional 500 sites had also linked to the Power Line story, sending so much traffic to the site that it caused the server to crash. Power Line co-founder John Hinderaker described the implications in a 2004 *Time* magazine interview: "I think it's fair to say that that post that Scott began is probably the most famous post in the young history of the blogosphere."[26] Following the lead of the blogosphere, the mainstream media started challenging the credibility of the documents. Journalists may have raised these questions on their own, but the speed of bloggers means that they cannot always raise these questions first.

Corey Pein, in an article for the *Columbia Journalism Review*, pointed out the flaws in this reasoning: "Newcomer begins with the presumption that the documents are forgeries, and as evidence submits that he can create a very similar document on his computer. This proves nothing—you could make a replica of almost any document using Word. Yet Newcomer's aggressive conclusion is based on this logical error."[27] In the end, document examiners could not conclusively determine the credibility of the documents, but the perception was already out there that the documents were forgeries. CBS had aired a story with documentation that could not be verified, and Dan Rather announced on November 23, 2004, that he would leave the anchor desk in March 2005. Pein reflects on the events, "While 2004 brought many stories of greater public import than how George W. Bush spent the Vietnam War, the year brought few of greater consequence for the media than the coverage of Memogate. When the smoke cleared, mainstream journalism's authority was weakened. But it didn't have to be that way."[28]

The presidential debate on September 30, 2004, raised questions from the blogosphere about whether Bush was wearing an earpiece. Evidence for this theory included the bulge on the back of Bush's jacket and a mid-sentence "now let me finish," when no one had apparently interrupted him. Starting October 2, 2004, several bloggers circulated the story of "The Bulge" for about a week before the *New York Times* addressed the issue on October 9, 2004.[29] Countless other news organizations then carried the story, including the *Washington Post*, the BBC, and the AP.[30] Theories for the Bulge proliferated, including a bullet-proof vest, a medical device, and a Secret Service transmitter. As blogger Chris Shaw told Jon Garfunkel of the Civilities blog:

In my opinion the Bulge "phenomenon" (and all its facets) was born and bred in the "blogosphere" . . . I also think the "blogosphere" was responsible for keeping the story alive so long. Every time the Bulge seemed to die, some great new "rumor" would get circulated and the Bulge would end up in the press again . . . I don't know why we never got the truth about the Bulge. I actually bothers me quite a bit. After all the hoopla, as I said on my site, the press never really asked any SERIOUS questions about the story.[31]

On October 17, 2004, Tim Russert, of *Meet the Press*, asked Bush's campaign manager Ken Mehlman about the allegations, with Mehlman laughing it off by saying that Bush was receiving secret signals from aliens in outer space.[32] ABC's Charlie Gibson asked Bush about the Bulge in a televised interview on *Good Morning America* a week before the election, with Bush saying it was a poorly tailored shirt.[33] As Shaw writes on the blog Bush Wired: "Most coverage was in a humorous light, or simply discussed the Internet debate. . .the absence of the media asking real questions about this possibly serious issue became very apparent."[34] This story, although it did receive mainstream media attention, was never deemed important by mainstream media in light of all the other stories during the campaign.

Corporations are also the target of bloggers, and unethical actions will rarely go unnoticed. Apple computer's popular "Switchers" campaign, featuring real people describing their switch from a PC to a Mac, motivated Microsoft, in response, to develop an online campaign titled "Confessions of a Mac to PC Convert" in 2002.[35] The ad featured a freelance writer who had switched from a Macintosh to a PC with Windows, even providing a photo of the woman. A poster to Slashdot questioned the authenticity of Microsoft's ad, calling them out for their use of a stock photo image.[36] After CNET News inquired about it, the company pulled the ad.[37] The Associated Press later determined that the "freelance writer" was actually an employee at a Microsoft public relations firm, learning her identity by examining personal data embedded in documents published with the ad.[38]

Not every story that emerges from the blogosphere and influences mainstream news coverage is intended to bring down politicians, journalists, or corporations. A webcam set up by an accountant on Hornby Island, near Vancouver, Canada, focused on an eagle's nest. More than 100 million people had checked in on the site, noting that one egg was missing and a second egg was overdue for hatching. Reporter Jonathan Brown of *The Independent* describes the nest as capturing the interest of many people online and offline "with the story developing into a major news event covered on television, newspapers, and online."[39]

Social media can also be helpful when full reporting is not possible. Twitter was used to provide information about an October 2007 earthquake in San Jose. The Twitterers were able to mobilize faster than any news organization in the area.[40] Another application of Twitter was to update San Diego residents of the status of wildfires in 2007.

THE BLOGGER/JOURNALIST

Bloggers are not the antithesis of journalists. In fact, many bloggers emerge from the ranks of journalism as an independent voice, with some of them returning to mainstream media organizations to work as bloggers for their online editions. Sullivan was an editor at *The New Republic* and a columnist for the *New York Times Magazine* before launching AndrewSullivan.com. His blog, The Daily Dish, now resides on the Web site for *The Atlantic*. Mickey Kaus is a former writer for *The New Republic* and *Newsweek*. His blog, Kausfiles, is now housed at Slate.com. Talking Points Memo's Marshall worked for *The American Prospect* as the Washington editor before launching his blog.

Media elites are also known consumers of blogs.[41] In addition to keeping tabs on the news in the blogosphere, journalists can also use blogs and social networks to learn more information about a public, or not so public, figure. For example, the boyfriend of Bristol Palin, daughter of 2008 vice presidential candidate Sarah Palin, had a MySpace account that became media fodder after it was revealed that Bristol was pregnant with his child. The *New York Post* referenced Levi Johnston's MySpace profile descriptions of himself ("I like to go camping and hang out with the boys, do some fishing, shoot some s- - - and just f - - -in' chillin' I guess.") and used his profile photo in its news story about the pregnancy.[42]

Time's Lev Grossman speculates on the future of bloggers:

> It's hard to imagine that bloggers will be content to remain media gadflies, sniping at the giants from below. In fact, it's entirely possible that they will ultimately be assimilated into the mainstream media they now openly despise. They'll start accepting advertising (Power Line already does), they'll go on Leno, they'll lose

their outsider cred and their aura of driven-snow purity. The best bloggers will be hired away by the hated MSM, bought off with Op-Ed columns and cable talk shows. And if bloggers do become Big Business, they will lose their free pass and become subject to the same scrutiny that *60 Minutes* is under.[43]

In 2004, bloggers received invitations to cover national political conventions for the first time, with 30 bloggers invited to the Democratic National Convention and about 15 to the Republican National Convention. The move gave bloggers legitimacy, or at least prompted discussions of their legitimacy, and attracted attention for their online ventures. Bloggers covering the 2004 Democratic National Convention included Ezra Klein of Pandagon.net, Jessamyn West of Librarian.net, Jeralyn Merritt, a criminal defense attorney who writes the blog TalkLeft, and Tom Burka of the satirical blog Opinions You Should Have.[44] The first bloggers for the Republican National Convention included Matt Margolis of Blogs for Bush, Captain Ed of Captain's Quarters, Scott Sala of Slant Point, and Hinderaker of Power Line.

NEWS REPORTING OF SOCIAL MEDIA

Mainstream media has not ignored the revolution of social media, and as a result, stories about social media are a hot topic in mainstream media. *Time* magazine, in fact, selected "You" as the Person of the Year in 2006, reflecting the intensified level of energy devoted to creating and sharing via the Internet. Also receiving news coverage was Merriam-Webster's word of the year in 2004: blog. *Time*'s Grossman details the story of 2006:

It's a story about community and collaboration on a scale never seen before. It's about the cosmic compendium of knowledge Wikipedia and the million-channel people's network YouTube and the online metropolis MySpace. It's about the many wresting power from the few and helping one another for nothing and how that will not only change the world, but also change the way the world changes.[45]

The *New York Times*, for example, increased its mentions of social media tools from 2007 to 2008. Stories that mention blogs are the most popular, up from 1,691 in 2007 to 2,127 in 2008. The social media applications of YouTube, MySpace, and Facebook have doubled in terms of the number of stories that mention them, up from 267 to 770 for YouTube, 155 to 355 for MySpace, and 299 to 568 for Facebook. *USA Today* also runs a number of stories about social media, with blog mentions increasing from 583 to 772 between 2007 and 2008. YouTube mentions increased from 266 to 327 during the same time period, MySpace mentions declined slightly from 211 to 172, and Facebook mentions grew from 119 to 157. Some of these increases may be attributed to the presidential campaign, which utilized social media to connect with voters.

At one time, what was popular online reflected what was popular in main-stream culture. Mainstream culture now looks to the Internet to determine newsworthy items. As Eric Deggans describes, "Now, YouTube interest brings news coverage, as the mainstream media cranes its neck into cyberspace to see what the kids are watching these days."[46] Several television programs, including the daytime talk show *Ellen*, feature segments with social media happenings. In 2006, VH1 partnered with iFilm to produce the program *Web Junk 20*, which counts down the hottest viral videos. After three cycles of weekly episodes that year, the show returned for a special episode in January 2008 called *Web Junk 40: Best of the New Crap*. The CW offered a viral video compilation program called *Online Nation*, but the show was canceled in October 2007. CNN's now-canceled *Judy Woodruff's Inside Politics* was the first show on cable or network television to provide a report from the blogosphere.[47] The four-minute segment called "Inside the Blog" has been expanded now that *Inside Politics* has been folded into *The Situation Room*.

THE FUTURE OF NEWS

Agenda-setting scholar Max McCombs describes in *Setting the Agenda: The Mass Media and Public Opinion* that there "is already evidence of a de facto oligopoly of news and information where a small number of sites command the largest proportion of the Internet users."[48] He is not convinced that the news agenda will be significantly altered because of online news and blogging, adding that the agenda will remain homogeneous across these sites until "someone invents a new kind of news that eclipses the traditional news audience. If that happens, it will be the result of journalistic creativity, not technology, and it will shift the agenda-setting influence of the news media to a new source."[49]

In the end, mainstream news organizations may be replaced by self-promoting capitalists posing as journalists as suggested by Bill Kovach and Tom Rosenstiel in their 2001 book *The Elements of Journalism*.[50] At the same time, the mainstream media may attempt to partner with bloggers and other citizen journalists by successfully bringing them under their corporate umbrellas and embracing a networked model of journalism. In the end, we need to recognize that news is not the domain of any one group of people. News gathering should be the responsibility for all citizens in an engaged and networked society.

Chapter 13

PRIMETIME SOCIAL MEDIA:
ADDING ONLINE TO STORY LINES

One could say that "life imitates art," but when social media appears in television programs, movies, or other products of the mass media, it is as if "art imitates life," online life, that is. This chapter will profile the television shows and other popular culture products that incorporate social media into story lines, receive creative inspiration from social media phenomena, or integrate the offline product with an online experience.

A History of Media Portrayals

The entertainment industry has produced many products about the media. Early movies include *Citizen Kane* (1941), which based its main character on newspaper publisher William Randolph Hearst; *All the President's Men* (1976), from the book by *Washington Post* reporters Bob Woodward and Carl Bernstein; *Network* (1976) with Faye Dunaway and William Holden; and *Broadcast News* (1987), starring William Hurt and Holly Hunter. A recent addition is *Good Night, and Good Luck* (2005), with David Strathairn portraying Edward R. Murrow. Countless television shows over the years have been set in media organizations, such as radio stations (*WKRP in Cincinnati*, *Frasier*, and *NewsRadio*), television stations (*The Mary Tyler Moore Show*, *Murphy Brown*, *Good Morning Miami*, *Sports Night*, and *Back to You*), and magazine offices (*Suddenly Susan* and *Just Shoot Me*).

When the Internet was still a new medium, several movies were released that embraced the Internet as a crucial plot element, including *The Net* (1995), *Hackers* (1995), and *You've Got Mail* (1998). *The Net*, starring Sandra Bullock, preyed on the public's fears of government surveillance and identity theft. The movie was followed by a 1998 television series that was canceled after one season. In the romantic comedy *You've Got Mail*, the characters, played by Tom Hanks and Meg Ryan, meet on the Internet and communicate via their AOL e-mail accounts. Later, they are shocked to find out that they are actually both booksellers, with Hanks's superstore threatening the closure of Ryan's cozy neighborhood bookshop. The cult classic *Hackers* follows a group of hackers as they learn of a dangerous computer virus that is set to be released and attempt to use their skills to build evidence for this plot while being pursued by the Secret Service and the evil creator of the virus. More recent releases include the 2002 film *Fear Dot Com*, where four people are found dead in New York City, with the connection among them being that they had all visited the Web site Feardotcom.com within 48 hours of their deaths. In another Internet thriller, the 2008 movie *Untraceable* follows actress Diane Lane as an FBI cybersleuth investigating a serial killer who shows videos of his murders on the Web site killwithme.com, committing crimes that get quicker and more violent the more hits the site receives.

SOCIAL MEDIA ON TELEVISION

The CollegeHumor Show, which premiered on MTV in February 2009, may be the first television show to be set in a social media organization. The show combines the "reality" of office antics with scripted sketches from the Web site, reminding the viewer at the beginning of the program that "these are the actual dorks who work here, and this is what they do all day long." As Brian Stelter describes in the *International Herald Tribune*, "The first half of the sentence is true, but the show is actually an exaggerated, fanciful version of a 20-something's workplace. In the first episode the actor-employees practice beer pong, install a taco truck in the office, and turn Van Veen's office into a children's ball pit (rules: 'no diving, no throwing, no playing')."[1]

Several new programs targeting youth prominently feature social media in their plots. Nickelodeon's *iCarly* features the young actress Miranda Cosgrove as Carly Shay, who, with her best friend, hosts a weekly webcast from her loft apartment in Seattle. The show also features viewer-submitted videos. A 2009 episode of *iCarly* featured Lucas Cruikshank, a.k.a. Fred, who is one of the most popular characters on YouTube. In the new version of *90210*, character Erin Silver maintains a blog where she posts videos featuring puppets of fellow students in an attempt to embarrass them.

The CW's *Gossip Girl* (based on the book series by the same name) is narrated by an unknown character whose blog of gossip and rumors about the main characters is widely read. Social networking and communication technologies, such as MySpace and texting, are featured in this program as well. The CW maintains a blog about the program at gossipgirl-blog.cwtv.com, which includes entries under the category of "Spotted" written in the style of the fictitious Gossip Girl as well as other entries such as character profiles and recaps. The "Spotted" entries have gained a following since the show's premiere, generating much discussion among blog readers and sometimes as many as 140 comments. Blog readers reflect the style of the Gossip Girl entries, often also using initials to refer to characters. Comments have had users debating the identity of P and H, expressing hope for B and C to get together, and eliciting surprise that S and N were hanging out over the summer.

The program *Secret Diary of a Call Girl* is based on a blog (belledejour-uk.blogspot.com) and book by an anonymous British call girl with the pen name Belle du Jour. *The Guardian*'s second British blog awards named Belle du Jour's blog as one of the three best written blogs of 2003. As Simon Waldman describes in *The Guardian*: "There's obviously a prurient and titillating element, but the quality of her writing took her blog well beyond that. Some judges were concerned it was a work of fiction, but even if it is, it remains an impressive piece of writing."[2] Belle has published two memoirs as well as the fictional novel *Playing the Game* with Orion Publishing Group. The eight-part television series that started on British television channel ITV2 was later rebroadcast on Showtime in the United States. The second season premiered in the United States in 2009.

A 2006 episode of *Law and Order* titled "Avatar" centered on a fictitious social networking site called BeFriends.com that served as the place where sex with a 16-year-old is offered in exchange for the murder of her mother. The episode cast social networking sites as a place where 20-something psychopathic sexual predators, bored teenagers, and computer geeks hang out. The ensuing trial on *Law and Order* determined that BeFriends.com was not at fault for the murder of the mother because, as was cited by the assistant district attorney to the girl's father, "Your daughter had a choice." In 2008, an episode of *Law and Order* titled "Babes" blended two news stories: a teenage pregnancy pack at Gloucester High School and a MySpace hoax that resulted in the suicide of the teenager being harassed. On this episode, the ringleader of the pregnancy pack commits suicide after becoming the target of online harassment by an unknown party.

An episode during the third season of *The West Wing* called "The U.S. Poet Laureate" featured a subplot involving a fan site devoted to character Josh Lyman. A real life situation involving *West Wing* writer and creator Aaron Sorkin and the TWoP forum was the impetus for this episode. The nasty exchange resulted in the episode that, as a *New York Times Magazine* article described, portrayed "hard-core Internet users as obese shut ins who lounge around in muumuus and chain-smoke Parliaments."[3] After Lyman responds to a post on LemonLyman.com, the users fight back with intense criticism, a situation that further escalates when a reporter from the *Washington Post* calls to question Lyman's statements on the site. White House Press Secretary C. J. Cregg describes the users as the cast of *One Flew Over the Cuckoo's Nest*, while Lyman likens the site to *The Lord of the Flies*.

An episode of *30 Rock* titled "Goodbye, My Friend" included a story of a pregnant teenager who was having difficulty communicating with her boyfriend. After not taking the girl's phone calls (which she knows he received because she has his voicemail password), the boyfriend texts the girl to say he is angry. She complains that his MyFace page still lists him as "horny" and that he should have the decency to Skype her face to face. Tina Fey's character responds with, "Man, there are just so many different devices for guys to not call you on now. When I was your age you could just be like, 'oh, he probably tried to call me but my line was busy,' and then just watch *Falcon Crest* and cry yourself to sleep."

During the summer of 2005, ABC ran a five-part series called *Hooking Up*, which followed 11 single women during a year of online dating. The show focused on how the women positioned themselves in their dating profiles, how they described the men they were looking for, and how they set up dates. The show, however, did not return for a second season.

Social news site Fark.com has twice sponsored a *Jeopardy* category, once on November 17, 2007, and again on January 9, 2009. Questions reflected the news-of-the-weird topics that are popular on the site. For example, one answer read: "'Noodle shop accused of aiding drunk driving. That's because nobody left the place' this buckwheat noodle." The question: "What is soba?" The search engine Google also receives mentions in television programs. On an episode of *Brothers and Sisters*, a character who is a soap opera star mentioned that his mother "Googles him once a week" to see what his fans and detractors are saying about him online.

TELEVISION SPOOFS OF SOCIAL MEDIA

Several television programs have provided references to social media phenomena as part of the plot. The writers of the *The Simpsons*, a program which has tapped popular culture for laughs for more than 20 years, recognized a popular YouTube video and were quick to create a parody. The target this time was Noah Kalina's six-year photo-a-day YouTube masterpiece, which has racked up more than 9 million views, 44,000 comments, and 57,000 favorites since he first posted it on YouTube in August 2006. During an episode titled "Eternal Moonshine of the Simpson Mind," photos flip through the 39 years of Homer's life, showing him as a baby to the present day and drawing to a close with the standard YouTube ending screen.[4] The concept was recreated for several commercials starring Kalina, including Dunkin' Donuts, Microsoft Istanbul, FSN Baseball, and the Melbourne Film Festival, which are featured on the blog Photoshelter.[5]

In another variation on his theme, Kalina was backstage at VH1's Big in '06 Awards, posing with celebrities. The images, which now reside on Kalina's Flickr page, were used to lead in and out of commercial breaks. Kalina expressed in an interview with Liz Kelly of the *Washington Post* blog Celebritology how the celebrities at the event were somewhat unaware of his concept. "[The producers] assured me that my video was so big and such a huge part of popular culture everyone would know who I was," describes Kalina. "Of course that was not the case."[6] The only two celebrities attending the award show to have ever heard of his project, according to Kalina, were Paris Hilton and Weird Al Yankovic. The audience may have been uninformed as well. "The funny thing is that they never explain it or even make mention of it during the show. If you never saw my video you would probably be scratching your head wondering who the hell I am. I think that was the best part," Kalina says.

"Chocolate Rain" singer Tay Zonday has received nods on television, including Tina Fey calling character Toofer "Chocolate Rain" in the 2007 premiere of *30 Rock*. Zonday also voiced his own character for an episode *South Park*, where he discussed "Chocolate Rain" and then died from a head explosion after falling victim to the stare of the dramatic prairie dog, the star of another popular YouTube video. When Steve Carell's character Michael Scott from *The Office* admitted that he had "watched 'Cookie Monster Sings Chocolate Rain' about a thousand times" after discovering YouTube, videos doing just that popped up online within days.

"Star Wars Kid," both an Internet meme and a pop culture reference, spawned hundreds of remixes. Spoofs have been featured on *American Dad*, *Arrested Development*, *Ned's Declassified School Survival Guide*, *Cory in the House*, and *South Park*. What Stephen Colbert of Comedy Central's *The Colbert Report* did with the meme created an intersection between mass and social media. The recreated segment with Colbert in front of a green screen allowed others to juxtapose Colbert's image with other videos. As Jeffrey Bardzell comments, "Colbert's use of intertextuality is particularly interesting, because rather than limiting himself to quoting earlier texts (however transgressively), his use of the green screen ensured that he would be quoted in future texts."[7] Colbert's "Green Screen Challenge" spurred new videos, such as Colbert vs. the Star Wars Kid, OK Go, and Nine Inch Nails. Others showed Colbert in an iPod commercial or playing Dance Revolution. These videos become mass media fodder when they are shown and talked about on *The Colbert Report*.

Memes from pop culture that enter the realm of social media do not always translate back in mainstream media, demonstrating the limits of online culture. When Daniel Day-Lewis shouted "I drink your milkshake" in the independent movie *There Will Be Blood*, the phrase sparked an onslaught of viral video parodies and mashups with the Kelis song "Milkshake" (with over 500,000 YouTube views), cementing those words as an online culture catchphrase. When *Saturday Night Live* parodied the phrase in a February 2008 episode, the audience reaction was described as "sheer bafflement."[8] As Josh Korr writes, "The sketch is a good reminder of how even the best pop culture blogs are still largely self-contained, inter-referential and off the general population's radar."[9]

SOCIAL MEDIA ON FILM

In August 2008, writer/producer Aaron Sorkin was negotiating a deal to write a screenplay for a movie about the founding of Facebook.[10] To prepare for the movie, Sorkin with his research partner Ian Reichbach created a Facebook page, which has attracted almost 10,000 friends and lots of commentary about the possibility of producing this movie.

A suicide attributed to MySpace cyberbullying that received much media attention will be the subject of a movie by independent production company Rocklin Entertainment. The film, titled *E-venge*, will tell the story of 13-year-old Megan Meier who committed suicide after being dumped by a purported MySpace love interest, who was actually a former friend and her mother posing as a teenage boy.[11]

The 2009 movie *Julie & Julia* blends the life story of Julia Child as per her autobiography written with Alex Prud'homme with the book *Julie & Julia: 365 Days, 524 Recipes, 1 Tiny Apartment Kitchen*, based on a blog by Julie Powell. Powell's project involved cooking all 524 recipes in Child's *Mastering the Art of French Cooking*, which she documented online and then on her popular blog, The Julie/Julia Project. The film represents the first major motion picture based on a blog.

Although not released in theaters, David Lehre's *MySpace: The Movie* deserves special recognition here. This MySpace parody is a collection of vignettes mocking the popular social networking site. In one, a guy poses in his bathroom, trying to capture a cool look for his profile photo. In another, a girl's profile photo is described as having "The Angles," a technique that uses awkward angles to hide an unattractive face. Another vignette involves a girl who argues with her boyfriend not including her among his "Top 8" friends. Even MySpace founder Tom Anderson is parodied at a wild party where he is everyone's friend. After a night of pizza, alcohol, and cocaine, Anderson is caught on camera in a bathroom over the toilet bowl, the resulting photo looking similar to his profile photo. Lehre also spoofed Facebook with *Facebook: The Movie*.

SOCIAL MEDIA ON THE STAGE

Several off-Broadway productions are tapping the creativity of bloggers for inspiration. In Marissa Kamin's *"The Fabulous Life of a Size Zero,"* which opened in June 2007, Anna Chlumsky spends several scenes reading from her fictional blog, which is composed of entries from real-life MySpace and LiveJournal blogs of young women. A contest to select the blog selections had been coordinated by the show's producers. Several characters in the play are also fascinated by celebrity gossip, and celebrity gossip blog Jossip.com provided tidbits of current gossip and accompanying photos to be projected onstage. Jossip received credit for its contribution and returned the favor by promoting *"Size Zero"* on its Web site. Although some productions might be criticized for blurring the distinctions between story and selling, producer Isaac Robert Hurwitz contends this concept works for such a storyline. Quoted in a *Variety* article in June 2007, Hurwitz argues, "With 'Size Zero,' the story we're telling already exists in the world of the Web. There can be a much more natural and expansive melding of product and marketing."[12]

Another stage production involving social media offers a script based on entries from MyFirstTime.com, a Web site founded in 1998 where more than 40,000 users have anonymously shared stories of their first sexual experiences.[13] "*My First Time*" opened July 17, 2007, and is currently the longest running off-Broadway play in years.[14]

The "*Impending Theatrical Blogging Event*" held June 3, 2007, incorporated blogging in a unique way. Fourteen bloggers sat among audience members in Brooklyn's Brick Theater and blogged about the experience, with these observations then being projected onto a large screen. This event was used to launch and promote the Pretentious Festival.[15]

SOCIAL MEDIA IN POPULAR FICTION

Several books targeted to teen girls either feature a blog as a major plot line or are written as a blog. *Something to Blog About* by Shana Norris, *Kiss and Blog* by Alyson Noel, *The Secret Blog of Raisin Rodriguez* by Judy Goldschmidt, and *Confessions of Boyfriend Stealer (a Blog)* by Robynn Clairday all figure prominently in this category.

Others have written books based on their blogs. The self-proclaimed first novel in blog format is *Diary of a Dysfunctional Flight Attendant: The Queen of Sky Blog* by Ellen Simonetti. Although fiction, Simonetti's book draws heavily on her adventures as a Delta flight attendant, chronicled in her own Queen of Sky blog. The blog eventually led to her firing, as she had posted "inappropriate" photos there of herself in her Delta uniform.

Salam Pax is a pseudonym for an Iraqi blogger whose blog, Where is Raed?, was started as a way to keep in touch with a friend, Jordan resident Raed Jarrar. After the invasion of Iraq in 2003, his blog generated widespread interest. Sometimes referred to as the "Baghdad Blogger," he became the most linked to diarist on the Web with over 20,000 regular readers.[16] Pax continued to write his blog entries until the regime blocked access to Blogger.com, where he had been maintaining his blog. Later, the Iraqis shut down all Internet access. Pax continued to write, but was relegated to using his computer if the generator was running or writing in a notebook. Eventually, he collected his writings and e-mailed them to blogger Diana Moon who posted them for him on his site.[17] In 2003, he published a book based on his posts called *The Baghdad Blog* that includes the posts for almost a year supplemented with footnotes.

Other forms of social media have also been featured in works of popular fiction. The social news site Slashdot has appeared in two books: Neil Gaiman's *Endless Nights* and Ken MacLeod's *Cosmonaut Keep*. Garry Trudeau, creator of the comic strip *Doonesbury*, has satirized Twitter. A March 2009 strip shows character Alex commenting on *Meet the Press* host David Gregory's tweet about eating a ham sandwich and shows character Roland Hedley sending a tweet. Trudeau even maintains a Twitter account for Roland.

SOCIAL MEDIA IN PRESIDENTIAL DEBATES

CNN and YouTube partnered to host the first-ever YouTube debate during the 2008 presidential campaign. In July 2007, the eight Democrats in the race at the time answered 40 questions chosen from approximately 3,000 submitted via YouTube.

Although the debate was helpful in involving young people, the format did not change the nature of the debate and perhaps even hampered debate as the taped questions did not provide an opportunity for the questioners to ask follow-up questions, according to Larry Sabato, director of the Center for Politics at the University of Virginia in a BBC report. He added the public may not be capable of asking questions that could highlight the nuances of the candidates' positions.[18] The format was repeated in November 2007 for the Republican candidates, albeit with less success after it was found that about 30% of the questions came from planted questioners with a Democratic bent.[19]

INTEGRATING THE ONLINE AND OFFLINE EXPERIENCE

In some cases, social media are used as the basis for a television show, providing a crucial interactive element. The DIY Network program *Blog Cabin* allows viewers to respond to blog posts and provide input to guide the building of a log cabin. During the first season in 2007, the audience cast more than 4 million votes for 13 elements of the Great Smoky Mountains cabin from the floor plan to the bathroom tile. The popular program returned for a second season in 2008 and a third season in 2009.

HGTV's *Rate My Space* integrates a social networking community into a television program. The Rate My Space community available at HGTV.com/rate-my-space allows users to post photos of rooms. Other users can then provide comments and ratings. On the television show, homeowners of low-rated spaces use the online community to find three rooms they admire. Designer Angelo Surmelis then uses elements from those rooms to redesign the space.

Fox's *Bones* used MySpace as a promotional stunt for an episode that aired in May 2007. Starting in April 2007 on MySpace, fans of the show could read the blog entries, watch videos, or become friends with the eight murder suspects. During the episode, the investigators scanned MySpace for clues, with Dr. Temperance Brennan declaring after looking at the murder victim's profile and her Top 8 friends, "I'm so used to victims being strangers."

Advertisers have started to bridge the gap between a television show and viewers, and are using social media to do so. Characters on the NBC hit program *Heroes* maintain blogs on the show's Web site. As part of Nissan's sponsorship of the program, a *Heroes* character demands a Nissan Versa at a rental car company and then later writes on his blog "Gotta love that Nissan Versa."[20] Back in 2004, NBC also used an interactive element for *Law & Order: Criminal Intent* when they asked viewers to cast votes online for the fate of character Nicole Wallace, a murderess played by Olivia d'Abo. The network saw a 460% increase in traffic to the Web site as more than 116,000 votes were cast.[21] Viewers voted to allow the character to live, and the character returned in the show's fifth season.[22]

When *Big Brother 1* launched, CBS created a relationship between the television program and its Web site. The online property offered a live, 24/7 video feed, which for many viewers, was their first experience with viewing video online.[23] On the show, the Web site was promoted as were reports of online activity from AOL. As June Deery describes, "This meant that Web material was part of the TV experience, even for those who never went online, and that audience reaction was, in this way, being sold back to viewers as broadcast material."[24] This integrated approach created a show that was consumed through two media.

To build buzz before and during the 2009 CBS drama *Harper's Island*, social entertainment company EQAL produced a social networking experience for the 13-part mystery series.[25] At harpersglobe.com, users were able to view special online episodes, content, and experiences. This multi-platform experience gave users an opportunity to experience the show both through the Web and on television.

An episode of CBS's *How I Met Your Mother* on November 20, 2006, centered on character Robin Scherbatsky's secret from her past—she was teen pop star "Robin Sparkles." After friend Barney finds a videotape of Robin's music video "Let's Go to the Mall," he says, "It'll be up and running on MySpace . . . right now." The show ended with a tag encouraging viewers to watch the full video on MySpace and CBS.com. Traffic on the sites showed that more than 300,000 people had viewed the video within the first 10 days. This social media promotion helped the show generate an estimated 600,000 additional viewers for the following week's episode.[26] CBS also integrated television with the Web for its crime drama *CSI*. To promote the two-part finale of *CSI* in 2006, CBS.com created an interactive site that allowed fans to examine the crime scene for clues.[27]

When actor Kal Penn, who played Dr. Lawrence Kutner on the popular television series *House*, was tapped by the Obama administration to serve as the associate director of the White House Office of Public Liaison, writers needed to find an explanation for his quick exit from the show. They chose suicide, and Fox created an online altar where fans could "grieve" his death. The plan backfired "with many fans insisting that the altar and flippant social media attempt was insensitive regarding the topic of suicide."[28] The memorial site has since been shut down.

SOCIAL MEDIA FOR ADVERTISING

The story behind the winner of the Doritos 2008 "Crash the Super Bowl" commercial contest further demonstrates the power of social media. Unlike the concept of the previous year to have entrants create a commercial for Doritos, the

2008 contest sought a musician to appear in its Super Bowl commercial. Winner Kina Grannis was already a social media phenomenon, having written and performed a song called "Gotta Digg" about the popular social news site Digg that received over 200,000 views on YouTube in just two days. As her song gained recognition in the Digg community, Grannis became known as the "Digg Girl." The Digg community members, excited about their "girl" having become a finalist in the Doritos contest, rallied around her and voted for her.[29] After winning, Grannis expressed her appreciation to her fans on her blog: "I just wanted to stop in briefly before the big moment to re-emphasize how completely grateful I am to have been supported by such an amazing community of people. Thank you all so much for all of your encouragement and support, and please know that regardless of the outcome, things will be going up, and having made it this far is winning enough for me."[30]

EA Sports created a commercial for the game Tiger Woods PGA Tour that begins with YouTube user Levinator 25 watching what he calls a new feature of the game—the ability of Tiger Woods to walk on water. The commercial responds with "Levinator 25, you seem to think your Jesus shot video was just a glitch in the game." Then, the commercial plays footage of a golf ball landing on a lily pad, Woods walking on extremely shallow water toward the ball, and then sinking the ball in the hole. The commercial ends with the tag: "It's not a glitch. He's just that good."

ONLINE CELEBRITIES IN AD CAMPAIGNS

People who have online followers have branded themselves in such a way that they are likely to be followed as they plug products for advertisers or sell their own products. Christine Dolce, a former cosmetologist with over 1 million MySpace friends, promotes herself through a sexually suggestive profile using the name "Forbidden." She now has a jeans company and online promotional deals with Axe body spray and Zippo lighters.[31]

A fall 2008 advertising campaign by Airwalk attempted to blur the boundaries between social media and print advertising by featuring several celebrities with strong MySpace followings, including rock band Lorene Drive that was discovered on MySpace and pro skateboarder Rodney Mullin, who is sponsored by Airwalk.[32] The print ads are designed to drive traffic to Airwalk.com, where consumers can continue to read more about "A Day in Our Life," the theme of the ad campaign, and add their own stories to the online conversation.

IMPLICATIONS OF SOCIAL MEDIA PORTRAYALS

The culture industry has begun to recognize the important role of social media in the lives of consumers. Plot elements involving social media are therefore being incorporated into television programs, movies, books, plays, and advertisements. Social media are also being used to prompt political debates, promote advertising contest entries, and allow viewers to direct the outcome of television programs. At this point, it is still too early to tell if the inclusion of social media is a promotional gimmick or a true reflection of what is going on in real life.

References to social media in pop culture products leads to the question of how social media are being portrayed. Television plots have depicted blogs as a way to anonymously gossip about others and social networks as a place where an unsuspecting person can be stalked. These derogatory portrayals may help to warn people of the dangers of social media, but also downplay the positive aspects.

CONCLUSION

This book tells the beginning of the synergistic story between social media and popular culture, a story that continues to unfold with unrelenting speed. Just as social media foster our fascination with popular culture, popular culture fuels much activity in social media. Scholar David Beer challenges us to consider the impact of Web 2.0 on culture as well as how culture impacts Web 2.0:

> As Web 2.0 applications move into the mainstream and restructure aspects of cultural production and consumption, it seems reasonable to conclude that cultural sociology, whatever type of culture it is concerned with, will need to begin to think in some detail both about the implications of Web 2.0 for each cultural sphere, and also about the possible ways in which each of these spheres might in turn come to affect that nature of the connections that make up Web 2.0 itself.[1]

This is the story of how bloggers, musicians, and video-creators emerged from the ranks of obscurity to become meaningful contributors to popular culture, whether a celebrity blogger like Perez Hilton, a news blogger like Josh Marshall of Talking Points Memo, a musician like Colbie Caillat, or a YouTube video star like Lucas Cruikshank. Some might argue, as Tom Shales of the *Washington Post* has done, that this phenomenon is detrimental to society:

> Outward signs are telltale indications of the new "real" reality are everywhere—indications that we are deeply into a major, fundamental role reversal, a reordering of the centuries-old relationship between who's onstage and who's watching, a devaluing of professionalism and a new premium on amateurism. There's been a kind of perverse democratization of mass media, fostered by the Internet and its blogs. At its worst, it trashes the idea of knowledgeable authority as being exclusionary or elitist—and holds up know-nothing opinionators as morally equal, or superior, sources of edification.[2]

Newcomers, however, are attracting increasingly smaller audiences online, making it difficult to become the next Perez, Colbie, or "Fred." Momus's prescient statement from a 1991 essay that "In the future everyone will be famous for fifteen people" rings true in this age of social media.[3]

This is also the story of how media organizations are taking control to avoid becoming irrelevant in modern times. As Richard Siklos of the *New York Times* describes, "Most ventures sound like logical extensions of existing media brands because, hey, media companies are all about attracting and keeping audiences and then figuring out ways to bring them closer to marketers."[4] Many social media companies have sold out, most notably MySpace to News Corp, and some mainstream media organizations marked their territory online by starting blogs or online communities. Social media opened up possibilities for those outside traditional media organizations or entertainment companies to establish an online presence, but the tide may be turning back to corporate control.

This is also the story of where popular culture exists today. Futurist Watts Wacker believes that our fast-moving society means that ideas, styles, and products move more quickly from the fringe to the mainstream, with the result being fewer cultural references that we share.[5] We have also seen many examples where popular culture is moved online and then online culture is moved back to popular culture. This phenomenon can be observed within the LOST-TV fan forums, where fans embraced this television program and then hoped to transform the product. Offline popular culture also changes when Web communities form more distinct cultures, as Garry Marshall describes:

> As Internet culture develops and moves farther from real-world culture, it becomes harder, not necessarily to gain access, but to join in effectively once access is gained. Besides this, there is the very real possibility of those with access to the network becoming cut off from their real-world history. They may have no interest in it: those who do may not share the technical and cultural interests of those with access. The consequence can be a separation of those who spend most of their time on the network from their own history, which can only serve to widen further the gulf between those with access and those without.[6]

This is the story of how social media moved the world, and then adapted to the new landscape.

NOTES

INTRODUCTION

1. Flamberg, Danny. "Making Sense of Social Media." *Social Media Insider*, November 20, 2008.

2. Morrissey, Brian. "Forrester: Social Web Now Mainstream." *AdWeek*, October 24, 2008.

3. AARP. "New Study Released by the Center for the Digital Future and AARP Shows Internet Users 50+ Are Rapidly Closing the Digital Divide with Booming Online Activity." June 19, 2008. http://www.aarp.org/research/press-center/presscurrentnews/new_study_released_by_the_center_for_the_digital_f.html.

4. RapLeaf. "Rapleaf Study of Social Network Users vs. Age." June 18, 2008. http://business.rapleaf.com/company_press_2008_06_18.html.

5. Lenhart, Amanda, and Mary Madden. "Teen Content Creators and Consumers." Pew Internet & American Life Project, December 12, 2005. http://www.pewinternet.org/pdfs/PIP_Teens_Content_Creation.pdf.

6. Center for Media Research. "Downloading TV and Watching Video Online Biggest Gainers in 2008." *Research Brief,* January 8, 2009.

7. Kelly, Kevin. "We Are the Web." *Wired*, August 2005. http://www.wired.com/wired/archive/13.08/tech.html?pg=3&topic=tech&topic_set=.

8. Beer, David, and Roger Burrows. "Sociology and, of and in Web 2.0: Some Initial Considerations." *Sociological Research Online* 12, no. 5 (2007).

9. Adorno, Theodor W. "Culture Industry Reconsidered." *The Culture Industry: Selected Essays on Mass Culture*, edited by J. M. Bernstein, 98–106. London: Routledge, 2001.

10. Ibid., p. 99.

11. Bernstein, J. M. *The Culture Industry: Selected Essays on Mass Culture*. London: Routledge, 2001.

12. Hinckley, David. "It Was You, Tony. It Was You." *New York Daily News*, June 10, 2007.

13. Donadio, Rachel. "You're an Author? Me Too!" *New York Times*, April 27, 2008.

14. Ibid.

15. Beer and Burrows. "Sociology and, of and in Web 2.0"

16. O'Reilly, Tim. "Not 2.0?" http://radar.oreilly.com/archives/2005/08/not-20.html.

17. O'Reilly, Tim. "What Is Web 2.0?" http://tim.oreilly.com/pub/a/oreilly/tim/news/2005/09/30/what-is-web-20.html?page=3.

18. Crumpler, Rob. "Social Networks: Show Me the Media." *MediaPost*, July 30, 2008. www.mediapost.com/publications/?fa=Articles.san&s=87505&Nid=45541&p=468709.

19. Kelly. "We Are the Web."

20. Ibid.

21. Reiss, Spencer. "Power to the People." *Wired*, December 1996. http://www.wired.com/wired/archive/4.12/esgage.html.

22. Technorati. "State of the Blogosphere." April 2007. http://technorati.com/weblog/2007/04/328.html.

23. Green, Heather. "With 15.5 Million Active Blogs, New Technorati Data Shows That Blogging Growth Seems to Be Peaking." *Business Week Online*, April 25, 2007. http://www.businessweek.com/the_thread/blogspotting/archives/2007/04/blogging_growth.html.

24. Donadio. "You're an Author? Me Too!"

25. Jensen, Mallory. "A Brief History of Weblogs." *Columbia Journalism Review* no. 5 (2003).

26. Ibid.

27. Levin, Todd. "Dear Diary." *Salon*, December 10, 1999. http://www.salon.com/tech/feature/1999/12/10/diaryland.

28. Jensen. "A Brief History of Weblogs."

29. Pilgrim, Mark. "What Is RSS?" http://www.xml.com/pub/a/2002/12/18/dive-into-xml.html.

30. O'Reilly. "What Is Web 2.0?"

31. Ibid.

32. Nielsen//NetRatings. "YouTube U.S. Web Traffic Grows 75 Percent Week over Week, According to Nielsen//NetRatings." July 21, 2006. http://www.nielsennetratings.com/pr/pr_060721_2.pdf.

33. Beer and Burrows. "Sociology and, of and in Web 2.0"

34. Google. "Google to Acquire YouTube for $1.65 Billion in Stock." October 9, 2006. http://www.google.com/press/pressrel/google_youtube.html.

35. comScore. "YouTube Surpasses 100 Million U.S. Viewers for the First Time." March 4, 2009. http://www.comscore.com/press/release.asp?press=2741.

36. Graham, Jefferson. "Video Websites Pop up, Invite Postings." *USA Today*, November 21, 2005.

37. Ibid.

38. La Monica, Paul R. "YouTube for Soccer Moms." *CNNMoney.com*, May 1, 2007. http://money.cnn.com/2007/04/30/technology/flipvideo/index.htm.

39. Ibid.

40. boyd, danah, and Nicole B. Ellison. "Social Network Sites: Definition, History, and Scholarship." *Journal of Computer-Mediated Communication* 13, no. 1 (2007): article 11.

41. Ibid.

42. Ibid.

43. Ibid.

44. Ibid.

45. Ibid.

46. O'Shea, William. "Six Degrees of Sexual Frustration: Connecting the Dates with Friendster.com." *Village Voice*, July 4, 2003. http://www.villagevoice.com/news/0323,oshea,44576,1.html.

47. boyd, danah. "Frienster Lost Steam. Is Myspace Just a Fad?" http://www.danah.org/papers/FriendsterMySpaceEssay.html.

48. Kurtzman, Cliff. "Marketing to the MySpace Generation (and the Economics of Social Networking)." www.marketingprofs.com/6/kurtzman1.asp?sp1#split.

49. Petrecca, Laura. "Marketers Get Their Mascots in on Action at MySpace." *USA Today*, August 30, 2006.

50. O'Malley, Gavin. "MySpace Blossoms into Major Web Portal." *Advertising Age*, July 17, 2006.

51. Li, Charlene. "How Consumers Use Social Networks." Forrester Research, 2007. http://www.forrester.com/Research/Document/Excerpt/0,7211,41626,00.html.

52. Nielsen. "Global Faces and Networked Places." March 2009. http://mashable.com/2009/03/09/social-networking-more-popular-than-email/?disqus_reply=7035992#comment-7035992.

53. Bowley, Graham. "The High Priestess of Internet Friendship." *Financial Times Weekend Magazine*, October 28, 2006.

54. Morrissey, Brian. "Beyond Clicks: Measuring Effects of Social Net Ads." *AdWeek*, 2007, 8.

55. "Facebook Surpasses 150 Million Users." *MediaPost*, January 8, 2009.

56. Nielsen. "Global Faces and Networked Places."

57. "Facebook Surpasses 150 Million Users."

58. Ibid.

59. Christensen, Ward. 1992. http://www.bbsdocumentary.com/software/AAA/AAA/CBBS/memories.txt.

60. Ibid.

61. Ibid.

62. MacManus, Richard. "Interview with Digg Founder Kevin Rose, Part 1." ZDNet, February 1, 2006. http://blogs.zdnet.com/web2explorer/index.php?p=108.

63. Ibid.

64. Ibid.

65. Adams, Richard. "Reddit.com." *Guardian*, December 8, 2005. http://www.guardian.co.uk/technology/2005/dec/08/innovations.guardianweeklytechnologysection1.

66. Ibid.

67. Arrington, Michael. "Breaking News: Condé Nast/Wired Acquired Reddit." TechCrunch, October 31, 2006. http://www.techcrunch.com/2006/10/31/breaking-news-conde-nastwired-acquires-reddit/.

CHAPTER 1

1. Walls, Jeannette. *Dish: The Inside Story on the World of Gossip*. New York: Avon Books, Inc., 2000.

2. Puente, Maria. "Britney's Collapse: Media Not Helping." *USA Today*, February 20, 2008, 4D.

3. Hopkins, Jessica. "A Brief History of Gossip: Five Hundred Years of Scandal." *Observer*, July 9, 2006. http://www.guardian.co.uk/media/2006/jul/09/pressandpublishing.woman.

4. Gardner, Ralph D. "The Age of Winchell." *Eve's Magazine*, 2001. http://www.evesmag.com/winchell.htm.

5. Walls. *Dish*.

6. Bessie, Simon Michael. *Jazz Journalism: The Story of the Tabloid Newspapers*. New York: E.P. Dutton, 1938.

7. Chandler, Curt. "The Glamour Shot: Photography a Flash Point for Image-Making." *Post-Gazette*, October 12, 1999. http://www.post-gazette.com/tv/19991012people4.asp.

8. Walls. *Dish*.

9. Anderson, Kurt. "Only Gossip." *New York Times*, March 3, 2002.

10. Bessie. *Jazz Journalism: The Story of the Tabloid Newspapers*.

11. Walls. *Dish*.

12. Ibid.

13. Ibid.

14. Ibid.

15. Ibid.

16. Ibid.

17. Hopkins. "A Brief History of Gossip."

18. Walls. *Dish*.

19. Ibid.

20. Ibid.

21. Gardner. "The Age of Winchell."

22. Walls. *Dish* p. 30.

23. Ibid.

24. HP-Time.com. "People's Premiere." *Time*, March 4, 1974. http://www.time.com/time/magazine/article/0,9171,944778,00.html.

25. Ibid.

26. Anderson. "Only Gossip."

27. Ibid.

28. McKinley, Jesse. "Spreading the Gossip at Snail Mail Speed." *New York Times*, August 7, 2005, 4.4.

29. Robertson, Campbell. "Hard, Shadowy Game of Gossip Rewards Ruthless." *International Herald Tribune*, April 9, 2006.

30. Bird, S. Elizabeth. *For Enquiring Minds: A Cultural Study of Supermarket Tabloids*. Knoxville: The University of Tennessee Press, 1992.

31. Gross, Michael Joseph. "Television/Radio: Famous for Tracking the Famous." *New York Times*, June 23, 2002, 2.1.

32. Ibid.

33. Anderson. "Only Gossip."

34. Ibid.

35. Gilsdorf, Ethan. "Celebrity Gossip's Siren Call Grows Louder." *Christian Science Monitor*, January 12, 2007.

36. Goodman, Lee-Anne. "Is Celeb Gossip Craze on the Wane? While Tongues Wag as Magazine Circulations Flag, Some Say Not So Fast." *Toronto Star*, April 1, 2008, L6.

37. Ibid.

38. Chang, Irene. "Celebrity Sites Offer Outlet for Brands with Irreverent Appeal." *PRWeek*, October 29, 2007.

39. Puente. "Britney's Collapse."

40. Heffernan, Virginia. "The Beautiful People, the Uglier the Better." *New York Times*, July 15, 2007, AR1.

41. Aspan, Maria. "A One-Two Punch at the Old Guard of Gossip." *New York Times*, February 12, 2007, C4.

42. Grigoriadis, Vanessa. "Everybody Sucks." *New York Magazine*, October 15, 2007.

43. Aspan. "A One-Two Punch at the Old Guard of Gossip."

44. Stelter, Brian. "In Race for Gossip, TV Shows Turn to Blogs." *New York Times*, January 5, 2008, C1.

45. Albiniak, Page. "New, Improved 'Access'." *Broadcasting and Cable*, September 10, 2007.

46. Ibid.

47. Stelter. "In Race for Gossip, TV Shows Turn to Blogs."

48. Albiniak. "New, Improved 'Access'."

49. Stelter. "In Race for Gossip, TV Shows Turn to Blogs."

50. Ibid.

51. Albiniak. "New, Improved 'Access'."

52. Gilsdorf. "Celebrity Gossip's Siren Call Grows Louder."

53. Garrison, Lawrence Mitchell. "From Blogs to Barnum & Bailey-Like Antics, 2005 Was a Bummer." *PRWeek*, January 9, 2006.

54. Fitzgerald, Toni. "As Paris Wept: The Story That Got Away." *Media Life Magazine*, June 21, 2007.

55. Tanaka, Wendy. "Celebrity 'Site-ings'." *Forbes*, September 17, 2008.

56. Nielsen//NetRatings. "Popular Celebrity News Sites Grow 40 Percent Year over Year, According to Nielsen//Netratings." March 29, 2007. http://www.nielsennetratings.com/pr/pr_070329.pdf.

57. Ibid.

58. Alexa, http://www.alexa.com.

59. Hitwise. "Perez Hilton Most Popular Blog." June 23, 2008. http://weblogs.hitwise.com/to-go-us/2008/06/perez_hilton_most_popular_blog.html.

60. Shafir, Doree. "The Truth About Perez Hilton's Traffic." *Gawker*, July 10, 2007. http://gawker.com/news/welcome-to-the-internet/the-truth-about-perez-hiltons-traffic-276369.php.

61. Technorati. "Top 100 Blogs." September 22, 2008. http://technorati.com/pop/blogs?type=faves&page=1.

62. Coen, Jessica. "If Paris Breaks a Nail, You'll Be There." *New York Times*, July 2, 2006.

63. Stelter. "In Race for Gossip, TV Shows Turn to Blogs."

64. comScore Media Metrix. "comScore Media Metrix Ranks Top 50 U.S. Web Properties for July 2008." http://www.comscore.com/press/release.asp?press=2399.

65. Jones, Vanessa E. "Believe the Hype: Frustrated with Mainstream Celebrity Sites, Fans of Black Stars Spread Their Own Gossip." *Boston Globe*, June 12, 2007, E1.

66. Ibid.

67. Chang. "Celebrity Sites Offer Outlet for Brands with Irreverent Appeal."

68. Semuels, Alana. "How Will Professional Bloggers Survive the Recession?" *Los Angeles Times*, October 6, 2008.

69. Mortensen, Torill. "Of a Divided Mind: Weblog Literacy." In *A Handbook of New Literacies Research*, edited by Julie Coiro, Michele Knobel, Colin Lankshear, and Donald J. Leu. Mahwah, NJ: Erlbaum, 2008.

70. Denton, Nick. "The Long and Illustrious History of Bile." October 14, 2007. http://nickdenton.org/5083258/the-long-and-illustrious-history-of-bile.

71. CNN.com. "Celeb Blogger: Publicist, Schmublicist." May 12, 2006.

72. Bosman, Julie. "In Web Era, Big Money Can't Buy an Exclusive." *New York Times*, June 12, 2006.

73. Ibid.

74. Ibid.

75. Bird. *For Enquiring Minds*.

76. Levin, Jack, Amita Mody-Desbarau, and Arnold Arluke. "The Gossip Tabloid as an Agent of Social Control." *Journalism Quarterly* 65, no. 2 (1988): 514–17.

77. Jones. "Believe the Hype: Frustrated with Mainstream Celebrity Sites, Fans of Black Stars Spread Their Own Gossip."

78. Schroeder, Fred E. H. "National Enquirer Is National Fetish! The Untold Story!" In *Objects of Special Devotion: Fetishes and Fetishism in Popular Culture*, edited by Ray B. Browne, 168–81. Bowling Green, Ohio: Bowling Green University Popular Press, 1982.

79. Turner, LaShelle. "Celebrity Blogging: The New Favorite American Pastime." The Student Operated Press, August 18, 2007. http://www.thesop.org/index.php?article=7072.

80. Gilsdorf. "Celebrity Gossip's Siren Call Grows Louder."

81. Goodman, Lee-Anne. "Gay Actors Still Feel Pressure to Stay in Closet: TV Stars More Likely Than Movie A-Listers to Reveal Homosexuality, but Blogs Changing That." *The Toronto Star*, April 23, 2008, E2.

82. Von Hahn, Karen. "The New Must-See Show: Lindsay at Starbucks." *Globe and Mail*, September 22, 2007, L3.

83. Levin, Mody-Desbarau, and Arluke. "The Gossip Tabloid as an Agent of Social Control."

84. Coen. "If Paris Breaks a Nail, You'll Be There."

85. Gross. "Television/Radio: Famous for Tracking the Famous."

86. Heffernan. "The Beautiful People, the Uglier the Better."

87. Schroeder. "National Enquirer Is National Fetish! The Untold Story!" p. 174.

88. Gould, Emily. "Coordinates of the Rich and Famous." *New York Times*, May 4, 2007, A23.

89. Beato, Greg. "From Film Factory to Gossip Factory: How the Internet Has Changed Hollywood." *National Post*, August 19, 2006, WP3.

90. CNN.com. "Celeb Blogger: Publicist, Schmublicist."

91. Goodman, Lee-Anne. "Britney's Baldness Is Boon for Celeb-Blogs." *Toronto Star*, February 23, 2007, D11.

92. McKinley. "Spreading the Gossip at Snail Mail Speed."

93. Gould. "Coordinates of the Rich and Famous."

94. Ibid.

95. Ibid.

96. Agrell, Siri. "Camera-Toting Partygoers Leave Paparazzi in the Dust." *Globe and Mail*, September 10, 2007, A1.

97. Gilsdorf. "Celebrity Gossip's Siren Call Grows Louder."

98. Ibid.

99. Turner. "Celebrity Blogging: The New Favorite American Pastime."

CHAPTER 2

1. Anderson, Kurt. "Only Gossip." *New York Times*, March 3, 2002.

2. Walls, Jeannette. *Dish: The Inside Story on the World of Gossip*. New York: Avon Books, Inc., 2000.

3. Anderson. "Only Gossip."

4. Walls. *Dish*.

5. Ibid.

6. Ibid.

7. Ibid.

8. Ibid.

9. Ibid.

10. Anderson. "Only Gossip."

11. Thompson, Clive. "Blogs to Riches: The Haves and Have-Nots of the Blogging Boom." *New York Magazine*, February 12, 2006.

12. Turner, LaShelle. "Celebrity Blogging: The New Favorite American Pastime." The Student Operated Press, August 18, 2007. http://www.thesop.org/index.php?article=7072.

13. Tenenbaum, Sara. "Through the Grapevine." PopMatters, June 9, 2009, http://www.popmatters.com/pm/feature/through-the-grapevine.

14. Dumenco, Simon. "From Media Darlings to Public Enemy No. 1 in Five Years or Less." *Advertising Age*, June 2, 2008.

15. Ibid.

16. Thompson. "Blogs to Riches."

17. Ibid.

18. Ibid.

19. Ibid.

20. Shirky, Clay. "Power Laws, Weblogs, and Inequality." *Networks, Economics, and Culture* Mailing List, February 8, 2003. http://shirky.com/writings/powerlaw_weblog.html.

21. Thompson. "Blogs to Riches."

22. Ibid.

23. Ibid.

24. Ibid.

25. "Interview: David Hauslaib." *PRWeek*, January 29, 2007.

26. Carlson, Erin. "Celeb-Gossip Blogger: It's Not a Job, It's a Lifeline." *Seattle Times (AP)*, November 8, 2006.

27. Ibid.

28. Hedegaard, Erik. "Perez Hilton: The Queen of Mean " *Rolling Stone*, November 1, 2007.

29. Ibid.

30. Ibid.

31. Ibid.

32. ABC Radio Networks. "ABC Radio Networks Announces Deal with 'C' Student Entertainment for Syndication of Perez Hilton." *PR Newswire*, April 21, 2008.

33. Tiffany, Laura. "The Gossip Artist." Entrepreneur.com, December 2007, http://www.entrepreneur.com/magazine/entrepreneur/2007/december/186508.html.

34. Dunn, Emily. "Hollywood's Gossip Queen Comes to Town." *Sydney Morning Herald*, April 11, 2007.

35. ABC Radio Networks. "ABC Radio Networks Announces Deal with 'C' Student Entertainment for Syndication of Perez Hilton."

36. Brand Republic. "Celebrity Blogger Perez Hilton Signs to Write for ITV Website." April 9, 2008.

37. Tiffany. "The Gossip Artist."

38. Ibid.

39. Hinds, Julie. "Celebrity Watcher Shows True Colors with His Pink Blog." *Detroit Free Press*, December 21, 2005.

40. Thompson. "Blogs to Riches."

41. Ibid.

42. Ibid.

43. "Interview: David Hauslaib."

44. Thompson. "Blogs to Riches."

45. Ibid.

46. Coen, Jessica. "David Hauslaib Abandons His Jossip Hobby." Gawker, December 12, 2005. http://gawker.com/news/jossip/david-hauslaib-abandons-his-jossip-hobby-142503.php.

47. Ibid.

48. Calderone, Michael. "Jossip Blogger to Join Page Six." *New York Observer*, September 21, 2006.

49. "Interview: David Hauslaib."

50. Arrington, Michael. "Sequoia Invests in Blog Network Sugar Publishing." *TechCrunch*, October 16, 2006. http://www.techcrunch.com/2006/10/16/sequoia-invests-in-blog-network-team-sugar.

51. Mugrabi, Sunshine. "Whose Gossip Is It Anyway?" *RedHerring.com*, January 18, 2007.

52. Arrington. "Sequoia Invests in Blog Network Sugar Publishing."

53. Grigoriadis. "Everybody Sucks."

54. Ibid.

55. Thompson. "Blogs to Riches."

56. Dewan, Shaila K. "Public Lives: Master of the Self-Referential Realm of Blogs." *New York Times*, December 23, 2003.

57. Ibid.

58. Grigoriadis, Vanessa. "Everybody Sucks." *New York Magazine*, October 15, 2007.

59. Dewan. "Public Lives: Master of the Self-Referential Realm of Blogs."

60. Spiers, Elizabeth. "About Elizabeth Spiers." 2006. http://www.elizabethspiers .com/about.html.

61. Ibid.

62. Dewan. "Public Lives: Master of the Self-Referential Realm of Blogs."

63. Ibid.

64. Spiers. "About Elizabeth Spiers."

65. Dumenco. "From Media Darlings to Public Enemy No. 1 in Five Years or Less."

66. Spiers. "About Elizabeth Spiers."

67. Sklar, Rachel. "Choire Sicha Returns to the Gawker Fold, Leaving the Observer: Mini-Shakeup at Gawker Media as Mohney Moves." *Huffington Post*, January 18, 2007. http://www.huffingtonpost.com/eat-the-press/2007/01/18/choire-sicha-returns-to-t_e_38960.html.

68. Pareene, Alex. "Choire Sicha to Radar." Gawker, August 22, 2008. http://gawker .com/5040739/choire-sicha-to-radar.

69. Balk, Alex. "Coen and Oxfeld, Together Again." Gawker, July 23, 2007. http:// gawker.com/news/alumni-notes/coen-and-oxfeld-together-again-281374.php.

70. Dumenco. "From Media Darlings to Public Enemy No. 1 in Five Years or Less."

71. "Best + Brightest: The Defamer." *Esquire*, December 1, 2005. http://www.esquire .com/features/ESQ1204DEFAMER_1.

72. Kois, Dan and Lane Brown. "Mark Lisanti Leaves Defamer: Our World Gets a Little Darker." *New York Magazine*, February 15, 2008.

73. Abramowitz, Rachel. "Feeding the Beast." *Los Angeles Times*, July 31, 2005. http://articles.latimes.com/2005/jul/31/entertainment/ca-gossip31.

74. Pierce, Tony. "Blogebrity's Top 10 Blogebrities of 2006." *LAist*, December 21, 2006. http://www.laist.com/2006/12/21/kyle_bunch_of_blogebritys_top_10_blogebrities_ of_2006.php.

75. Solway, Diane. "Poster Girl." *W*, May 2008.

76. Thompson. "Blogs to Riches."

77. Solway. "Poster Girl."

78. Ibid.

79. Wolf, Josh. "Huffington Post Doesn't Plan to Pay Its Bloggers." *CNET News*, September 26, 2007. http://news.cnet.com/8301-10784_3-9785908-7.html.

80. Arango, Tim. "Huffington and Brown: Paths Intertwine in the Blog Thicket." *New York Times*, October 27, 2008.

81. Wolf, Josh. "Huffington Post Doesn't Plan to Pay Its Bloggers."

82. Dumenco, Simon. "Pay the Talent? Sorry, Suckas, That's Not the Huffpo Financial Model: New CEO Betsy Morgan's Endgame Should Include Compensating Bloggers Who Give Website Credibility." *Advertising Age*, October 8, 2007.

83. Elber, Lynn. "TMZ.com Makes Jump from Online to On-Air." *SFGate.com (AP)*, September 7, 2007.

84. comScore Media Metrix. "More Americans Reading Entertainment News Online with Much of It Occurring During Work Hours." July 1, 2009, http://ir.comscore.com/ releasedetail.cfm?ReleaseID=393477.

85. Mugrabi. "Whose Gossip Is It Anyway?"

86. Tabloid Baby. "Tabloid Baby's 2007 Journalist of the Year." December 30, 2007, http://tabloidbaby.blogspot.com/2007/12/tabloid-babys-2007-journalist-of-year.html.

87. Hopkins, Jim. "TMZ.com Lets Readers Talk to the Blog." *USA Today*, September 19, 2007.

88. Stelter, Brian. "Celebrities Off Guard? 'TMZ' Is a Hit." *New York Times*, October 15, 2007.

89. Maynard, John. "TMZ: No Boundaries in the 30-Mile Zone." *Washington Post*, September 18, 2007.

90. Elber. "TMZ.com Makes Jump from Online to On-Air."

91. Stelter. "Celebrities Off Guard? 'TMZ' Is a Hit."

92. Ibid.

93. Ibid.

CHAPTER 3

1. Dehnart, Andy. "About reality blurred." http://www.realityblurred.com/realitytv/about.

2. Keller, Richard. "A History of Reality Television." TVSquad, July 9, 2008. www.tvsquad.com/2008/07/09/a-history-of-reality-television-part-one-the-beginning.

3. Ibid.

4. Crossen, Cynthia. "Reality Shows Today Evolved from Contest of Competing Misery." *Wall Street Journal*, February 4, 2008.

5. Ibid.

6. Keller. "A History of Reality Television."

7. Ruoff, Jeffrey. *An American Family: A Televised Life*. Minneapolis: University of Minnesota Press, 2001.

8. Keller. "A History of Reality Television."

9. Barovick, Harriet. "Reality TV." *Time*, September 19, 2008.

10. Podrazik, Walter J. "The Reality of Reality TV." Electronic House, November 2, 2007. http://www.electronichouse.com/article/the_reality_of_reality_tv.

11. Keller. "A History of Reality Television."

12. Ibid.

13. Keveney, Bill. "MTV's 'Real World' Launched a Revolution." *USA Today*, October 9, 2007.

14. Ibid.

15. Schechner, Sam. "This Writers' Strike Feels Like a Rerun from 1988." *The Wall Street Journal*, November 12, 2007.

16. Keller. "A History of Reality Television."

17. Ibid.

18. Deggans, Eric. "Best Television of 2007: You've Got to Get Cable." *St. Petersburg Times*, December 21, 2007.

19. Podrazik. "The Reality of Reality TV."

20. Ibid.

21. Hirschorn, Michael. "The Case for Reality TV." *Atlantic Monthly*, May 2007.

22. Ibid.

23. Rushkoff, Douglas. "Who Are the Real Subjects of These Twisted Psych Experiments?" *Discover Magazine*, May 23, 2007.

24. Dehnart, Andy. E-mail communication. March 17, 2009.

25. Ibid.

26. Ibid.

27. Ibid.

28. Federated Media Publishing. "Reality Blurred." http://federatedmedia.net/authors/realityblurred.

29. Reality TV World. "About Reality TV World." http://www.realitytvworld.com/realitytvworld/about.shtml.

30. Ibid.

31. dingoRUE. "About the Site." http://www.dingorue.com/about.

32. Howell, Matt. "About RTV." http://www.realtelevision.net/about/.

33. Grosvenor, Carrie. "About.com Guide to Game Shows." http://gameshows.about.com/mbiopage.htm.

34. Blackmon, Joe. "Reality TV Magazine Readership Soars." March 14, 2005. http://www.prweb.com/releases/2005/03/prweb217818.htm.

35. Weisenthal, Joseph. "SheKnows Acquires RealityTVMagazine.com." January 30, 2008. http://www.atomiconline.com/media/files/news/paidcontent_sheknows_acquires_realitytvmagazine.pdf.

36. Ibid.

37. Fahs, Joe. E-mail communication. May 5, 2008.

38. Ibid.

39. Ibid.

40. Adalian, Josef. "Bravo Nabs Popular TV Web Site." *Variety*, March 13, 2007.

41. Ibid.

42. Ariano, Tara. "Announcement from the Founders." Television Without Pity, March 6, 2008. http://www.televisionwithoutpity.com/telefile/2008/03/announcement-from-the-founders.php.

43. Weisenthal, Joseph. "Comcast Buying Entertainment Community Site BuddyTV." *PaidContent.org*, September 16, 2007.

44. Ibid.

45. Ibid.

46. Alderman, Tom. "Shame TV: Why Humiliation Sells on 'American Idol' and Others." *Huffington Post*, February 13, 2008. http://www.huffingtonpost.com/tom-alderman/shame-tv-why-humiliation_b_86500.html.

CHAPTER 4

1. Yael, Aviva. "Celebrity Blogs: The Good, the Bad, and the Ugly." *Fast Company*, August 2007.

2. Zacharek, Stephanie. "Attack of the Celebrity Blogs." Salon, March 19, 2005. http://dir.salon.com/story/ent/feature/2005/03/19/celebrity_blogs/index.html.

3. Sweetser, Kaye D. "Celebrity Weblogs: Investigation in the Persuasive Nature of Two-Way Communication." PhD diss., University of Florida, 2004.

4. Wheaton, Wil. http://wilwheaton.typepad.com/wwdnbackup/the-hooters-incident.html.

5. Zacharek. "Attack of the Celebrity Blogs."

6. Ibid.

7. Yael. "Celebrity Blogs: The Good, the Bad, and the Ugly."

8. Ibid.

9. Armstrong, Jennifer, Marc Bernardin, Leah Greenblatt, Lindsay Soll, Tim Stack, Tanner Stransky, Ken Tucker, and Margeaux Watson. "The 20 Best and Worst Celebrity Blogs," *Entertainment Weekly*, July 20, 2007. http://www.ew.com/ew/article/0,,20041669_20041686_20045660,00.html.

10. Yael. "Celebrity Blogs: The Good, the Bad, and the Ugly."

11. Ingram, Mathew. "There's Way More to Jeff Bridges Than Meets the Eye." *Globe and Mail*, January 10, 2008.

12. Macartney, Jane. "Chinese Actor Tops Blog Chart." *Australian*, July 24, 2007.

13. Ibid.

14. Armstrong. "The 20 Best and Worst Celebrity Blogs."

15. Porter, Rachel, and Polly Dunbar. "Our Not-So-Secret Diaries." *Express*, January 26, 2007, 22.

16. Yael. "Celebrity Blogs: The Good, the Bad, and the Ugly."

17. Armstrong et al. "The 20 Best and Worst Celebrity Blogs."

18. Steinberg, Jacques. "An Anchor by Evening, a Blogger Any Time" *New York Times*, August 25, 2005.

19. O'Connor, Joe. "NHL Promoting Its Star Factor with Online Blogs." *National Post*, April 12, 2007, S3.

20. Ibid.

21. Guynn, Jessica. "Cut! Actors Take Five to Twitter Their Fans: Celebrities Using the Blogging Site to Mold Their Online Image Might Help the Service Hit the Mainstream. But Can It Make Money?" *Los Angeles Times*, March 3, 2009, B1.

22. Ibid.

23. MacMillan, Douglas. "Social Media: The Ashton Kutcher Effect." *BusinessWeek*, May 3, 2009.

24. Ibid.

25. Guynn, Jessica. "Cut! Actors Take Five to Twitter Their Fans."

26. MacMillan, Douglas. "Social Media: The Ashton Kutcher Effect."

27. Guynn, Jessica. "Cut! Actors Take Five to Twitter Their Fans."

CHAPTER 5

1. Boorstin, Daniel. *The Image: A Guide to Pseudo-Events in America.* New York: Atheneum, 1961.

2. Smiley, Jane. *Charles Dickens: A Penguin Life.* New York: Viking, 2002.

3. Lodge, David. "Dickens Our Contemporary." *Atlantic Monthly*, May 2002.

4. Smiley. *Charles Dickens.*

5. Lodge. "Dickens Our Contemporary."

6. Ibid.

7. "People & Events: Jenny Lind, 1820–1887." PBS. http://www.pbs.org/wgbh/amex/foster/peopleevents/p_lind.html.

8. James, Clive. *Fame in the 20th Century.* New York: Random House, 1993.

9. Trebay, Guy. "She's Famous (and So Can You)." *New York Times*, October 28, 2007.

10. Halpern, Jake. *Fame Junkies: The Hidden Truths Behind America's Favorite Addiction.* Boston: Houghton Mifflin, 2007.

11. Ingram, Mathew. "Aiming for Fame on the Web? One Million Hits Won't Do It." *Globe and Mail,* October 27, 2007.

12. comScore. "YouTube Attracts 100 Million U.S. Online Video Viewers in October 2008." December 9, 2008.

13. della Cava, Marco R. "Searching the Web for the Next Big Thing." *USA Today,* May 30, 2008, A1.

14. "Star Wars Kid Is Top Viral Video." BBC, November 27, 2006. http://news.bbc .co.uk/2/hi/entertainment/6187554.stm.

15. Baio, Andy. "Star Wars Kid: The Data Dump." May 22, 2008, http://waxy.org/ 2008/05/star_wars kid the data_dump/.

16. Ibid.

17. Wallace, Bruce. "YouTube Star Funtwo Rocks Stages." *Los Angeles Times,* March 21, 2008.

18. Ibid.

19. Bruno, Antony. "YouTube Stars Don't Always Welcome Record Deals." *Reuters,* February 25, 2007.

20. Smith, Ethan, and Peter Lattman. "Download This: YouTube Phenom Has a Big Secret." *Wall Street Journal,* September 6, 2007.

21. Goodman, Elizabeth. "YouTube Phenom Mia Rose Has Her Thorns?" *Rolling Stone,* January 25, 2007.

22. Dwyer, Michael. "The Rise of the Faux Internet Indie." *Age,* February 8, 2007.

23. Korr, Josh. "SNL's 'Milkshake' Miss and the Limits of Viral Video Fads." *tbt*,* February 26, 2008.

24. Milian, Mark. "YouTube Video Creators Make Money, but Not a Fortune." *Los Angeles Times,* January 11, 2009.

25. Sullivan, Mark. "Greatest Hits of Viral Video." http://tech.msn.com/products/ articlepcw.aspx?cp-documentid=5841669&GT1=10736.

26. "Star Wars Kid Is Top Viral Video."

27. Raphael, J. R. "A Decade of Internet Superstars: Where Are They Now?" *PC World.*

28. Sullivan, Laurie. "Geico Gecko Dancing in Numa Numa YouTube Video." *MediaPost,* March 26, 2009.

29. Sullivan. "Greatest Hits of Viral Video."

30. Raphael. "A Decade of Internet Superstars."

31. della Cava. "Searching the Web for the Next Big Thing."

32. Stelter, Brian. "YouTube Videos Pull in Real Money." *New York Times,* December 10, 2008.

33. Ibid.

34. Powers, Nicole. "Philip Defranco Is sXephil." *Suicide Girls,* January 2, 2009.

35. Ibid.

36. Wallenstein, Andrew. "HBO Offshoot Launches Web Video Series." *Reuters,* September 8, 2008.

37. Jurgensen, John. "Moguls of New Media." *Wall Street Journal Online,* July 29, 2006.

38. Ibid.

39. Tedeschi, Bob. "New Hot Properties: YouTube Celebrities." *New York Times,* February 26, 2007.

40. Sarno, David. "YouTube Sensation Fred to Guest Star on 'iCarly' Next Monday." *Los Angeles Times,* February 9, 2009.

41. Clark, John. "Web Auteur Takes the Leap from YouTube to Boob Tube." *New York Times,* February 11, 2007.

42. Jurgensen. "Moguls of New Media."

43. Raphael. "A Decade of Internet Superstars."

44. Jurgensen. "Moguls of New Media."

45. Tedeschi. "New Hot Properties."

46. McCarthy, Sean. "Reign of Dane Began with the Web." *Daily News,* September 21, 2007, 47.

47. "Social Networking Web Sites." http://www.2facts.com/TempFiles/ i1100310.htm.

48. Tedeschi. "New Hot Properties: YouTube Celebrities."

49. Hutcheon, Stephen. "Caitlin Raps Her Way to YouTube Success." *The Age,* September 4, 2006.

50. Hardy, Michael. "The Self-Made Star." *Boston Globe,* June 27, 2006.

51. McCarthy. "Reign of Dane Began with the Web."

52. della Cava. "Searching the Web for the Next Big Thing."

53. Ibid.

54. Ibid.

55. Ibid.

56. Ibid.

57. Cassidy, Mike. "Looking Back through the Numbers." *MediaPost,* December 18, 2007.

58. Holahan, Catherine. "Web Video: Move Over, Amateurs." *BusinessWeek,* November 20, 2007.

59. Stelter, Brian. "YouTube Said to Be Near Hollywood Deal." *New York Times,* January 29, 2009.

60. Ibid.

61. Sarno, David. "On YouTube, 'Popular' No Longer Means the Thing Everyone's Watching." *Los Angeles Times,* February 4, 2009.

CHAPTER 6

1. Howard-Spink, Sam. "Grey Tuesday, Online Cultural Activism, and the Mash-up of Music and Politics." *First Monday* 9, no. 10 (2004).

2. Taylor, Catharine P. "My Morning Listening to Radiohead Remixes." *Social Media Insider,* April 23, 2008.

3. Bardzell, Jeffrey. "Creativity in Amateur Multimedia: Popular Culture, Critical Theory, and HCI." *Human Technology* 3, no. 1 (2007): 12–33.

4. O'Brien, Damien, and Brian Fitzgerald. "Mashups, Remixes, and Copyright Law." *Internet Law Bulletin* 9, no. 2 (2006): 17–19.

5. Manuel, Peter. *Cassette Culture: Popular Music and Technology in North India.* Chicago: The University of Chicago Press, 1993.

6. McLeod, Kembrew. "Confessions of an Intellectual (Property): Danger Mouse, Mickey Mouse, Sonny Bono, and My Long and Winding Path as a Copyright Activist-Academic." *Popular Music and Society* 28, no. 1 (2005): 79–93.

7. Ibid.

8. Ibid.

9. Ibid.

10. Ibid.

11. Morley, Paul. *Words and Music*. London: Bloomsbury, 2003.

12. Howard-Spink. "Grey Tuesday, Online Cultural Activism, and the Mash-up of Music and Politics."

13. Ibid.

14. Ibid.

15. Begun, Bret. "Bootylicious Beats." *Newsweek*, June 10, 2002, 12.

16. Taylor, Charles. "A Love Song to Bastard Pop." Salon, August 9, 2003. http://www.salon.com/ent/music/feature/2003/08/09/mashups_taylor/index_np.html.

17. Hebdige, Dick. *Subculture: The Meaning of Style*. London: Methuen & Co. Ltd, 1979.

18. Dawkins, Richard. *The Selfish Gene*. Oxford: Oxford University Press, 1976.

19. Silby, Brent. "What Is a Meme?" Department of Philosophy, 2000. http://www.def-logic.com/articles.

20. Ibid.

21. Hodge, Karl. "It's All in the Memes." *Guardian*, August 10, 2000.

22. Marshall, Garry. "The Internet and Memetics." http://pespmc1.vub.ac.be/Conf/MemePap/Marshall.html.

23. Hodge. "It's All in the Memes."

24. Ibid.

25. Ibid.

26. Ibid.

27. Fraser, Matthew, and Soumitra Dutta. "Obama and the 'Facebook Effect'." *MediaPost*, November 17, 2008.

28. Ibid.

29. Douglas, Nick. "The 12 Internet Memes that Took Obama to the Nomination." Gawker, May 8, 2008. http://gawker.com/388332/the-12-internet-memes-that-took-obama-to-the-nomination.

30. Booth, William. "Obama's On-the-Wall Endorsement." *Washington Post*, May 18, 2008, M01.

31. YouChewPoop. http://youchewpoop.com/news/faq/.

32. McKay, Niall. "Movie Mashups Take on Trailers." *Wired*, May 1, 2006.

33. McLeod. "Confessions of an Intellectual (Property)."

34. Frere-Jones, Sasha. "1+1+1=1." *New Yorker*, January 10, 2005.

35. Ibid., 84.

36. McLeod. "Confessions of an Intellectual (Property)."

37. McAvan, Em. "'Boulevard of Broken Songs': Mash-Ups as Textual Re-Appropriation of Popular Music Culture." *M/C Journal* 9, no. 6 (2006).

38. Taylor. "My Morning Listening to Radiohead Remixes."

39. Bruno, Antony. "New Web Site Encourages Fan Remixes and Interaction." *Reuters*, December 9, 2007.

40. McAvan. "'Boulevard of Broken Songs'."

41. Taylor, Catharine P. "Must-See Online TV: Kutiman's Mother of All Mashups." *Social Media Insider*, March 11, 2009.

42. Carthy, Roi. "Kutiman Killed the Video Star." TechCrunch, March 11, 2009. http://www.techcrunch.com/2009/03/11/kutiman-killed-the-video-star/.

43. Holson, Laura M. "Hollywood Asks YouTube: Friend or Foe?" *New York Times*, January 15, 2007.

44. Graham, Renee. "Jay-Z, the Beatles Meet in 'Grey' Area." *Boston Globe*, February 10, 2004.

45. Ibid.

46. Howard-Spink. "Grey Tuesday, Online Cultural Activism, and the Mash-up of Music and Politics."

47. Frere-Jones. "1+1+1=1."

48. O'Brien and Fitzgerald. "Mashups, Remixes, and Copyright Law."

49. Ibid., p. 3.

50. Shiga, John. "Copy-and-Persist: The Logic of Mash-up Culture." *Critical Studies in Media Communication* 24, no. 2 (2007): 93–114.

51. Howard-Spink. "Grey Tuesday, Online Cultural Activism and the Mash-up of Music and Politics."

52. McLeod. "Confessions of an Intellectual (Property)."

53. Rojas, Pete. "Bootleg Culture." Salon, August 1, 2002.

54. Fisher, William W. *Promises to Keep: Technology, Law, and the Future of Entertainment*. Palo Alto, CA: Stanford University Press, 2004.

CHAPTER 7

1. Kaye, Barbara K., and Thomas J. Johnson. "From Here to Obscurity?: Media Substitution Theory and Traditional Media in an On-Line World." *Journal of the American Society for Information Science and Technology* 54, no. 3 (2003): 260–73.

2. Dimmick, John, Susan Kline, and Laura Stafford. "The Gratification Niches of Personal E-Mail and the Telephone." *Communication Research* 27, (2000): 227–48.

3. Kang, Mee-Eun, and David J. Atkin. "Exploring the Role of Media Uses and Gratifications in Multimedia Cable Adoption." *Telematics and Infomatics* 16, (1999): 59–74.

4. Lin, Carolyn A. "Audience Attributes, Media Supplementation, and Likely Online Service Adoption." *Mass Communication & Society* 4, (2001): 19–38.

5. Negroponte, Nicholas. *Being Digital*. New York: Vintage Books, 1995.

6. Coffey, Steve, and Horst Stipp. "The Interactions between Computer and Television Usage." *Journal of Advertising Research* 37, no. 2 (1997): 61–67.

7. Kaye and Johnson. "From Here to Obscurity?."

8. Ibid., p. 271.

9. Coffey and Stipp. "The Interactions between Computer and Television Usage."

10. Ibid.

11. Kaye and Johnson. "From Here to Obscurity?"

12. Walsh, Mark. "Study: Web Video Viewers Will Continue to Increase Consumption." *MediaPost*, February 26, 2008.

13. "blinkx Survey of TV and Online Video Habits Reveals Surprising User Behavior." *BusinessWire*, February 28, 2008.

14. comScore Video Metrix. "U.S. Internet Users Viewed 10 Billion Videos Online in Record-Breaking Month of December, According to comScore Video Metrix." February 8, 2008. http://www.comscore.com/press/release.asp?press=2051.

15. Walsh. "Study: Web Video Viewers Will Continue to Increase Consumption."

16. Associated Press. "New Data Reveal Online Video Views Are Soaring." April 17, 2008.

17. O'Malley, Gavin. "U.S. Online Video Viewing Increases 64% vs. Year Ago." *MediaPost,* May 13, 2008.

18. comScore. "YouTube Attracts 100 Million U.S. Video Views in October 2008." December 9, 2008.

19. Associated Press. "YouTube Popularity Eclipses, and Influences, Fall TV Season." August 8, 2006.

20. Horowitz Associates. "Study Tracks Broadband Video Consumption on Multiple Platforms." December 1, 2007. http://www.horowitzassociates.com/bcspr.html.

21. Ibid.

22. Madden, Mary. "Online Video." Pew Internet & American Life Project, July 25, 2007. http://www.pewinternet.org/pdfs/PIP_Online_Video_2007.pdf.

23. "blinkx Survey of TV and Online Video Habits Reveals Surprising User Behavior."

24. O'Malley, Gavin. "Lost Tops for Online TV, Viewership on Upswing." *Online MediaDaily,* February 13, 2009. http://www.mediapost.com/publications/index.cfm?fa=Articles.showArticle&art_aid=100246.

25. Ipsos MediaCT. "PC Encroaching On TV's Dominance in Share of Screen Time with Digital Video Users." May 30, 2008. http://www.ipsosmediact.com/knowledge/pressrelease.aspx?id=3941.

26. Center for Media Research. "Three Screen Viewing Reaches New Heights." *Research Brief,* March 3, 2009.

27. Ibid.

28. Vorhaus, Mike. "Younger Demos Shift Focus from TV Screens to YouTube." *Advertising Age,* October 8, 2007.

29. Madden. "Online Video."

30. Ibid.

31. Center for Media Research. "Video on PCs Captures Share of TV Screen Time." June 13, 2008.

32. O'Malley, Gavin. "Survey: Web Video Beats TV among Respondents Ages 18-24." *MediaPost,* January 16, 2009.

33. Teinowitz, Ira. "Skit's Web Popularity: That's Rich." *TelevisionWeek* 26, no. 1 (2007).

34. Associated Press. "YouTube Popularity Eclipses, and Influences, Fall TV Season."

35. Buckman, Adam. "Paris Hot on YouTube." *New York Post,* October 2, 2007.

36. Mudhar, Raju. "Never-Kissed Singer an Instant Web Star." *Toronto Star,* April 15, 2009. http://www.thestar.com/News/World/article/618583.

37. Khan, Urmee. "'Britain's Got Talent' Church Worker Susan Boyle Becomes YouTube Hit." *The Daily Telegraph,* April 14, 2009. http://www.telegraph.co.uk/culture/tvandradio/5152638/Britains-Got-Talent-church-worker-Susan-Boyle-becomes-YouTube-hit.html.

38. Mudhar, Raju. "Never-Kissed Singer an Instant Web Star."

39. Dobuzinskis, Alex. "Susan Boyle Breaks Past 100 Million Online Views. " *Reuters,* April 20, 2009. http://blogs.reuters.com/fanfare/2009/04/20/susan-boyle-breaks-past-100-million-online-views.

40. Karnes, Jeff. "The Revolution Will Be Downloaded." *MediaPost*, October 28, 2008.

41. Woodson, Alex. "MySpace, TMZ Launch Web Channel." *The Hollywood Reporter*, February 27, 2008.

42. Goetzl, David. "NBC Airs '30 Rock' New Season Online First." *MediaPost*, October 13, 2008.

43. Carter, Bill. "Sitcom Given up for Dead Hits the Web. It's Alive!" *New York Times*, July 3, 2006, E1.

44. Rose, Frank. "Hollywood Has Finally Figured out How to Make Web Video Pay." *Wired*, July 21, 2008.

45. Keveney, Bill. "Women on Web May Find Dating Brad a Tall Order." *USA Today*, June 12, 2008, D3.

46. Ohanian, Tom. "Google Addresses Video Concerns." *MediaPost*, July 16, 2008.

47. Tedeschi. Bob. "New Hot Properties: YouTube Celebrities." *New York Times*, February 26, 2007.

48. Vascellaro, Jessica E. "Video's New Friends. Social-Networking Sites Ramp up Original Online Series to Lure Users, Advertisers and Compete with YouTube." *Wall Street Journal*, February 28, 2008.

49. Ibid.

50. Ibid.

51. Ibid.

52. O'Malley, Gavin. "MySpace Users Invited to Get Hitched on New Web Series." *OnlineMediaDaily*, January 20, 2009.

53. Sullivan, Laurie. "MySpace Debuts 'BFF' Online Game Show Series." *MediaPost*, April 2, 2009.

54. Cassidy, Mike. "P&G: From Soap Operas to Online/Mobile Shows." *Video Insider*, October 23, 2007.

55. Rose. "Hollywood Has Finally Figured out How to Make Web Video Pay."

56. Learmonth, Michael. "Web Series Still Struggle to Hold on to Audiences." *Advertising Age*, January 26, 2009.

57. O'Malley, Gavin. "Research Contradicts Myths About Online TV Shows." *MediaPost*, May 19, 2008.

58. Stelter, Brian. "You've Seen the YouTube Video; Now Try the Documentary." *New York Times*, May 10, 2008.

59. Stelter, Brian. "Can NBC Do for 'Quarterlife' What YouTube Could Not?" *New York Times*, December 24, 2007.

60. Ibid.

61. Rose. "Hollywood Has Finally Figured out How to Make Web Video Pay."

62. Zap2It. "NBC Logs Off 'Quarterlife'." February 28, 2008. http://www.zap2it.com/tv/news/zap-nbcpullsquarterlife,0,4836180.story.

63. Chong, Kevin. "YouTube to Boob Tube." *CBC*, March 28, 2008. http://www.cbc.ca/arts/media/onlinesitcoms.html.

64. Strauss, Gary. "CollegeHumor.com Laughs All the Way to a TV Series." *USA Today*, February 5, 2009, D3.

65. Ibid.

66. Stelter. "Can NBC Do for 'Quarterlife' What YouTube Could Not?"

67. Schneider, Michael. "ABC Orders 'Motherhood' Episodes." *Variety*, September 5, 2008.

68. Wu, Tim. "Outdated Copyright Rules Make Us All Lawbreakers." Salon, 2007.

69. Associated Press. "New Data Reveal Online Video Views Are Soaring."

70. Greenberg, Andy. "YouTube's Doppelganger." *Forbes*, November 29, 2006.

71. Ibid.

72. Shields, Mike. "Viacom, YouTube Strive for Accord." *MediaWeek*, October 31, 2006.

73. Steinberg, Jacques. "Censored 'SNL' Sketch Jumps Bleepless onto the Internet." *New York Times*, December 21, 2006.

74. Hall, Sarah. "PTC Puts NBC on Naughty List" E! Online, December 22, 2006. http://www.eonline.com/uberblog/b54026_PTC_Puts_NBC_on_Naughty_List.html.

75. Ibid.

76. Kaufman, Gil. "'SNL' Star Behind Timberlake's Raunchy Hit Hopes to 'Box' up Full LP." VH1, December 20, 2006. http://www.vh1.com/artists/news/1548607/20061220/timberlake_justin.jhtml.

77. Associated Press. "YouTube Popularity Eclipses, and Influences, Fall TV Season."

78. Steinberg. "Censored 'SNL' Sketch Jumps Bleepless onto the Internet."

79. Associated Press. "New Data Reveal Online Video Views Are Soaring."

80. Ibid.

81. Patterson, Thom. "Is the Future of TV on the Web?" CNN.com, 2008.

82. Learmonth, Michael. "Hulu Now No. 2 Online-Video Site, Behind YouTube." *Advertising Age*, March 12, 2009.

83. O'Malley, Gavin. "NBC Announces News Chapters of Webisodes for NBC.com." *MediaPost*, April 3, 2008.

84. Franchi, Eric. "What Disney's Hulu Investment Means." *VideoInsider*, May 4, 2009.

85. "Hulu Who?" *Economist.com*, February 5, 2009.

86. Franchi. "What Disney's Hulu Investment Means."

87. MacMillan, Douglas. "Online TV Sites Battle for Viewers." *BusinessWeek*, January 19, 2009.

88. Learmonth. "Hulu Now No. 2 Online-Video Site, Behind YouTube."

89. Franchi. "What Disney's Hulu Investment Means."

90. O'Malley. "NBC Announces News Chapters of Webisodes for NBC.com."

91. Stone, Brad. "Video Site Joost Reboots as a Hulu Clone." *New York Times*, October 13, 2008.

92. MacMillan. "Online TV Sites Battle for Viewers."

93. Hefflinger, Mark. "CBS TV Clips on YouTube Viewed 30 Million Times." Digital Media Wire, November 21, 2006. http://www.dmwmedia.com/news/2006/11/21/cbs-tv-clips-on-youtube-viewed-30-million-times.

94. Adegoke, Yinka. "YouTube Starts Running Full-Length CBS Shows." *Reuters*, October 10, 2008.

95. Patterson. "Is the Future of TV on the Web?"

96. Ibid.

97. Woodson. "MySpace, TMZ Launch Web Channel."

98. Walsh. "Study: Web Video Viewers Will Continue to Increase Consumption."

99. Patterson. "Is the Future of TV on the Web?"

100. Madway, Gabriel. "Yahoo Unveils Partners for Web TV Push at CES." *Reuters*, January 8, 2009.

CHAPTER 8

1. boyd, danah, and Nicole B. Ellison. "Social Network Sites: Definition, History, and Scholarship." *Journal of Computer-Mediated Communication* 13, no. 1 (2007): article 11.

2. Cohn, David. "Bands Embrace Social Networking." *Wired*, May 18, 2005.

3. Michaels, Sean. "Gorillaz Most Popular Band on MySpace." *Guardian.co.uk*, December 24, 2008.

4. Dhar, Vasant, and Irene Chang. "Does Chatter Matter? The Impact of User-Generated Content on Music Sales." 2007. https://archive.nyu.edu/handle/2451/23783.

5. Grace, Julia, Daniel Gruhl, Kevin Haas, Meena Nagarajan, Christine Robson, and Nachiketa Sahoo. "Artist Ranking through Analysis of Online Community Comments." IBM, October 25, 2007. http://domino.research.ibm.com/library/cyberdig.nsf/papers/E50790E56F371154852573870068A184/$File/rj10421.pdf.

6. Ibid.

7. Stelter, Brian. "MySpace to Showcase Music and Sell Performance Videos." *New York Times*, December 4, 2007.

8. "Arctic Monkeys in Concert." *NPR*, March 27, 2006. http://www.npr.org/templates/story/story.php?storyId=5293452.

9. Barton, Laura. "The Question: Have the Arctic Monkeys Changed the Music Business?" *Guardian*, October 25, 2005.

10. Beer, David. "Making Friends with Jarvis Cocker: Music Culture in the Context of Web 2.0." *Cultural Sociology* 2, no. 2 (2008): 222–41.

11. Ingram, Mathew. "Record Labels Fear MySpace May Soon Be Calling the Tunes." *Globe and Mail*, September 7, 2006, B11.

12. Valisno, Jeffry O. "Musical Girl Power: MySpace Discovery." *BusinessWorld*, 2008.

13. Caillat, Colbie. http://www.myspace.com/colbiecaillat.

14. Weingarten, Abby. "Hometown Men among Kings." *Sarasota Herald-Tribune*, September 27, 2007.

15. Hoye, Sarah. "Record Label Hires Guitarist after Seeing His MySpace Page." *Tampa Tribune*, October 5, 2008.

16. Cridlin, Jay. "Signed Via MySpace? Worked for Matt Hires." *tbt**, March 20, 2009, 24.

17. Frere-Jones, Sasha. "High and Mighty: Lil Wayne Takes over Hip-Hop." *New Yorker*, August 13, 2007.

18. Harrington, Richard. "Soulja Boy Cranks it up Big-Time." *Washington Post*, December 21, 2007.

19. Cordor, Cyril. "Soulja Boy Tell Em Biography." AllMusic, http://allmusic.com/cg/amg.dll?p=amg&sql=11:0nfrxqerldje~T1.

20. Ibid.

21. Adib, Desiree, and Stephanie Dahle. "Boston Needed Lead Singer, Found One Online." ABC.com, http://www.abcnews.go.com/GMA/story?id=4971065&page=1.

22. Greene, Andy. "Q&A: Journey's Arnel Pineda." *Rolling Stone*, October 2, 2008. http://www.rollingstone.com/news/story/23180978/qa_journeys_arnel_pineda.

23. Serpick, Evan. "Foos, Weezer Try MySpace." *RollingStone.com*, November 3, 2005.

24. Walsh, Mark. "Bands Outnumber Brands on Facebook Pages." *MediaPost*, May 16, 2008.

25. Plagenhoef, Scott. "Interview: Lily Allen." Pitchfork, http://www.pitchforkmedia.com/article/feature/39534-interview-lily-allen.

26. Salmon, Chris. "Click to Download." *The Guardian*, April 25, 2008. http://www.guardian.co.uk/music/2008/apr/25/popandrock3.

27. Kee, Tameka. "R.E.M. to Debut Album Exclusively on iLike." *MediaPost*, March 12, 2008.

28. O'Malley, Gavin. "Madonna Launches New Album on MySpace." *MediaPost*, April 25, 2008.

29. Serpick. "Foos, Weezer Try MySpace."

30. Lev-Ram, Michal. "MySpace Music Service to Launch in September." *Fortune.com*, July 23, 2008.

31. Goffman, Erving. *The Presentation of Self in Everyday Life*. New York: Doubleday, 1959.

32. Ibid., p. 252.

33. Döring, Nicola. "Personal Home Pages on the Web: A Review of Research." *Journal of Computer-Mediated Communication* 7, no. 1 (2006).

34. Karlsson, Anna-Malin. "Selves, Frames, and Functions of Two Swedish Teenagers' Personal Homepages." In *6th International Pragmatics Conference*, Reims, 1998. http://www.nordiska.su.se/personal/karlsson-a-m/ipra.htm.

35. Ellison, Nicole, Rebecca Heino, and Jennifer Gibbs. "Managing Impressions Online: Self-Presentation Processes in the Online Dating Environment." *Journal of Computer-Mediated Communication* 2, (2006): 415–41.

36. Perreta, Heather. "Presentation of Self in MySpace.com, an Online Social Networking Site." Master's thesis. State University of New York Institute of Technology, 2007.

37. Beer. "Making Friends with Jarvis Cocker," p. 236.

38. Ibid.

39. Aune, Sean P. "New Pennywise Album Is Free for Two Weeks on MySpace." Mashable, March 23, 2008. http://mashable.com/2008/03/23/new-pennywise-album-is-free-for-two-weeks-on-myspace/.

40. Netherby, Jennifer. "Social Networking Sites for Major Artists." *Billboard.com*, April 4, 2008.

41. Ibid.

42. Ibid.

43. Dubner, Stephen J. "What's the Future of the Music Industry? A Freakonomics Quorum." *New York Times* Freakonomics blog, September 20, 2007.

44. IFPI. "Digital Music Report 2007." January 17, 2007. http://www.ifpi.org/content/section_resources/digital-music-report.html.

45. Chmielewski, Dawn C. "Digital Music Downloads Set Record But Fail to Make Up for Decline in CD Sales." *Los Angeles Times*, January 1, 2009. http://articles.latimes.com/2009/jan/01/business/fi-music1.

46. Klaasen, Abbey, and Jonathan Lemonnier. "MySpace Milks Music for Monetization." *Advertising Age*, April 7, 2008.

47. Kot, Greg. "Billy Corgan Dishes on the Smashing Pumpkins: The Past Is Dead to Me." *The Chicago Tribune*, December 9, 2008.

48. Stelter. "MySpace to Showcase Music and Sell Performance Videos."

49. Warner Music Group. "MySpace, Sony BMG Music Entertainment, Universal Music Group and Warner Music Group Partner in Landmark Joint Venture: MySpace Music." April 3, 2008.

50. McCarthy, Caroline. "Catching up with MySpace Music." *CNET News*, March 11, 2009.

51. Morrissey, Brian. "MySpace Moves into Music." *BrandWeek*, September 25, 2008.

52. Ostrow, Adam. "imeem Retools as MySpace Music Looms." Mashable, October 1, 2008. http://mashable.com/2008/10/01/imeem-free-streaming-music.

53. Holahan, Catherine. "The Record Labels' Digital Future." *Business Week Online*, April 4, 2008.

54. Galupo, Scott. "Looking for Friends: Big Record Labels Reach out to MySpace for New Revenues." *Washington Times*, April 4, 2008.

55. Bruno, Antony. "In with the New." *Billboard*, 2008.

56. Holahan. "The Record Labels' Digital Future."

57. Harding, Cortney. "Whose Space?" *Billboard*, 2008.

58. Garrahan, Matthew. "Independent Labels Rail at MySpace Music." *Financial Times*, September 25, 2008.

59. Bruno, Antony. "MySpace Music Expands Content." *Billboard*, January 16, 2009.

60. Van Buskirk, Eliot. "MySpace Music: What Went Wrong, and What's Being Done About It." *Wired*, April 1, 2009.

61. Weiner, Jonah. "Tila Tequila for President." *Slate.com*, April 11, 2006.

62. Galupo. "Looking for Friends."

63. Associated Press. "Huge Hits Don't Spell Success for New Rap Stars." October 19, 2007. http://www.msnbc.msn.com/id/21365044.

CHAPTER 9

1. Bulik, B. S. "The Man Moves in on MySpace: Businesses Flock to Teen-Socializing Site to Network, Trend Watch and Get the Word Out." *Advertising Age*, June 12, 2006.

2. Bowley, Graham. "The High Priestess of Internet Friendship." *Financial Times Weekend Magazine*, October 28, 2006.

3. Petrecca, Laura. "Marketers Get Their Mascots in on Action at MySpace." *USA Today*, August 30, 2006, B3.

4. Hansell, Saul. "Joining the Party, Eager to Make Friends." *New York Times*, October 16, 2006.

5. Ibid.

6. "Case Study." *Advertising Age*, March 21, 2008, 46.

7. Li, Charlene. "How Consumers Use Social Networks." Forrester Research, 2007. http://www.forrester.com/Research/Document/Excerpt/0,7211,41626,00.html.

8. Hansell. "Joining the Party, Eager to Make Friends."

9. "Case Study."

10. Walsh, Mark. "MySpace Top Draw for Young Movie Fans." *MediaPost*, October 29, 2008.

11. Bowles, Scott. "Is This the Next Monster Hit?" *USA Today*, January 17, 2008.

12. Gladkova, Svetlana. "MySpace Launches Promotional Campaign for 'High School Musical 3' Today." September 2, 2008. http://profy.com/2008/09/02/myspace-launches-promotion-high-school-musical-3-today.

13. "Case Study."

14. Walsh. "MySpace Top Draw for Young Movie Fans."

15. Li. "How Consumers Use Social Networks."

16. Ibid.

17. "MySpace and Isobar Debut First Comprehensive Research Study on Social Networks and Marketing." April 23, 2007. http://home.businesswire.com/portal/site/google/index.jsp?ndmViewId=news_view&newsId=20070423005453&newsLang=en.

18. Elkin, Toby. "MySpace Exec: Teen Users Promote Brands." *MediaPost*, March 29, 2006.

19. Hempel, Jessi, and Paula Lehman. "The MySpace Generation." *BusinessWeek*, December 12, 2005.

20. Salzman, Marian, Ira Matathia, and Ann O'Reilly. *Buzz: Harness the Power of Influence and Create Demand*. Hoboken, NJ: John Wiley and Sons, 2003.

21. Bowley. "The High Priestess of Internet Friendship."

22. Ibid.

23. Hagel, John, III, and Arthur G. Armstrong. *Net Gain: Expanding Marketing through Virtual Communities*. Cambridge, MA: Harvard Business School Press, 1997, p. 2.

24. Schultz, Don E. "Social Call." *Marketing Management* 16, no. 4 (2007): 10–11.

25. Dou, Wenyu, and Sandeep Krishnamurthy. "Using Brand Websites to Build Brands Online: A Product Versus Service Brand Comparison." *Journal of Advertising Research* 47, no. 2 (2007): 193–206.

26. Johnson, Grace, Gordon C. Bruner II, and Anand Kumar. "Interactivity and its Facets Revisited." *Journal of Advertising* 35, no. 4 (2006): 35–52.

27. McMillan, Sally J., and Jang Sun Hwang. "Measures of Perceived Interactivity: An Exploration of the Role of Direction of Communication, User Control, and Time in Shaping Perceptions of Interactivity." *Journal of Advertising* 31, no. 3 (2002): 29–42.

28. Cho, Chang-Hoan, and John D. Leckenby. "Internet-Related Programming Technology and Advertising." In *Proceedings of the 1997 Conference of the American Academy of Advertising*, edited M. Carole Macklin. Cincinnati, OH: American Academy of Advertising, 1997.

29. McMillan and Hwang. "Measures of Perceived Interactivity."

30. Thorson, Kjerstin S., and Shelly Rodgers. "Relationships between Blogs as eWOM and Interactivity, Perceived Interactivity, and Parasocial Interaction." *Journal of Interactive Advertising* 6, no. 2 (2006).

31. McCormick, Andrew. "Social Network Advertising " *New Media Age*, May 10, 2007.

32. Morrissey, Brian. "Beyond Clicks: Measuring Effects of Social Net Ads." *AdWeek*, April 23, 2007.

33. Rosen, Emanuel. *The Anatomy of Buzz: How to Create Word-of-Mouth Marketing*. New York: Doubleday, 2000, p. 43.

CHAPTER 10

1. Bielby, Denise D., C. Lee Harrington, and William T. Bielby. "Whose Stories Are They? Fans' Engagement with Soap Opera Narrative in Three Sites of Fan Activity." *Journal of Broadcasting and Electronic Media* 43, no. 1 (1999): 35–51.

2. Harrington, C. Lee, and Denise D. Bielby. *Soap Fans: Pursuing Pleasure and Making Meaning in Everyday Life*. Philadelphia: Temple University Press, 1995.

3. Jenkins, Harold. *Textual Poachers: Television Fans and Participatory Culture*. New York: Routledge, 1992.

4. Thorne, Scott, and Gordon C. Bruner II. "An Exploratory Investigation of the Characteristics of Consumer Fanaticism." *Qualitative Market Research* 9, no. 1 (2006): 51–72.

5. Bielby, Harrington, and Bielby. "Whose Stories Are They?"

6. Ibid.

7. Ibid.

8. Ibid.

9. Jenkins. *Textual Poachers*, p. 271.

10. Ibid.

11. Lo, Malinda. "Fan Fiction Comes out of the Closet." *AfterEllen*, January 4, 2006. http://www.afterellen.com/Print/2006/1/fanfiction.html.

12. Bielby, Harrington, and Bielby. "Whose Stories Are They?"

13. Ibid.

14. Kuppers, Petra. "Quality Science Fiction: 'Babylon 5's' Metatextual Universe." In *Cult Television*, edited by Sara Gwenllian-Jones and Roberta E. Pearson, 45–59. Minneapolis: University of Minnesota Press, 2004.

15. Interpublic Media Group. "Ad*Vizr New Media Audit 2006/2007."

16. Andrejevic, Mark. "Watching Television without Pity." *Television & New Media* 9, no. 1 (2008): 24–46.

17. Ibid., p. 33.

18. Borah, Rebecca Sutherland. "Apprentice Wizards Welcome: Fan Communities and the Culture of Harry Potter." In *The Ivory Tower and Harry Potter: Perspectives on a Literary Phenomenon*, edited by Lana A. Whited. Columbia: University of Missouri Press, 2004.

19. Bielby, Harrington, and Bielby. "Whose Stories Are They?"

20. Walsh, Mark. "Fox Creates Online Community for Viewers." *MediaPost*, June 23, 2008.

21. Sella, Marshall. "The Remote Controllers." *New York Times Magazine*, October 20, 2002.

22. Bradberry, Grace. "Get a Shave, Carter." *Guardian*, January 5, 2003.

23. Ibid.

24. Atkinson, Claire, and Abbey Klaasen. "Wanting Conversation, TV Nets Beef up Web Presence." *Advertising Age*, October 23, 2006.

25. Sella. "The Remote Controllers," p. 68.

26. Ibid., p. 62.

27. Deery, June. "TV.com: Participatory Viewing on the Web." *Journal of Popular Culture* 37, no. 2 (2003): 161–83.

28. Bielby, Harrington, and Bielby. "Whose Stories Are They?"

29. D'Acci, Julie. "The Case of 'Cagney & Lacey'." In *Boxed In: Women and Television*, edited by H. Baehr and G. Dyer. New York: Pandora, 1987.

30. Jenkins. *Textual Poachers*.

31. Wyatt, Edward. "CBS Bringing 'Jericho' Back after Protests from Fans." *New York Times*, June 7, 2007, C4.

32. Deery. "TV.com: Participatory Viewing on the Web."

33. Bird, S. Elizabeth. "Chatting on Cynthia's Porch: Creating Community in an E-Mail Fan Group." *Southern Communication Journal* 65, (1999): 49–65.

34. Menon, Siddhartha. "A Participation Observation Analysis of the 'Once & Again' Internet Message Bulletin Boards." *Television & New Media* 8, no. 4 (2007): 341–74.

35. Ibid., p. 384.

36. Costello, Victor J., and Barbara Moore. "Cultural Outlaws: An Examination of Audience Activity and Online Television Fandom." *Television & New Media* 8, (2007): 124–43.

37. Gates, David, and Devin Gordon. "One Ring to Lure Them All." *Newsweek*, January 29, 2001.

38. Deery. "TV.com: Participatory Viewing on the Web."

39. Andrejevic. "Watching Television without Pity."

40. Ibid.

41. Ibid.

42. Menon. "A Participation Observation Analysis of the 'Once & Again' Internet Message Bulletin Boards."

43. Andrejevic. "Watching Television without Pity."

44. Dohery-Farina, Stephen. *The Wired Neighborhood*. New Haven, CT: Yale University Press, 1996.

45. Bird. "Chatting on Cynthia's Porch: Creating Community in an E-Mail Fan Group."

46. Bakardjieva, Maria. "Virtual Togetherness: An Everyday-Life Perspective." *Media, Culture & Society* 25, (2003): 291–313.

47. Baym, Nancy. "The Emergence of Community in Computer-Mediated Communication." In *Cybersociety: Computer-Mediated Communication and Community*, edited by Steve Jones, 138–63. Thousand Oaks, CA: Sage, 1995.

48. Baym, Nancy. *Tune In, Log On: Soaps, Fandom, and Online Community*. Thousand Oaks, CA: Sage, 2000.

49. Deery. "TV.com: Participatory Viewing on the Web."

50. Costello and Moore. "Cultural Outlaws."

51. DiGiovanna, James. "Losing Your Voice on the Internet." In *High Noon on the Electronic Frontier: Conceptual Issues in Cyberspace*, edited by Peter Ludlow and Mike Godwin, Cambridge, MA: MIT Press, 1996.

52. McKinley, E. Graham. *Beverly Hills, 90210: Television, Gender, and Identity*. Philadelphia: University of Pennsylvania, 1997, p. 83.

53. Baym. *Tune In, Log On*.

54. Menon. "A Participation Observation Analysis of the 'Once & Again' Internet Message Bulletin Boards," p. 348.

55. Andrejevic. "Watching Television without Pity."

56. Costello and Moore. "Cultural Outlaws."

57. Deery. "TV.com: Participatory Viewing on the Web."

58. Ibid., p. 174.

59. Nielsen Media. "'House' and 'Lost' Show Greatest Gains from DVR Playback, Nielsen Reports." April 25, 2007.

60. Caslin, Sam. "Compliance Fiction: Adorno and Horkheimer's 'Culture Industry' Thesis in a Multimedia Age." *Fast Capitalism* no. 2.2, 2007. http://www.uta.edu/huma/agger/fastcapitalism/2_2/caslin.html.

CHAPTER 11

1. Baym, Nancy K. "The New Shape of Online Community: The Example of Swedish Independent Music Fandom." *First Monday* 12, no. 8 (2007).

2. Ibid.

3. Ibid., p. 6.

4. Dann, Gabrielle. "'American Idol'. From the Selling of a Dream to the Selling of a Nation." *Mediations* 1, no. 1: 15–21.

5. Franck, Egon, and Stephan Nüesch. "Avoiding 'Star Wars': Celebrity Creation as Media Strategy." Kyklos 60, no. 2 (2007): 211–230.

6. "'Idol' Finale Sets Fox Ratings Records." Zap2It, September 4, 2002. http://tv.zap2it.com/tveditorial/tve_main/1,1002,271%7C77956%7C1%7C,00.html.

7. Carter, Bill. "Fox Mulls How to Exploit the Mojo of 'American Idol'." *New York Times*, May 23, 2003.

8. Ibid.

9. Ibid.

10. Drama 2.0. "The Future of Media Is Integrated." July 28, 2007. http://www.drama20show.com/2007/07/28/the-future-of-media-is-integrated/.

11. Flamm, Matthew. "An American Phenomenon." *Crain's New York Business*, May 5, 2006.

12. Ibid.

13. Ibid.

14. Stelter, Brian. "Voting for the Worst on 'American Idol' Makes Money for an Entrepreneur." *New York Times*, March 17, 2008, C4.

15. Ibid.

16. Ibid.

17. della Cava, Marco R. "From Living in His Car to Living out His Dream, Leming's Songs Strike Sad Note." *USA Today*, May 27, 2008, D1.

18. Cullen, Steve. "Antonella Barba: Victim or Social Media Genius?" *Media Relations and SEO PR* blog, February 26, 2007. http://www.endgamepr.com/blog/2007/02/26/antonella-barba-social-media-genius.

19. Carter. "Fox Mulls How to Exploit the Mojo of 'American Idol'."

20. *People*. "Clay Aiken Biography." http://www.people.com/people/clay_aiken/biography.

21. Keveney, Bill. "Rooting for Ruben or Clay?" *USA Today*, May 20, 2003. http://www.usatoday.com/life/television/news/2003-05-19-clay-ruben_x.htm.

22. Gazan, Ali. "The Best and Worst of Reality TV." *TV Guide*, August 8, 2005. http://www.tvguide.com/news/battle-reality-stars-41379.aspx.

23. Ryfle, Steve. "Is There Life After 'American Idol'?" Netscape Celebrity. http://webcenters.netscape.compuserve.com/celebrity/becksmith.jsp?p=bsf_afteridol.

24. Lazzaro, Stephanie. "Fans' Most Anticipated Album Worth All-Nighters." *NinerOnline*, October 23, 2003. http://www.nineronline.com/2.5292/1.554908.

25. Ibid.

26. Kylene. E-mail communication. March 28, 2009.

27. Ibid.

28. Ibid.

CHAPTER 12

1. Emery, Michael, Edwin Emery, and Nancy L. Roberts. *The Press in America: An Interpretive History of the Mass Media.* 9th ed. Boston: Allyn & Bacon, 1997.

2. Ibid.

3. Bowman, Shayne, and Chris Willis. "We Media: How Audiences Are Shaping the Future of News and Information." The Media Center at the American Press Institute, July 2003. http://www.hypergene.net/wemedia/download/we_media.pdf.

4. Ibid., p. 10.

5. Ibid.

6. Rainie, Lee et al. "One Year Later: September 11 and the Internet." Pew Internet & American Life Project, September 5, 2002. http://www.pewinternet.org/pdfs/PIP_9-11_Report.pdf.

7. Schwartz, John. "3,000 Amateurs Offer NASA Photos of Columbia's Demise." *New York Times*, April 19, 2003.

8. Kuntz, Tom. "Word for Word/FreeRepublic.com: From Excitement to Horror: Columbia's Last Flight Online." *New York Times*, February 9, 2003.

9. Fallows, Deborah, and Lee Rainie. "The Internet as a Unique News Source." Pew Internet & American Life Project, July 2004. http://www.pewinternet.org/pdfs/PIP_News_Images_July04.pdf.

10. Ibid.

11. Taylor, Catharine P. "The New York Times and National Public Radio Get Social." *MediaPost*, October 8, 2008.

12. Bowman and Willis. "We Media: How Audiences Are Shaping the Future of News and Information."

13. CurrentTV. "About Current." http://current.com/s/about.htm.

14. Learmonth, Michael. "CNN Shells out $750k for iReport.com Domain." Huffington Post, January 18, 2008. http://www.huffingtonpost.com/2008/01/18/cnn-shells-out-750k-for-_n_82210.html.

15. Project for Excellence in Journalism. "The Latest News Headlines—Your Vote Counts." September 12, 2007. http://www.journalism.org/node/7493.

16. Ibid.

17. Morley, Brian, and Chris Roberts. "Biting the Hand That Feeds: Blogs and Second-Level Agenda Setting." April 27, 2005. http://bryanmurley.com/site/wp-content/uploads/2007/01/murley-roberts605.pdf.

18. Krugman, Paul. "The Other Face." *New York Times*, December 13, 2002.

19. Ibid.

20. Smith, Robert. "Talking Points Site Kept Attorneys Story Alive." NPR, March 22, 2007. http://www.npr.org/templates/story/story.php?storyId=9083501.

21. Cohen, Noam. "Blogger, Sans Pajamas, Rakes Muck and a Prize." *New York Times*, February 25, 2008.

22. Grossman, Lev. "Blogs Have Their Day." *Time*, December 19, 2004.

23. Sullivan, Andrew. "Blogs and Bragg." The Daily Dish, May 28, 2003. http://sullivanarchives.theatlantic.com/index.php.dish_inc-archives.2003_05_01_dish_archive.html.

24. Taylor, Chris. "10 Things We Learned About Blogs." *Time*, December 19, 2004. http://www.time.com/time/personoftheyear/2004/poymoments.html.

25. Pein, Corey. "Blog-Gate." *Columbia Journalism Review*, January/February 2005. http://cjrarchives.org/issues/2005/1/pein-blog.asp.

26. Grossman. "Blogs Have Their Day."

27. Pein. "Blog-Gate."

28. Ibid.

29. Garfunkel, Jon. "Theories of the Bulge: The Timeline." January 9, 2005. http://civilities.net/BushBulgeTimeline.

30. Shaw, Chris. "Bulge History . . . The Story." Bush Wired, November 21, 2004. http://bushwired.blogspot.com/2004/11/bulge-history-story.html.

31. Garfunkel, Jon. "Theories of the Bulge." *Civilities*, January 9, 2005. http://civilities.net/BushBulge.

32. Garfunkel. "Theories of the Bulge: The Timeline."

33. Ibid.

34. Shaw. "Bulge History . . . The Story."

35. Fried, Ian. "Microsoft 'Regrets' Mac-to-PC Ad." *CNET News*, October 14, 2002. http://news.cnet.com/2100-1001-961994.html.

36. Jamie. "Microsoft PR Rep Is the Switcher." Slashdot.com, October 14, 2002. http://slashdot.org/articles/02/10/15/0044255.shtml?tid=109.

37. Fried. "Microsoft 'Regrets' Mac-to-PC Ad."

38. Jamie. "Microsoft PR Rep Is the Switcher."

39. Brown, Jonathan. "Unlikely Hits of the Internet." *The Independent*, May 4, 2006.

40. Hopkins, Mark. "California Earthquake: Twitter First, Take Cover Later." Mashable, October 30, 2007. http://mashable.com/2007/10/30/california-quake-twitter-first-take-cover-later/.

41. Columbia University-Euro RSCG Magnet Study of the Media. "Rebuilding Trust: Credibility in the Newsroom and the Boardroom." 2004.

42. Goldsmith, Samuel, and Clemente Lisi. "Palin Admits Her 17-Year-Old Daughter Is Pregnant." *New York Post*, September 1, 2008.

43. Grossman. "Blogs Have Their Day."

44. Fenton, Justin. "Bloggers Bring New Perspective to Convention." *USA Today*, July 23, 2004.

45. Grossman, Lev. "Time's Person of the Year: You." *Time*, December 13, 2006.

46. Deggans, Eric. "Increased YouTube-rity Brings a Jolt of Reality." *St. Petersburg Times*, September 20, 2007, E1.

47. Johnson, Peter. "It's Prime Time for Blogs on CNN's 'Inside Politics'." *USA Today*, March 20, 2005.

48. McCombs, Maxwell. *Setting the Agenda: The Mass Media and Public Opinion.* Cambridge, UK: Polity, 2004, p. 149.

49. Ibid., p. 149.

50. Kovach, Bill, and Tom Rosenthiel. *The Elements of Journalism: What Newspeople Should Know and the Public Should Expect.* New York: Three Rivers Press, 2001.

CHAPTER 13

1. Stelter, Brian. "Dudes! Time for Beer Pong! CollegeHumor.com Invades MTV." *International Herald Tribune*, February 6, 2009.

2. Waldman, Simon. "The Best of British Blogging." *Guardian.co.uk*, December 18, 2003. http://www.guardian.co.uk/technology/2003/dec/18/weblogs11.

3. Sella, Marshall. "The Remote Controllers." *New York Times Magazine,* October 20, 2002.

4. Morgan, Spencer. "D'oh-Tube! Internet Sensation Scores Big Simpsons Moment." *The New York Observer,* December 18, 2007.

5. Hulin, Rachel. "Noah Kalina Had a Really Good Idea." Photoshelter, March 18, 2008. http://blog.photoshelter.com/2008/03/object-width425-height355param.html.

6. Kelly, Liz. "He Oughta Be in Pictures." Washingtonpost.com Celebritology, December 2006. http://blog.washingtonpost.com/celebritology/2006/12/he_oughta_be_in_pictures.html.

7. Bardzell, Jeffrey. "Creativity in Amateur Multimedia: Popular Culture, Critical Theory, and HCI." *Human Technology* 3, no. 1 (2007).

8. Korr, Josh. "SNL's 'Milkshake' Miss and the Limits of Viral Video Fads." *tbt**, February 26, 2008.

9. Ibid.

10. Havenstein, Heather. "'West Wing' Creator May Be Writing Movie About Facebook." *Computerworld,* August 28, 2008.

11. Irwin, Tanya. "MySpace Suicide Case to Be Subject of Movie." *MediaPost,* February 3, 2009.

12. Blankenship, Mark. "Bloggers Find 'Life' on N.Y. Stage." *Variety,* June 11, 2007.

13. Ibid.

14. "My First Time the Play: About the Show." http://www.myfirsttimetheplay.com/about.htm.

15. Blankenship. "Bloggers Find 'Life' on N.Y. Stage."

16. McCarthy, Rory. "Salam's Story." *Guardian*, May 30, 2003.

17. Ibid.

18. Smith-Spark, Laura. "YouTube Debate: Hype or History?" *BBC News,* July 24, 2007.

19. Malkin, Michelle. "Digging out More CNN/YouTube Plants." November 29, 2007. http://michellemalkin.com/2007/11/29/digging-out-the-cnnyoutube-plants-abortion-questioner-is-edwards-supporter/.

20. Steinberg, Brian. "Nissan's Upfront Bet Pays Off: NBC's 'Heroes' Turns into Hit." *Wall Street Journal*, November 15, 2006.

21. NBC. "More Than 116,000 Viewers Cast Vote on Fate of Nicole Wallace, 'Law & Order: Criminal Intent's' Recurring Murderess Guest-Star." October 21, 2004.

22. NBC. "Olivia d'Abo to Guest Star on NBC's 'Law & Order: Criminal Intent's Season Debut." September 21, 2005.

23. Deery, June. "TV.com: Participatory Viewing on the Web." *The Journal of Popular Culture* 37, no. 2 (2003).

24. Ibid., p. 171.

25. Friedman, Wayne. "CBS, lonelygirl15 Launch Social Net for 'Harper's Island'." *MediaDailyNews*, June 13, 2009.

26. Whitney, Daisy. "MySpace Video a Boon to 'Mother': CBS Sitcom Parlays Internet Ploy into Viewership Surge." *Television Week*, December 4, 2006.

27. TeevBlogger. "'CSI' Finale Goes Interactive." *BlogCritics Magazine*, May 15, 2006.

28. Leggio, Jennifer. "Nine Worst Social Media of 2009. . .Thus Far." ZDNet, May 22, 2009. http://blogs.zdnet.com/feeds/?p=1204.

29. Carcutt, John. "Digg Voters Influence Super Bowl Ad." Applied SEO, February 4, 2008. http://www.appliedseo.com/archives/digg-voters-influence-superbowl-ad/.

30. Grannis, Kina. http://www.twoweeksforkina.com/blog/index.html.

31. Jurgensen, John. "Moguls of New Media." *Wall Street Journal*, July 29, 2006. http://online.wsj.com/public/article/SB115412710465720901-Ah3MvEIHa-4T2Ck8IgsXrr01znUw_20070728.html?mod=rss_free.

32. Newman, Eric. "Airwalk Print Lauds MySpace Celebrities." *Brandweek*, March 10, 2008.

CONCLUSION

1. Beer, David. "Making Friends with Jarvis Cocker: Music Culture in the Context of Web 2.0." *Cultural Sociology* 2, no. 2 (2008).

2. Shales, Tom. "Amateur Power: Novices Steal the Show as Television Plays Who Wants to Be a Star." *Washington Post*, September 2, 2007, M1.

3. Momus. "Pop Stars? Nein Danke!" *Grimsby Fishmarket*, 1992. http://imomus.com/index499.html.

4. Siklos, Richard. "Big Media's Crush on Social Networking." *New York Times*, January 21, 2007, 3.1.

5. Wacker, Watts, and Ryan Mathews. *The Deviant's Advantage: How to Use Fringe Ideas to Create Mass Markets.* New York: Three Rivers Press, 2004.

6. Marshall, Garry. "The Internet and Memetics." http://pespmc1.vub.ac.be/Conf/MemePap/Marshall.html.

INDEX

ABOUT THE AUTHOR

Kelli S. Burns, Ph.D. is an assistant professor in the School of Mass Communications at the University of South Florida. She holds a doctorate in mass communication from the University of Florida, a master's degree in mass communication from Middle Tennessee State University, and a bachelor's degree in mathematics from Vanderbilt University. She is a pop culture and social media junkie who reads gossip blogs and tabloids; watches YouTube videos and reality shows; has attended two Clay Aiken concerts; likes to comment about television shows on message boards and blogs; maintains Facebook, MySpace, Twitter, YouTube, and LinkedIn accounts; and writes several blogs.